spreads the butter really thin

letters
1) no private letter
2) occasion is part of letter
3) gift accompany letter

54 - what was the purpose of letters?

76. central element in Xtian friendship is Xt

105 - Gualdes O'Donnell: the figurative use of
language is the natural one

133 - she finds ep. 23 witty

_____

Mined for historical info -
    monasticism
    friendship
    classical forms
fact of letters - "letter" in antiquity
sought to extract ideas or images
A. not remembered for his letters

- mannered -

clearness
history
theology

OXFORD EARLY CHRISTIAN STUDIES

General Editors

Gillian Clark   Andrew Louth

THE OXFORD EARLY CHRISTIAN STUDIES series includes scholarly volumes on the thought and history of the early Christian centuries. Covering a wide range of Greek, Latin, and Oriental sources, the books are of interest to theologians, ancient historians, and specialists in the classical and Jewish worlds.

Titles in the series include:

Pelagius' Commentary on St Paul's Epistle to the Romans
Translated with introduction and commentary
T. S. de Bruyn (1993)

The Desert Fathers on Monastic Community
Graham Gould (1993)

Arator on the Acts of the Apostles
A Baptismal Commentary
Richard Hillier (1993)

Origen and the Life of the Stars
A History of an Idea
Alan Scott (1991) paperback (1994)

Athanasius and the Politics of Asceticism
David Brakke (1995)

Jerome's *Hebrew Questions on Genesis*
Translated with an introduction and commentary by
C. T. R. Hayward (1995)

Ambrose of Milan and the
End of the Nicene-Arian Conflicts
Daniel H. Williams (1995)

Arnobius of Sicca
Religious Conflict and Competition in the Age of Diocletian
Michael Bland Simmons (1995)

Gregory of Nyssa's Treatise
on the Inscriptions of the Psalms
Ronald E. Heine (1995)

Ascetics and Ambassadors of Christ
The Monasteries of Palestine 314–631
John Binns (1994) paperback (1996)

Paulinus Noster

Self and Symbols in the Letters of Paulinus of Nola

CATHERINE CONYBEARE

OXFORD
UNIVERSITY PRESS

OXFORD
UNIVERSITY PRESS

Great Clarendon Street, Oxford ox2 6DP

Oxford University Press is a department of the University of Oxford.
It furthers the University's objective of excellence in research, scholarship,
and education by publishing worldwide in

Oxford New York

Athens Auckland Bangkok Bogotá Buenos Aires Calcutta
Cape Town Chennai Dar es Salaam Delhi Florence Hong Kong Istanbul
Karachi Kuala Lumpur Madrid Melbourne Mexico City Mumbai
Nairobi Paris São Paulo Shanghai Singapore Taipei Tokyo Toronto Warsaw

with associated companies in Berlin Ibadan

Oxford is a registered trade mark of Oxford University Press
in the UK and in certain other countries

Published in the United States
by Oxford University Press Inc., New York

British Library Cataloguing in Publication Data

Data available

Library of Congress Cataloging in Publication Data

Conybeare, Catherine.
Paulinus Noster : Self and symbols in the letters of Paulinus of Nola / Catherine Conybeare.
p. cm. — (Oxford early Christian studies)
Includes bibliographical references and indexes.
1. Paulinus, of Nola, Saint, ca. 353–431. 2. Self. 3. Church history—Primitive and early church, ca. 30–
600. I. Title. II. Series.
BR1720.P3 C66 2000
270.2'092–dc21   00–029668

ISBN 0–19–924072–8

1 3 5 7 9 10 8 6 4 2

Typeset in Ehrhardt
by Kolam Information Services Private Limited, Pondicherry, India.
Printed in Great Britain
on acid-free paper by
Biddles Ltd., Guildford & King's Lynn

*For Gabriel
and in memory of Celsa*

PREFACE

I was charmed by Paulinus of Nola from the moment I first met him, through his correspondence with Ausonius, and I shall always feel grateful to Jocelyn Hillgarth for introducing us. Initially, Paulinus represented to me the accommodation of classical ideas and *mores* to Christianity in which I was particularly interested; as I read his letters, though, I discovered that something both more dramatic and more subtle was going on: the invention and enactment of ideas that were to prove, directly or indirectly, incredibly influential upon the direction which Christianity took at a crucial period in its development. These ideas—on Christian friendship, on symbolic thought as a stepping stone from the material realm to the spiritual, and on personal identity—proved utterly inter-dependent, and, along with a discussion of how the epistolary medium itself helped to generate these ideas, they form the substance of the present work.

A book on Paulinus needs little excuse, as there have been to date so few—though the new biography by Dennis Trout will surely prompt more. This one would not have taken its present form without the encouragement and guidance, at an early stage, of Brian Stock whose own broad scope led me to explore so many different avenues of Paulinus' thought. My study is not, however, aimed at specialists on Paulinus—a small though, as I have discovered, exceedingly select band—but at those interested more generally in the history of ideas and the development of Christian thought. My mother, Virginia Conybeare, has kindly embodied for me that elusive entity known as 'the general reader', and I hope that others too will find this text accessible.

This book began life as a doctoral thesis at the University of Toronto, Canada: my work in Canada was supported by a scholarship offered by the Canadian Government under the Commonwealth Scholarship and Fellowship Plan, to which I am naturally extremely grateful. Thanks are also due to the staff of the library of the Pontifical Institute of Mediaeval Studies, especially Nancy Kovacs, who answered many an urgent bibliographic request. The seeds of Chapters 4, 5, and 6 were presented at different times to research seminars in Toronto, Leeds, and Manchester, and to a symposium at Kalamazoo: my thanks severally to Jo

Goering, George Rigg, Jim Ginther, Kate Cooper, and Eugene Vance for inviting me to address those sessions, and to their audiences for their various and constructive responses. Giselle de Nie, with extraordinary kindness, read through an entire early draft of this work and made most useful comments, especially on the then-nascent 'symbolism' sections: I wish I had the expertise to follow her directives more fully.

I have had particularly good fortune in my immediate colleagues: at Toronto, Alison Fizzard and Barbara Mann generously supplied bibliography in the visual arts of late antiquity; Harriet Sonne and Miguel Torrens supplied more general help and support; and the conversation of Andrew Gillett and Bob Stanton, especially, was always stimulating and helped me to clarify my thoughts on various topics. Specific suggestions from other colleagues are acknowledged at the appropriate places in the text. Back in England, the warm collegiality of the Department of Classics at the University of Manchester has proved a marvellous environment in which to bring this book to fruition.

There are a few people to whom my deeper debt runs through almost every page of this text. The enchanting conversation of Mark Vessey, and his deep engagement with the textual culture of late antiquity, have prompted several exciting and profitable trains of thought. Dennis Trout, Paulinian *par excellence*, has been from the first beginnings of our acquaintance unfailingly generous with expertise and offprints. As a reader for Oxford University Press, he offered many useful and detailed comments to enhance my argument here; and, most valuable of all, he allowed me to read the manuscript of his work on Paulinus in its entirety while it was still in pre-publication stages, which has been instrumental in speeding the preparation of this study. Finally, Gillian Clark has been a veritable fairy godmother to the work. She read an early version, and made unfailingly perspicacious editorial suggestions upon it; she then, as one of the General Editors of this series, suggested its inclusion and—with her fellow-editor, and the second reader, Jill Harries—made further helpful and generous comments. I need hardly say that none of the above should bear the slightest blame for such deficiencies and elisions as remain in this work.

Almost at the last—as is traditional; but how significantly so in this case—comes my husband Kevin Marsh, without whose constant loving presence, intellectual stimulation, and expertise with the computer this work would truly have been impossible. To him I hope one day to dedicate a worthier tome; but this first foray is for Gabriel, with whose gestation, birth, and growth the parallel stages in the preparation of this volume have been so intimately linked.

C. C.

Manchester, 1999

CONTENTS

ABBREVIATIONS

ACW	Ancient Christian Writers
Blaise	Albert Blaise, *Dictionnaire Latin-Français des auteurs chrétiens* (reissued Turnhout 1993)
CP	*Classical Philology*
CQ	*Classical Quarterly*
CCSL	Corpus Christianorum (Series Latina)
CSEL	Corpus scriptorum ecclesiasticorum Latinorum
Green	*The Works of Ausonius*, ed. with Introduction and Commentary by R. P. H. Green (Oxford, 1991)
Hartel, Praef.	Preface to Hartel's edition of Paulinus *Epistulae* (see main bibliography)
JbAC	*Jahrbuch für Antike und Christentum*
JECS	*Journal of Early Christian Studies*
JMLat	*Journal of Medieval Latin*
JRS	*Journal of Roman Studies*
JThS	*Journal of Theological Studies*
Lampe	G. W. H. Lampe, *A Patristic Greek Lexicon* (Oxford, 1961)
Lewis and Short	Charlton T. Lewis and Charles Short, *A Latin Dictionary* (Oxford, 1879)
MEFRA	*Mélanges d'archéologie et d'histoire de l'École Française de Rome, Antiquité*
MGH	Monumenta Germaniae Historica
Nat.	*Natalicium*
OCT	Oxford Classical Text
OLD	*Oxford Latin Dictionary*
PCPS	*Proceedings of the Cambridge Philological Society*
PG	Patrologia Graeca
PL	Patrologia Latina
PLRE I	A. H. M. Jones, J. R. Martindale, and J. Morris, *The Prosopography of the Later Roman Empire*, vol. 1 (Cambridge, 1971)
RBén	*Révue bénédictine*
RÉA	*Revue des études anciennes*

RÉAug	*Revue des études augustiniennes*
RecAug	*Recherches augustiniennes*
RÉL	*Revue des études latines*
RE	*Paulys Real-Encyclopädie der Classischen Altertumswissenschaft*
SC	Sources chrétiennes
SP	*Studia Patristica*
TAPhA	*Transactions of the American Philological Association*
TLG	*Thesaurus Linguae Graecae*
TLL	*Thesaurus Linguae Latinae*
Trout, *Paulinus*	Dennis E. Trout, *Paulinus of Nola: Life, Letters, and Poems* (Berkeley/Los Angeles, 1999)
VChr	*Vigiliae Christianae*
Walsh, *Letters*	*Letters of Saint Paulinus of Nola*, tr. and ann. P. G. Walsh (2 vols.) ACW 35 and 36 (New York NY/Ramsey NJ, 1966/7)
Walsh, *Poems*	*The Poems of Paulinus of Nola*, tr. and ann. P. G. Walsh, ACW 40 (New York, NY/Ramsey, NJ, 1975)

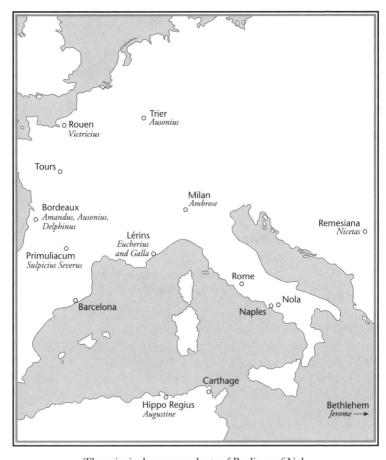

The principal correspondents of Paulinus of Nola

Introduction

In his own time—the late fourth and early fifth centuries—Paulinus of Nola was viewed as the emblematic example of aristocratic conversion to ascetic Christianity. The politicking bishop Ambrose wrote of the event to his episcopal colleague Sabinus with ill-concealed exultation: he exclaims, 'what will the leading men say when they hear this? That someone from that family, that lineage, that stock, and endowed with such tremendous eloquence has migrated from the senate, and that the line of succession of a noble family has been broken: it cannot be borne.'[1] Sulpicius Severus puts praise of his longstanding friend Paulinus for his renunciation of secular wealth into the mouth of St Martin:

[Martin's] conversation with us was simply that worldly enticements and secular burdens should be abandoned, to follow the Lord Jesus free and unencumbered: he adduced to us as the most outstanding example of this in present times the aforementioned glorious Paulinus, who, almost alone in these times, rejected the highest wealth, followed Christ, and fulfilled the teachings of the gospel. . .'[2]

Even the irascible *presbyter* Jerome, despite being notoriously un-impressed by others' interpretations of Christianity, wrote in a hortatory letter, 'look at the holy man Pammachius and the ardent faith of the priest Paulinus: they offered not just their riches, but their actual selves to the Lord. . .'[3]

---

[1] Ambrose and Sabinus were Bishops of Milan and Piacenza respectively. The quote is from Ambrose, *Letter* 6. 27 (=Maur. 58). 3, written in 395: 'haec ubi audierint proceres viri, quae loquentur? ex illa familia, illa prosapia, illa indole, tanta praeditum eloquentia migrasse a senatu, interceptam familiae nobilis successionem: ferri hoc non posse.' The translations of all texts cited in this work are my own, unless otherwise stated.

[2] Sulpicius Severus, *Vita S. Martini* 25. 4: 'sermo autem illius non alius apud nos fuit, quam mundi inlecebras et saeculi onera relinquenda, ut Dominum Iesum liberi expediti sequeremur: praestantissimumque nobis praesentium temporum inlustris viri Paulini, cuius supra fecimus mentionem, exemplum ingerebat, qui summis opibus abiectis Christum secutus solus paene his temporibus evangelica praecepta conplesset.' Paulinus also appears in the *Vita* when Martin cures him of an eye infection, 19. 3; and in Sulpicius' *Dialogues* 1. 23. 4 and 3. 17. 3.

[3] Jerome, *Letter* 118. 5: 'respice sanctum virum Pammachium et ferventissimae fidei Paulinum presbyterum, qui non solum divitias, sed se ipsos domino obtulerunt. . .'

Above all, the letters of St Augustine contain repeated rapturous *testimonia* to the sanctity of Paulinus; from them we may select the one most literally suggestive of rapture, his account of his monks' reception of Paulinus' first letter: 'each person who reads it, carries it away, because he is carried away when he reads it'.[4] For Augustine too, Paulinus' renunciation of wealth and position was exemplary: he is mentioned prominently, for example, in the first book of the *City of God*: 'My friend Paulinus, bishop of Nola, from the most opulent riches voluntarily became exceedingly poor and abundantly holy; when the barbarians devastated Nola and he was held captive by them . . . he prayed, "Lord, let me not be tortured for the sake of gold and silver; for you know where all my possessions are".'[5] Augustine's synopsis also shows another characteristic of those who wrote to and about Paulinus: all his life, he was someone with whom people wished to claim association. 'My friend Paulinus'—'Paulinus noster': the invocation seems to confer a reflected sanctity upon the writer. Someone as apparently remote as the Spanish priest Eutropius felt entitled to use the possessive;[6] Eucherius of Lyons, who probably had more right to it, transfers the 'noster' to make of Paulinus 'a particularly blessed example to our Gaul', also pointing out that Paulinus moved over to 'our way of thinking';[7] each, once again, focuses on 'their' Paulinus' exemplary disbursement of riches. Ambrose dispenses with the 'noster' altogether, but starts his above-mentioned letter with a bald 'Paulinum' which presumes a certain intimacy.[8]

---

[4] 'quotquot eas legerunt, rapiunt, quia rapiuntur, cum legunt'. Augustine, *Letter* 27. 2.

[5] Augustine, *City of God* 1. 10: ' . . . Paulinus noster, Nolensis episcopus, ex opulentissimo divite voluntate pauperrimus et copiosissime sanctus, quando et ipsam Nolam barbari vastaverunt, cum ab eis teneretur . . . precabatur: 'Domine, non excrucier propter aurum et argentum; ubi enim sint omnia mea, tu scis.'

[6] 'Istud sibi sepulcrum et Paulinus noster nuper ipse divitiis cum sua matrefamilias comparavit, qui conversatione saeculi morientes, a mundialibus operibus iam quiescunt, dicente Apostolo: Mortui enim estis, et vita vestra abscondita est cum Christo in Deo [Col. 3: 3].' Letter of Eutropius *presbyter* to the daughters of Geruntius, *De Contemnenda Haereditate*: PL 30, col. 50B.

[7] 'Paulinus . . . Nolanus episcopus, *peculiare et beatum Galliae nostrae exemplum*, ingenti quondam divitiarum censu uberrimo eloquentiae fonte; ita *in sententiam nostram* propositumque migravit, ut etiam cunctas admodum mundi partes eloquio operibusque resperserit'. Eucherius of Lyons, hortatory letter to his relation Valerianus, *De Contemptu Mundi et Saecularis Philosophiae*: PL 50, cols. 718D–19A.

[8] Peter Brown comments on the use of 'noster' by Augustine, and observes, 'Throughout his life, Paulinus remained something of an exhibit'. Brown, *The Cult of the Saints: Its Rise and Function in Latin Christianity* (Chicago, 1981), 54.

Meropius Pontius Paulinus was born of a distinguished and wealthy family[9] not later than AD 355,[10] and brought up near Bordeaux in Aquitaine.[11] He was apparently tutored at Bordeaux by the *grammaticus* Decimus Magnus Ausonius, who was subsequently tutor at the imperial court to the future emperor Gratian, and attained the consulship in 379; despite a discrepancy of some forty years between their ages, the two men formed a close literary friendship which was severed only at Paulinus' insistence on a committed, ascetic Christianity.[12] Initially, Paulinus followed the expected public career for a man of his parentage—aided, apparently, by an influential set of men at Rome which included not only Ausonius but also the prominent aristocrat and subsequent *praefectus urbi Romae*, Symmachus:[13] he was appointed *consul suffectus* no later than 378[14] and governor *(consularis)* of Campania in 381.[15] Here he first took part in the celebrations for the feast day of St Felix of Nola, whose cult he was later to do so much to develop and adorn.[16] Probably in late 383, Paulinus returned to Gaul: this was to prove the first move in a protracted transformation of his way of life, though his return may originally have been

---

[9] Paulinus' family as senatorial: *Poem* 21. 458. Familial distinction and wealth: see the *praeteritio* of Uranius, *De Obitu* 9: 'Taceamus generis nobilitatem, paternis maternisque natalibus in senatorum purpuras admirabiliter rutilantem . . .' See also the letter of Ambrose, cited at n. 1 above.

[10] Probably 352/3 (the date espoused by Trout, *Paulinus*, 287). The date is based on the first letter of Paulinus to Augustine, when he describes his physical age as the same as that of the man cured by the Apostles at the Porta Speciosa (Acts 4: 22). The man's age was 'amplius quadraginta'; the letter is dated 395.

[11] Paulinus offers us his own, highly compressed and allusive, autobiographies at *Letter* 5. 4–5 and *Poem* 21. 365–487: compared and analyzed at Trout, *Paulinus*, 15–21.

[12] For Ausonius, see Robert A. Kaster, *Guardians of Language: The Grammarian and Society in Late Antiquity* (Berkeley/Los Angeles/London, 1988), 247–9, and R. P. H. Green's introduction to his edition of *The Works of Ausonius* (Oxford, 1991). On his relationship with Paulinus, see Trout, *Paulinus*, 28–30. Further on Paulinus' education, see Chapter 1, n. 6 and text. The disseverance of the friendship between Paulinus and Ausonius is discussed at some length in Chapter 6.

[13] Symmachus was *praefectus urbi Romae* in 384/5 (*PLRE* I 867–8). See Trout, *Paulinus*, 34–40 for a full account of Paulinus' probable associates at Rome in the late 370s.

[14] The rank is inferred from Ausonius' reference to Paulinus' *trabea*, which at this period seems to have designated specifically a consular robe: Ausonius, *Letter* 21. 60 (Green's numeration).

[15] See Trout, *Paulinus*, 47–9 on Paulinus' interpretation of his consular duties.

[16] The second *Natalicium* for St Felix, written for his feast day in 396, records that it was three *lustra*—fifteen years—since Paulinus had first participated in the festivities: hence the dating of the governorship. Paulinus, *Poem* 13. 7–9. In addition, the thirteenth *Natalicium* recalls Paulinus' first encounter with Felix: *Poem* 21. 367–73.

prompted by the threat to Gaul—and to his personal estates—of the imperial usurper Maximus.[17] Soon afterwards, he married the devout Spanish heiress Therasia,[18] and there ensued a period in Aquitaine which Paulinus later styled his 'otium ruris'.[19] This period, though entirely undocumented bar retrospectively, was probably a significant one of reflection and spiritual development for Paulinus, for when we next hear of him he is presenting himself for baptism. He was baptized at Bordeaux in 389 by Bishop Delphinus,[20] having been prepared for baptism by the priest Amandus;[21] shortly thereafter, Paulinus and Therasia moved to Spain.

Paulinus, however, subsequently barely alludes to his baptism: for him, it seems, the significant spiritual step was the beginnings of his renunciation of property and, ultimately, the removal to Nola. In this, he undoubtedly prepared the way for those who insisted on seeing the rejection of his worldly goods as the most important thing about him. It was in Spain that Paulinus and Therasia seem to have begun the slow process of divestment of their considerable property, with a view to leading more truly Christian lives. At around this time, Paulinus' brother met a violent death, and there was a second, perhaps closely linked, crisis in which his property was threatened by a *sector*.[22] Paulinus himself presents these as the turning points in his secular renunciation;[23] but, although his earliest surviving letters respond to his *consolationes* on his brother's death from Delphinus and Amandus, he tells us almost nothing of the circumstances.[24]

---

[17] Who murdered Gratian in August 383. See Trout, *Paulinus*, 50–1 for this suggestion.

[18] Paulinus married in Spain: *Poem* 21. 398–403. More on Therasia: see again Ambrose, *Letter* 6. 27. 2. 'Devout' is inferred from the fact that Ausonius resentfully attributed to her Paulinus' increased 'Christianization': Ausonius, *Letter* 22. 31 'Tanaquil tua' (Paulinus rebuffs the insinuation, *Poem* 10. 192: 'nec Tanaquil mihi, sed Lucretia, coniunx'). Further on the relationship of Paulinus and Therasia, see Chapter 3, text to nn. 95–99.

[19] 'otium ruris': Paulinus *Letter* 5. 4. See Jacques Fontaine, 'Valeurs antiques et valeurs chrétiennes dans la spiritualité des grands propriétaires terriens à la fin du IVe siècle occidental', in *Epektasis: mélanges patristiques offerts au Cardinal Jean Daniélou* (Paris, 1972), 571–95; reprinted in idem, *Études sur la poésie latine tardive d'Ausone à Prudence* (Paris, 1980), 241–65.

[20] Paulinus, *Letter* 3. 4 to Alypius: 'a Delphino Burdigalae baptizatus...'

[21] In *Letter* 2. 4 to Amandus, Paulinus describes himself as 'de vobis...et per vos deo natus in Christo'.

[22] A *sector*: one who purchased at public auction property which had been confiscated by the state.

[23] See Paulinus, *Poem* 21. 416–27.

[24] Paulinus, *Letters* 35 and 36. This is a traditional view: Trout doubts the connection, and thinks that Paulinus probably had more than one brother, and that the *consolationes* address the death of the second (*Paulinus*, 65).

Paulinus and Therasia's desire for withdrawal seems to have been cemented by the death in infancy of their beloved son, Celsus.[25] On Christmas Day 394,[26] Paulinus was ordained 'subito' as *presbyter* by Bishop Lampius at Barcelona,[27] and after Easter he and Therasia began the journey to their estates in Campania. They travelled via Rome, where they met with a disappointingly chilly reception from Pope Siricius,[28] and by the autumn were settled at Nola. There they were to remain for the rest of their lives, founding a monastery and more or less reinventing the cult of Saint Felix, through their very public celebration of his festival[29] (which included the annual composition and performance of Paulinus' poems, the *Natalicia*) and their expansive ecclesiastical building projects. There Paulinus succeeded (by 412) the somewhat nebulous figure of Paul as Bishop of Nola;[30] there they were called on by many distinguished figures from their past who, like Paulinus and Therasia, had parlayed worldly wealth into ostentatiously spiritual resources. In the thirty-five years until his death, Paulinus apparently left Nola only to attend the festival of the apostolic saints Peter and Paul at Rome each June. From Nola, too, Paulinus wrote (often in his wife's name as well) almost all the letters which survive to us.[31]

Paulinus' correspondents included those who had been influential on him as he developed his ideas of an appropriate Christian way of life,

---

[25] He was only eight days old. Paulinus recalls his death in a poem of consolation for the death of another boy named Celsus, *Poem* 31. 599–610 and 619–20.

[26] Following the dating for which Dennis Trout argues (himself following Fabre), 'The dates of the ordination of Paulinus of Bordeaux and his departure for Nola', *RÉAug* 37 (1991), 237–60.

[27] *Letter* 3. 4 to Alypius.

[28] See *Letter* 5. 14: 'urbici papae superba discretio'. (In the light of Trout's emphasis (*Paulinus*, 106–8) on the brief outbreak of paganism in Italy immediately preceding Paulinus' arrival, could Paulinus' previous association with Symmachus and others of his like have prompted the pope's suspicion?) The slight was subsequently compensated for by Siricius' successor, Anastasius.

[29] The festival commemorating Felix's death, 14 January.

[30] See Trout, *Paulinus*, 120 on the obscure dating of Paulinus' rise to the episcopate. Presumably he had been acting as *de facto* spiritual leader at Nola for some time, though one of the inscriptions for his new basilica does acknowledge Paul's authority: *Letter* 32. 15 mentions the dedication of *atria* by 'Paulus antistes'.

[31] These letters are not, unfortunately, representative of his entire time at Nola: they appear to be concentrated in time between 395 and 408. The letters of Paulinus are cited from the edition of Hartel, CSEL 29 (Vienna, 1894), corrected against the suggestions in Walsh, *Letters*, and Giovanni Santaniello, *Paolino di Nola: Le Lettere* (Naples, 1992), 2 vols. (summary of emendations at 1. 151).

notably Delphinus, the aforementioned Bishop of Bordeaux, and Amandus his successor.[32] With these may be placed his lifelong friend Sulpicius Severus, who had undergone a similar process of conversion and renunciation under the influence of Saint Martin of Tours, of whom he was to write the celebrated biography;[33] he settled at Primuliacum in Southern Gaul, and vied with Paulinus for achievement in asceticism and church-building.[34] Another contact of Paulinus who had probably been his associate in the secular world as well was the senator Pammachius, to whom Paulinus wrote a *consolatio* on the death of his wife Paulina;[35] Melania the Elder, almost certainly a relation of Paulinus', does not actually receive a (surviving) letter, but does form the centre of a marvellous piece of hortatory reportage when she arrives, in all her ascetic anti-pomp, at Nola.[36]

But after retiring to Nola, Paulinus also made contact with some of the most prominent Christians of the day: several letters on either side survive from his correspondence with Augustine, which was initiated by Augustine's lifelong friend and associate in North Africa, Alypius;[37] three letters to Paulinus from Jerome bear witness to another important contact, though it seems that Jerome swiftly became disenchanted with the man

---

[32] Recipients respectively of Paulinus, *Letters* 10, 14, 19, 20, 35 and 2, 9, 12, 15, 21, 36.

[33] For Sulpicius' exquisite oblique compliment to the exemplary Paulinus in his *Vita S. Martini*, see text to n. 2 above. On Paulinus' relations with Sulpicius, see Clare Stancliffe, *Saint Martin and his Hagiographer: History and Miracle in Sulpicius Severus* (Oxford, 1983), 16–19 and 30–47. Sulpicius received Paulinus, *Letters* 1, 5, 11, 17, 22–24, 27–32; unfortunately, none of his side of the correspondence survives.

[34] For the church-building, see especially Paulinus, *Letter* 32; for the course of the epistolary friendship between the two men, see Chapter 3, especially the text to nn. 100–15.

[35] *Letter* 13. Jerome, too, wrote rather belatedly to the bereaved Pammachius: Jerome, *Letter* 66.

[36] Melania's relationship with Paulinus: *Letter* 29. 5: 'noster sanguis'. Her arrival at Nola reported: *Letter* 29. 5–14.

[37] Paulinus, *Letters* 4, 6, 45, and 50 are addressed to Augustine; *Letter* 3 to Alypius. Augustine addressed to Paulinus *Letters* 27, 31, 42, 45 (with Alypius), 80, 95, and 149. The letters of Augustine are cited from the editions by Goldbacher, CSEL 34, 44, 57, and 58 (1895–1923), and by Divjak, CSEL 88 (1981). For a suggested reconstruction of the correspondence between Augustine and Paulinus, see Pierre Courcelle, *Recherches sur les 'Confessions' de S. Augustin* (new edn., Paris, 1968), 29–32, and 'Les lacunes dans la correspondance entre s. Augustin et Paulin de Nole', *RÉA* 53 (1951), 253–300. The standard biography of Augustine is still that of Peter Brown, *Augustine of Hippo* (London, 1967); see also the new overview by Garry Wills, *Saint Augustine* (Harmondsworth, 1999), with the enthusiastic response by Brown, 'A New Augustine', *New York Review of Books* (24 June 1999, 45–50).

he had originally embraced as a promising protégé.[38] Paulinus' political adroitness is shown, however, by the fact that he managed to remain in communication with Jerome while maintaining cordial relations with Rufinus, Jerome's chief opponent in the Origenist controversy.[39] We know that he communicated with Ambrose, Bishop of Milan, by whom he was 'semper... dilectione ad fidem innutritus' ('always lovingly nurtured for the faith'), and, apparently, claimed as a member of his clergy.[40] Although no actual letters between the two survive, we do know that Ambrose sent relics of Saints Gervasius and Protasius to Paulinus.[41] We also have letters from Paulinus to such prominent figures as Victricius of Rouen,[42] Eucherius of Lyons and his wife Galla; this last is an important early source for Lerinian monasticism.[43]

This galaxy of prominent epistolary addresses should be augmented with the named auditors of some of the *Natalicia*, notably Nicetas, Bishop of Remesiana, who toured Paulinus' new basilica in 403;[44] and Melania the Younger with her husband Pinian, her mother Albina, and an

[38] Jerome, *Letters* 53, 58, and 85. The letters of Jerome are cited from the edition of Hilberg, CSEL 54–56 (1910–18). On the relations between Paulinus and Jerome, see Stefan Rebenich, *Hieronymus und sein Kreis* (Stuttgart, 1992), 220–40, especially 229–30 (the mutual attempt to cast Paulinus as *patronus* to Jerome's *magister*); see also Yves-Marie Duval, 'Les premiers rapports de Paulin de Nole avec Jérôme: moine et philosophe? poète ou exégète?' *Studi tardoantichi* 7 (1989), 177–216.

[39] Paulinus to Rufinus: *Letters* 46 and 47. On the potentially precarious relationship with Rufinus, see Trout, *Paulinus*, 223–7; for the Origenist controversy, see Elizabeth Clark, *The Origenist Controversy: The Cultural Construction of an Early Christian Debate* (Princeton, 1992).

[40] Paulinus, *Letter* 3. 4 to Alypius again: for comment, see Trout, *Paulinus*, 49–50.

[41] Paulinus, *Letter* 32. 17. The letters of Ambrose are cited from the edition of Faller, CSEL 10. 1–3 (1968–82). He has recently received a long-awaited modern biography: Neil B. McLynn, *Ambrose of Milan: Church and Court in a Christian Capital* (Berkeley/Los Angeles/London, 1994).

[42] Paulinus to Victricius of Rouen: *Letters* 18 and 37; for new work on Victricius, see Gillian Clark, 'Victricius of Rouen: *Praising the Saints*' and David Hunter, 'Vigilantius of Calagurris and Victricius of Rouen: Ascetics, Relics, and Clerics in Late Roman Gaul', in *JECS* 7 (1999), 365–99 and 401–30 respectively.

[43] Paulinus, *Letter* 51. Further on Lérins: see Leclercq's article ad loc. in the Dictionnaire d'archéologie chrétienne et de liturgie 8.2. cols. 2596–2627.

[44] Paulinus *Poem* 27 (*Nat.* 9) conducts Nicetas round the buildings at Nola. *Poem* 17, a propemptikon, is written to despatch Nicetas after his first visit to Nola in 400: see André Basson, 'A Transformation of Genres in Late Latin Literature: Classical Literary Tradition and Ascetic Ideals in Paulinus of Nola' in Ralph W. Mathisen and Hagith S. Sivan (eds.), *Shifting Frontiers in Late Antiquity* (Aldershot/Brookfield VT, 1996), 267–76.

extensive further entourage, who took part in the celebrations of Felix's feast-day in 407 and to whom Paulinus' fullest autobiography was addressed.[45]

Soon after the death of Paulinus on 22 June 431 (Therasia having apparently died some years before[46]), his presbyter Uranius wrote an account of his passing, which juxtaposes the events of his last days with an extended hagiographic description of his merits.[47] The saintliness of Paulinus is confirmed by a conversation before his death with his *fratres*, Januarius, Neapolitan bishop and martyr, and Saint Martin of Tours (thus embracing his claims both to Gallic and to Campanian sanctity); and at his death there is a 'privatus in cellula . . . terrae motus', a private earthquake in his cell—which, explains Uranius, is far from incredible, as 'in cuius obitu totus pene orbis ingemuit' ('almost the whole world groaned over his death').[48] Two aspects of Paulinus are particularly singled out for comment: upon his conversion, he opened his barns and treasury to the poor— the 'riches' theme yet again; and he was always loved by all. Paulinus' emblematic status is completed, in Uranius, by his adoption of the best qualities of each of the patriarchs.[49]

Paulinus' position as emblem persisted after his death: writers continued, though less frequently, to dwell primarily upon his miraculous renunciation of wealth and status. There is the famous story in Gregory the Great's *Dialogues* about Paulinus' encounter with pirates,[50] and Gregory of Tours continues in the tradition of seeing Paulinus as an emblematic figure, choosing the Bishop of Nola for the final *vita* in his *Lives of the Confessors*, and his patron Saint Felix as the culmination for his *Lives of the Martyrs*.[51] But there is nothing to parallel those rapturous *testimonia* which Paulinus received in his own lifetime: clearly the power of sanctity by association with Paulinus was fast evaporating. Emblems

---

[45] I.e. *Poem* 21, *Nat.* 13: the gathering is celebrated in ll. 60–83 and 203–331. Further on Melania the Younger, see Elizabeth Clark, *The Life of Melania the Younger* (New York/ Toronto, 1984).

[46] Between 408 and 415: Trout, *Paulinus*, 120.

[47] *De Obitu Paulini*: PL 53, cols. 859–66. For the date of Paulinus' death, see *De Obitu* 4. 12. There is now a convenient English translation in Trout, *Paulinus*, 293–8.

[48] Januarius and Martin: *De Obitu* 3 (col. 861A); the private earthquake: *De Obitu* 4 (col. 862A).

[49] List of patriarchs: *De Obitu* 8 (col. 863B–C).

[50] Gregory, *Dialogues*, 3. 1. 1–10. The 'private earthquake' survives too in this sensational story.

[51] Gregory of Tours, *In Gloria Confessorum* 108 (Paulinus); *In Gloria Martyrum* 103 (Felix).

have the disadvantage of being both irreducibly topical—their validity restricted to a certain historical moment—and necessarily two-dimensional.[52] It is perhaps for this reason that until recently there have been relatively few significant modern studies of Paulinus—particularly studies drawing on his prose letters; his metrical works, apparently because of their more obvious appeal to traditional classicists, have fared rather better. Paulinus remains exemplary, and hence, though of utility in developing the master narrative of declining empire, of only limited interest. W. H. C. Frend concludes his study 'The Two Worlds of Paulinus of Nola' with the words, 'Paulinus of Nola, Romano-Gallic aristocrat, Christian man of letters, and seeker after perfection, fully represented the spirit of his times'.[53] In this and an earlier study of Paulinus,[54] Frend uses Paulinus as *exemplum* to elaborate the thesis, famously espoused by Momigliano (after Gibbon),[55] that Christianity played the villain in the downfall of the Roman Empire, seducing aristocrats away from their proper role of defending the Empire against barbarian incursions. This argument has also been made by the translator of Paulinus' works, P. G. Walsh.[56] Joseph Lienhard, in his careful study of the contribution of Paulinus to early Western monasticism, resists the temptation to make him emblematic, but still, in a modified form, finds him exemplary: 'His importance in [the monastic] movement should not be exaggerated; nor, however, should it be underestimated. Paulinus is not himself a link in a rigid chain of tradition. But he is an example, a good example and an instructive one, of the hesitant beginnings of monasticism in the West.'[57]

[52] On Paulinus as emblematic figure, and its limitations, see Dennis Trout, 'History, Biography, and the Exemplary Life of Paulinus of Nola', *SP* 32 (1997), 462–7: he calls for a more nuanced and multi-dimensional reading of Paulinus—a call he has himself now answered (see below).

[53] 'The Two Worlds of Paulinus of Nola', in J. W. Binns (ed.), *Latin Literature of the Fourth Century* (London/Boston, 1974), 100–133; quote from 127.

[54] W. H. C. Frend, 'Paulinus of Nola and the Last Century of the Western Empire', *JRS* 59 (1969), 1–11. This ends even more uncompromisingly: 'Paulinus . . . was truly representative of the deeper psychological causes that led to the fall of the Roman Empire in the West.'

[55] See A. Momigliano, 'Christianity and the Decline of the Roman Empire', in idem, *Paganism and Christianity in the Fourth Century* (Oxford, 1963), 1–16.

[56] Walsh, 'Paulinus of Nola and the Conflict of Ideologies in the Fourth Century', in P. Granfield and J. A. Jungmann (eds.), *Kyriakon: Festschrift Johannes Quasten* (2 vols.: Münster, 1970), 2. 565–71.

[57] Joseph T. Lienhard, *Paulinus of Nola and Early Western Monasticism* Theophaneia 28: Beiträge zur Religions- und Kirchengeschichte des Altertums (Cologne/Bonn, 1977).

Such has been the pressure of the traditional image of Paulinus as *exemplum* and as legendary disburser of wealth that only two monographs this century, as far as I am aware, form true precursors to this study of his letters qua letters and of the ideas contained in them. The first is a doctoral dissertation from the turn of the century, Paul Reinelt's *Studien über die Briefe des hl. Paulinus von Nola*—which would perhaps have been more aptly entitled *Prolegomena zu Studien*. . . :its first part crisply surveys the collection as a whole, including offering a then-revisionary dating of the letters; the second, the intellectual background to the letters ('das Bibelstudium der Zeit', 'das literarische Ideal der zeitgenössischen Aszetik', for example) and its instantiation in and significance for the letters.[58] The second monograph concentrates on one of the themes adumbrated and explored in the letters of Paulinus, that of Christian friendship. Fabre's *Saint Paulin de Nole et l'amitié chrétienne* charts in considerable detail the course of individual friendships for Paulinus, but leaves almost entirely out of account the theological aspects of friendship, or, for that matter, its role in a broader Christian world-view.[59] In preparing his study, Fabre also wrote an account of the chronology of Paulinus' work which, though intermittently challenged, remains generally accepted.[60]

Paulinus' hitherto unsatisfactory biographical situation has, at the time of writing, dramatically changed. Dennis Trout has just published a study of Paulinus which should lay to rest for ever the two-dimensional *exemplum* notable only for replacing earthly riches with treasure in heaven.[61] The germ of the study lay in Trout's doctoral thesis,[62] in which he emphasized both the processual and the visible nature of Paulinus' withdrawal, firmly contradicting Momigliano's position:[63] 'when Paulinus renounced the world in 394, he did not forget it; nor did he wish it to forget him.'[64] From this has now grown a remarkably full account of Paulinus' life and times, with an extensive development of the external,

[58] Paul Reinelt, *Studien über die Briefe des hl. Paulinus von Nola* (Breslau, 1903). Dating, 58–9; 'Bibelstudium', 84–91; 'literarische Ideal', 99–103.

[59] Pierre Fabre, *Saint Paulin de Nole et l'amitié chrétienne* (Paris, 1948).

[60] Pierre Fabre, *Essai sur la chronologie de l'oeuvre de saint Paulin de Nole* (Paris, 1948). See further my Appendix on the dating of Paulinus' letters.

[61] Dennis E. Trout, *Paulinus of Nola: Life, Letters, and Poems* (Berkeley/Los Angeles/London, 1999).

[62] Dennis E. Trout, *Secular Renunciation and Social Action: Paulinus of Nola and Late Roman Society* (PhD thesis: Duke University, 1989).

[63] Trout makes this explicit, *Secular Renunciation*, 364.

[64] Ibid., 360. Trout summarizes Paulinus' attitude to secular renunciation at 287: 'His developed theoretical position is founded upon several principles rich in traditional nuances:

political significance of many of Paulinus' actions, decisions, and writings.
Trout especially emphasizes, for example, the provocative nature of
Paulinus' withdrawal—often characterized (not least, as we have seen, in
Paulinus' own time) as a matter of simply slipping into a pre-existent role,
rather than as the ongoing invention of that role amidst a proliferation of
competing discourses and positions.[65] Paulinus, in Trout's account, is
constantly sensitive to the pressures towards continuity upon those
around him; he is endlessly resourceful in his accommodation of them,
while always insisting upon the importance of a reorientation towards
Christ.

My own study should be seen as in many ways complementary to that of
Trout: while not expressly developed in dialogue with it, the correspond-
ences in many places have emerged as extremely fruitful, and will be
repeatedly signalled in my notes. In counterpoise with Trout's portrayal
of a politically embattled Paulinus—his troubled encounters with Vigilantius, Origenism, Pelagianism—I trace Paulinus' spiritualization of
experience: his attempts to interpret and reframe the murky complexities
of human life in a truly theological light. This is far from a contradiction of
the socio-political engagement upon which Trout insists: it is an elucida-
tion of another approach, one which emphasizes interiority, and which is
arguably—if the survival of the body of his letters is not to be attributed
purely to chance—one for which Paulinus was particularly appreciated in
his own time.

Notwithstanding their slender interpretative tradition, the letters of
Paulinus are of particular interest for a number of reasons. The range of
his correspondents is extraordinary: directly or indirectly, he was connected with practically every important figure of the Christian Latin West
in his time. His letter collection is therefore significant as an entrée to
other epistolary exchanges between the Western fathers of the Church. It
also straddles the classical and Christian traditions, the converting aristo-
cracy and the converted middle classes, in a most remarkable manner.

Above all, the letters repay reading in their own right. They bear
witness to Paulinus' literary enactment of his commitment to Christianity

an adamant insistence on the dangerous and deceptive nature of worldly goods; a subordination of all other elements of conversion to the absolute necessity of a total inner reorientation,
and a correlative emphasis on mental detachment from possessions; and an advocacy of the
proper use of riches, not their heedless rejection.'

[65] Trout's new declaration of intent is that he aims 'to centre Paulinus' life within the
complicated nexus of political, military, cultural, and spiritual forces shaping the late antique
world'. Trout, *Paulinus*, 104.

and his realization of an individual mode of Christian expression. Paulinus' intellectual and spiritual influence upon those to whom he wrote well exceeds any previous estimation. His obliquity of style is notorious, and I have intermittently resorted, as a heuristic device, to 'reading' Paulinus' ideas through the more precisely-articulated words of Augustine; this device is, however, more than justified when in the final chapter we see how crucially influential Paulinus' overall notion of Christian selfhood was upon Augustine. The sense of an ongoing conversation between Paulinus and Augustine extends well beyond the coincidence that this is the only section of Paulinus' prose correspondence of which both sides, albeit in part, survive,[66] and significantly develops the tentative picture of interaction previously sketched by other scholars.[67]

My emphasis on the intellectual and spiritual significance of the letters, as opposed to the metrical works, is deliberate, and—with the exception of the metrical epistolary exchange with Ausonius—it will be seen that Paulinus' poems very much take second place here. There are several reasons for this. First, I shall be arguing that the epistolary medium—its flexibility, and its particular fusion of the public and private spheres—is ideally suited to the development and enactment of Paulinus' ideas. Moreover, it had especial significance, both historically and in the fourth century, for the creation and reinforcement of a sense of community within the Christian Church. Second, the ideas and stylistic traits which I shall be examining, while also frequently evinced in the poems, are undoubtedly present in their most distilled form in the prose letters. Third, with especial reference to the group of poems known as the *Natalicia*, to which I shall refer most often, these works raise their own issues of performance, audience, and context; their purpose was broadly similar to that of the prose letters, in the promulgation of a particular set of ideas of Christian community, but their distinctive nuances need independent treatment elsewhere.

The letters gain particular importance from the fact that it is clear that Paulinus was renowned for them in his own lifetime. Sanctus provides him with an 'adnotatio epistolarum', a catalogue of his own letters; Paulinus writes to reprove Amandus for so exaggerating his merit that

---

[66] Pierre Courcelle has attempted to fill in the gaps: 'Les lacunes dans la correspondance entre s. Augustin et Paulin de Nole', *RÉA* 53 (1951), 253–300.

[67] See, for example, J. J. O'Donnell's edition of Augustine *Confessions* (Oxford, 1992), 2. 362: '. . . the text of [Paulinus'] letters . . . is a tissue of scriptural language to an even greater degree than is true of *conf.* A[ugustine] must have been impressed by this, and it was surely one element in the forging of the distinctive style of *conf.*'

their mutual mentor Delphinus has requested from him a letter—for why, he demands, would Delphinus have thought him capable of writing something spiritually worthy if Amandus had not been so persuasive?[68] Notwithstanding the brevity of the account in the *Epistola de Obitu S. Paulini*, Paulinus' letters are twice mentioned as crucial points of contact with the great man. Everyone had wished to see and know him; and 'qui corpore eum videre non poterant, saltem eius epistolas contingere cupiebant. Erat enim suavis et blandus in litteris...' ('those who could not see him in person wished at least to make contact with his letters. For he was sweet and charming in his letters...').[69]

However, it is equally clear that Paulinus kept no record or copies of his own letters. The same letter to Sanctus qualifies the mention of the letters with 'quas meas esse indicastis', 'which you have told me are mine', and goes on, 'nam vere prope omnium earum ita inmemor eram, ut meas esse non recognoscerem, nisi vestris litteris credidissem' ('For I had certainly so forgotten almost all of them, that I wouldn't have recognized them as mine if I hadn't believed your letter').[70] This is in marked contrast to Paulinus' own correspondent, Augustine, who made a habit of keeping copies of his own letters—and, presumably, the letters of several of his correspondents: witness the letters from Paulinus, Nebridius, and Jerome to be gleaned from the Augustinian collection[71]—and intended to catalogue and comment on them in his *Reconsiderations*.[72] Augustine's care over his own letters at least begins to account for the fact that a far more extensive and arguably more representative sample of Augustine's correspondence remains to us. For example, a significant proportion of the

---

[68] *Letter* 41. 1 replies to Sanctus; Paulinus' reproof to Amandus, *Letter* 9. 1. Delphinus' request is fulfilled in *Letter* 10.

[69] *De Obitu* 9 (col. 864B); see also col. 864A: Paulinus 'alios epistolis, alios sumptibus adiuvabat'.

[70] Paulinus, *Letter* 41. 1. Typically, Paulinus attaches significance to Sanctus' gesture as a proof of *caritas*: 'unde maius accepi documentum caritatis vestrae, quia plus me vobis quam mihi notum esse perspexi'.

[71] Further evidence is supplied by a remark in a letter to Seleuciana, who appears to have misconstrued a point of doctrine: '...exemplum epistulae tuae, ne forsitan tu non habeas, misi tibi, in quo diligentius consideres ad ea me respondere, quae inveni in litteris tuis...' *Letter* 265. 1. See also Hans Lietzmann, 'Zur Entstehungsgeschichte der Briefsammlung Augustins', in *Kleine Schriften*, Texte und Untersuchungen zur Geschichte der altchristlichen Literatur 67 (Berlin, 1958).

[72] See Augustine, *Letter* 224. 2, written in 428, four years before his death, to Quodvultdeus: 'Et duo iam volumina absolveram retractatis omnibus libris meis... restabant epistulae, deinde tractatus populares, quas Graeci homilias vocant. Et plurimas iam epistularum legeram, sed adhuc nihil inde dictaveram...'

letters is concerned with the minutiae of church administration, a further
sheaf with his confrontations with Donatism or Pelagianism; yet despite
the fact that Paulinus too was a bishop and presumably had similar
concerns, such topics are entirely unrepresented in his surviving
letters. Our only hint, for example, that Paulinus may have held *audientia
episcopalis* comes from a brief allusion in the *De Obitu Paulini*;[73] we
have no idea whether he ever publicly combatted heresy (despite an urgent
letter from Augustine and Alypius on the subject of Pelagianism[74]), or
was asked for doctrinal advice. His response, indeed, to a question
of Augustine's about resurrection would suggest that he was uncomfort-
able with formal theological discussion, though it may imply that he was a
more accomplished adviser 'de praesenti vitae . . . statu' ('on the present
way of life').[75] For that matter, we are indebted to the Augustinian
corpus for the fullest preservation of the epistolary exchange between
Augustine and Paulinus.[76] As we have seen, this is a particularly
happy accident of survival, and the exchange will be frequently referred
to.

The boundaries of letter-collections from the fourth century are per-
force ill-defined, owing to the publication techniques of the period.
Certainly there was no technique which reflected the modern one of
simultaneously releasing on to the market multiple copies of a single
work.[77] In a sense, any written work, once directed to a recipient, became
'published' automatically, for it seems to have been assumed that sending
out such a work conferred the right to communicate its contents and,
indeed, to take copies.[78] Often, the 'publication' of a treatise entailed
merely sending it to another party, under a covering letter bestowing the

---

[73] *De Obitu* 7 (col. 863): 'nunquam in iudicio sine misericordia sedit . . . et . . . tenebat
rigorem in examinatione iustitiae, misericordiam autem in definitione sententiae profere-
bat.'
[74] Augustine, *Letter* 186.
[75] See Paulinus, *Letter* 45. 4.
[76] Hartel, Praef., xvi: 'uberrimam messem novarum epistularum corpus S. Augustini
obtulit, in quo epistulae 3, 4, 6, 7, 8, 45, 50 exstabant.' See again Lietzmann, 'Entstehungsgeschichte', 278; and the discussion of manuscripts of Paulinus in my Appendix.
[77] H.-I. Marrou, 'La technique de l'édition à l'époque patristique', *VChr* 3 (1949), 208–24:
question of parallel to modern publication posed, 216; answered in the negative, 221. The
argument in this paragraph is indebted to this article.
[78] The prologue to Augustine's *Reconsiderations* betrays a strong sense of the irreversibility
of publication: 'scribere autem ista mihi placuit, ut haec emittam in manus hominum, a
quibus ea quae iam edidi *revocare emendanda non possum.*' *Retr.* Prol. 3. See further the
discussion of public/private in Chapters 2 and 6 below.

right—or even the obligation—to publicize its contents.[79] How, then, in this instance would the treatise be considered as published and the letter not? Few authors of the fourth century were as textually aware as Augustine, with his public revision, in the *Reconsiderations*, of texts already released; there is no internal evidence to suggest that Paulinus would have considered it necessary to collect or reissue his own letters after their first 'publication', their simple direction to a recipient.

It must be acknowledged, then, that any reference to the 'corpus' or 'collection' of Paulinus' letters probably invokes a latter-day construct, and not a body of writing which Paulinus himself would have recognized. Although Paulinus' fame survived his death, it seems to have been preserved anecdotally and not through continued attention to his literary works—least of all his letters. Perhaps the themes of the letters became dated or superseded; perhaps their Latinity was too complex for later generations. At any rate, Reinelt concludes: 'In general, Paulinus' heroic renunciation, his love of neighbour, and the miracles ascribed to him counted for much more than his letters.'[80] We may infer that Paulinus' letters, left uncollected in his own lifetime, are likely to have been somewhat haphazardly and partially gathered after his death.[81]

The probable lack of a single archetype for the manuscripts of Paulinus' letters, and the fragmentary nature of the correspondence drawn from other sources, bear one extremely important implication for this study. We must take into account the possibility that these letters were selected for preservation for precisely the characteristics which we are to explore: for their significance in the burgeoning genre of Christian literature as exquisite expressions of Christian friendship, as texts for meditation, and

---

[79] See C. Lambot, 'Lettre inédite de S. Augustin relative au *De Civitate Dei*', *RBen* 51 (1939), 109–121. Marrou comments: 'Rien de plus clair: l'exemplaire de la *Cité de Dieu* adressé à Firmus *n'est pas destiné qu'à lui*' (my emphasis), 'Technique', 219. The letter to Firmus is now conveniently printed as a prefatory text to the CCSL edition of *De Civitate Dei* (iii–iv).

[80] 'Im allgemeinen aber galten die heroische Entsagung Paulins, seine Nächstenliebe und die ihm zugeschriebenen Wunder viel mehr als seine Briefe.' Reinelt, *Studien*, 68. Reinelt also gathers together (68–70) the negative modern (i.e. nineteenth-century) opinions on Paulinus, ending with the scathing judgement of Kaufmann on Paulinus' 'Heuchelei' and 'Koketterie'!

[81] Hartel says, 'epistulae...mox post Paulini mortem ab amicis collectae fuisse videntur...' (Praef., v), but offers no firm corroborating evidence beyond the suggestion from *Letter* 41 to Sanctus. See Appendix for more detailed observations on the manuscript tradition of Paulinus' letters, and the way in which they appear to have been collected.

as fine exemplars of the process of Christian communication.[82] If this is the case, it far from vitiates the work—indeed, it would show the contemporary importance of the phenomena which we shall isolate for discussion; but it does mean that extrapolation to the generality of late antique Latin letters should, and will, be made with caution.

We shall start from a close reading of the letters of Paulinus, to produce what is essentially a thematic commentary upon them. Chapter 1 begins with a systematic examination of the circumstances of delivery of letters in late antiquity: the chapter discusses such issues as the norms (or their contravention) for composing letters, and the role of the letter-carrier in augmenting their message. This leads directly in to Chapter 2, which discovers a sacramental purpose to Christian epistolography, and concludes that the process of composition and distribution of letters has important implications for ideas about the distribution of public and private spheres in late antiquity, and for appreciation of the texture and philosophical basis of Christian life at the period.

The third chapter takes its cue from this dynamic to study ideas of Christian friendship as they are developed and played out in epistolary exchange. Letters express the love of friends, which reflects and is enriched by Christ's love; in loving a friend more fully, one will also love Christ more fully, and hence become more fully Christian. We shall see that the entire process of communication surrounding the composition of the physical letters constantly explores and re-enacts this experience. Chapter 4 explores the patterns of thought with which this perpetual relation of the spiritual to the temporal, the invisible to the visible, is accomplished, and concludes that it is due to an essentially imagistic (and hence non-linear) manner of framing experience and making connections. This assertion is based on the many densely imagistic passages in Paulinus: it is developed, in Chapter 5, in a detailed reading of two extended examples of these passages. We shall take the opportunity of reading these imagistic passages alongside the similar characteristics to be found in the

---

[82] Perhaps this, combined with the lack of interest in literary posterity which apparently led Paulinus to preserve neither his own letters nor those of his correspondents, may explain the preservation of Paulinus' letters in the face of the loss of Sulpicius'. Note Stancliffe's comments on Sulpicius' very different prose style, *Saint Martin*, 38–41: although she suggests that his letters may have been written in a style closer to that of Paulinus—especially with regard to his techniques of biblical allusion—the only evidence on which Stancliffe bases this idea is the perceived 'literalism' of Sulpicius' biblical interpretation in an extremely vexed passage at Paulinus *Letter* 23. 27 (*Saint Martin* 43; For my own discussion of this passage, see Chapter 5, nn. 2 and 5).

visual arts of the period, as well as exploring in greater depth the theological implications of this figural style.

The sixth, and concluding, chapter investigates ideas of the self and of personal identity that the conclusions of the preceding studies entail. 'Personal identity' is considered as not necessarily coextensive with either the philosophical self or the soul, but as something closer to the modern, untechnical 'sense of self'. This chapter finds that the self in late antiquity is, in a most thoroughgoing sense, relational. The implications for the interactions of individuals, both within monasteries and in the broader Christian community, are immense, and form indirectly Paulinus' most important contribution to Christian thought. There are, moreover, important consequences for the notion of the transformation wrought by conversion, which will be explored in a detailed reading of the correspondence between Ausonius and Paulinus. The self is always configured as completed by God; yet, despite some conscientious attempts—for good historical reasons—to think of the self as purely spiritual, it remains strongly associated with a physical entity.

Several themes are suggested which span the divisions artificially imposed on this study by the arrangement of the chapters. Most importantly, there is the theme of striving for understanding of the relationship between the temporal and spiritual realms, so often framed in an appreciation of symbolic value in things, events, or people. This is inseparable from the theological project, prompted by dwelling on the significance of Christ's incarnation, of assigning value to material things. Since the assignment of symbolic value to the temporal realm is founded in the habituation to imagistic patterns of thought, the two chapters on images, while in many ways the most speculative in this work, also form the pivot of my argument. They try to recreate the significance of the Christian attachment to finding meaning in paradox—another theme which runs throughout the study; and their explanatory force is tested in their attempt to make less rebarbative the extensive imagistic *jeux d'esprit* to be found in Paulinus' letters, which have tended to disgust or to mystify modern taste. Also of importance are the effects of an ideally communitarian existence on patterns of thought and responses. That such an existence should be significant for the way in which friendships are formulated and sustained should be immediately apparent; but, as I shall argue, a sense of community is of equal significance in formulating a sense of self. Finally, the impression of a conscious creation and enactment of new ideas about how to live a Christian life pervades the letters of Paulinus and his correspondents. These are often based upon the notion of imitation as a positive, creative concept—an oddity in this age which prizes 'originality', but, as we shall see, a fundamental aspect of engagement with Christ for Paulinus and his peers. While these Christian ideas are inevitably linked to antecedent modes of thought, they strive, severally and collectively, towards the expression of Christianity.

I

Ipsae litterae: the actual letters

A study of the ideas in the letters of Paulinus of Nola must begin by establishing the nature of the letters themselves. What constitutes a 'letter' has been interminably discussed and redefined.[1] Scholars of the New Testament have been especially assiduous in their quest for schematic distinctions between types of and typical themes in letters;[2] but so, of course, were those few who wrote on the subject in late antiquity.[3] It is not my purpose here to enter this debate: it is clear that Paulinus and his correspondents had a working notion of *litterae* or *epistulae*, and my purpose in the first two chapters is to teaze out, from internal evidence in the letters, the contents of this working notion. That this on occasion includes what have subsequently been designated as theological treatises is a possibility I am willing to embrace, and which will be illuminated by discussions to follow.[4]

In brief: my interest in these chapters lies above all with the letters as historical events. By speaking of letters as 'historical events', I attempt to include far more than merely the textual traces of the correspondence: the letters of late antiquity, though abundant, are imperfectly and incompletely preserved; the superscriptions indicating recipients, which might be

---

[1] Reviewed in brief by Giles Constable, *Letters and Letter-Collections*, Typologie des Sources du Moyen Age Occidental 17 (Turnhout, 1976), 11–25; useful caveats against 'a modern frame of reference and anachronistic criteria' for judging antique and medieval letters, 12–13. For an overview of the tradition in antiquity and (briefly) the early Christian period, see 'Epistolographie', *RE* Supplementband v, 185–220.

[2] Dating at least from Deissmann's letter/epistle distinction, which is entirely unhelpful for the letters of late antiquity (and increasingly regarded as of questionable value even for the letters of Paul: see recently Harry Y. Gamble, *Books and Readers in the Early Church* (New Haven and London, 1995), esp. 32–40).

[3] These sources have been usefully gathered by Abraham J. Malherbe, *Ancient Epistolary Theorists*, Society of Biblical Literature Sources for Biblical Study 19 (Atlanta 1988); note especially the contribution of Pseudo-Libanius, 66 ff.

[4] We may in any case note the observation of Marrou, that methods of publication in the fourth century account for 'la frontière indécise qui, dans la littérature patristique, sépare lettres et traités'. He also cites instances of patristic uncertainty about whether to categorize a work as letter or treatise. 'Technique', 221 and 222 respectively.

thought to be the most reliable indicators of their epistolary status, do not reliably survive. What must also be taken into account is the entire nexus of communication which surrounded these textual traces, the written documents. This could include everything from supplementary notes, which have not survived, through gifts of one sort or another sent with the letter, to verbal messages brought by the letter-carriers.[5] Indeed, I shall argue that what we refer to as a letter was often a relatively insignificant part of this more general and various communication. My first chapter will set out what this communication seems to have entailed, and explore the various mechanisms operating around the letters' carriage and exchange; Chapter 2 will concern itself with the wider implications of the form and function of the letters, and lay the groundwork to applying them for the study of Paulinus and of late antiquity more generally.

A variety of models for letters would have been available to a writer such as Paulinus, whose increasing commitment to Christianity belied his classical training.[6] As a Christian, his obvious model was the letters of Saint Paul to the early Christian communities, letters marked by their tension between the personal and the preaching voice, their studied simplicity and directness, and their combination of Christian instruction, admonishment, and reflective exposition. Paulinus drew heavily on many of Saint Paul's themes and phrases, as will be seen; but his inspiration for the form of epistolary composition seems to have come for the most part from elsewhere. His pagan education would certainly have included a familiarity with the letters of Cicero and Seneca, and he would probably have had some knowledge of Pliny;[7] we know, not least from echoes in his verse correspondence with Ausonius, that he had read the lyric poetry of

---

[5] As John Matthews has pointed out in his study of the letters of Symmachus: 'It is clear . . . that the letters were not always intended to say everything that we might expect of them.' He discusses the extra-textual aspects of the letters in 'The Letters of Symmachus', in J. W. Binns (ed.) *Latin Literature of the Fourth Century* (London/Boston, 1974), 63–4.

[6] We know little specifically of Paulinus' education; for some careful reconstruction, see Trout, *Paulinus*, 28–30. What we know of his mentor Ausonius' career and reading (see the references in Introduction, n. 12) may supply some guide, though it is apparent that Paulinus' Greek was very much inferior to that of Ausonius, and he was probably never at home reading in the language. Werner Erdt tries to trace Paulinus' attitude to classical education through a commentary on his letter to the pagan Jovius, *Christentum und heidnisch-antike Bildung bei Paulin von Nola mit Kommentar und Übersetzung des 16. Briefes*, Beiträge zur Klassischen Philologie 82 (Meisenheim, 1976). More generally, see H.-I. Marrou, *Histoire de l'éducation dans l'antiquité* (6th edn., Paris, 1965).

[7] On the survival of Pliny into late antiquity, and his likely appeal to such epistolographers as Ausonius and Symmachus, see Alan Cameron, 'The Fate of Pliny's Letters in the Late Empire', *CQ* NS 15 (1965), 289–98.

Horace, and he may well have had some knowledge of Horace's hexameter epistles too. (Certainly, Paulinus wrote several letters that enact the assumption that letters may be written in metrical form as well as prose:[8] this will be discussed further below.) Cicero had set the model for a letter as half of a conversation between friends, a purportedly informal purveyor of news and gossip[9]—yet at the same time, optionally a vehicle for self-advertisement and political advancement; Seneca had written a set of didactic philosophical essays on moral improvement, all addressed to a single 'pupil', Lucilius, which make no pretence of representing a private correspondence. The letters of Pliny, however, set a pattern for an ambiguity of public and private voice which, as we shall see, resonates closely with the practice of Paulinus: his collection begins with a dedicatory note to the equestrian Septicius Clarus, 'Frequenter hortatus es ut epistulas, si quas paulo curatius scripsissem, colligerem publicaremque' ('You have often encouraged me to collect and publish any letters which I have written with rather more care than usual').[10] This lays the claim that the letters had their origin in a genuine correspondence, while acknowledging both Pliny's editorial and arranging hand, and his care for polished composition in the first place. Pliny also insists on the need for brevity in correspondence, and prefers that each letter should explore a single theme.[11]

With this literary context, the letters of late antiquity established a certain rhetoric of epistolary norms to which they frequently advert. I speak of 'norms' rather than theory because reading epistolary theory, however contemporaneous, back into the letters of late antiquity leads to awkward confusions and elisions.[12] However, as we shall see, this

[8] *Letter* 16, to Jovius, is paralleled by *Poem* 22, to the same; *Letter* 8, to Licentius, is supplemented with a long metrical treatment of the same theme. *Poems* 1 and 2 are very early, pre-renunciation examples of epistolary poems; *Poems* 10 and 11 Paulinus' side of the famous correspondence with Ausonius. *Poem* 24, by far the longest of the Christian epistolary poems, is addressed to the Aquitanian noble Cytherius, and has many thematic similarities with *Letter* 23.

[9] A typical epistolary phrase from Cicero: 'Ego, etsi nihil habeo, quod ad te scribam, scribo tamen, *quia tecum loqui videor*', *Ad Atticum* 12. 53. Cicero prefers the use of *sermo quotidianus*; he also insists on the need for jocularity in private letters.

[10] Pliny, *Letter* 1. 1. 1.

[11] Sherwin-White summarizes the letters which form exceptions to this rule: see A. N. Sherwin-White, *The Letters of Pliny: A Historical and Social Commentary* (Oxford, 1966), 3–4.

[12] And, ultimately, statements like the following, which are simply not borne out by the letters of late antiquity: 'Letter writers such as Basil, Gregory of Nyssa, Gregory of Nazianzus, Synesius, Ambrose, Jerome, and Augustine tend to follow the "textbooks" on rhetoric and epistolary theory.' Stanley K. Stowers, *Letter-Writing in Greco-Roman Antiquity* (Philadelphia, 1986), 24. The inverted commas are revealing: what 'textbooks' on epistolary theory?

rhetoric tends to be invoked negatively, in circumstances asserted as a departure from its restrictions. A reading of the internal evidence from the letters is invaluable in investigating the practices of epistolary composition. This rhetoric of epistolary norms is seen exquisitely expressed in the intricate and minimalist letters of Paulinus' pagan contemporary Symmachus. Symmachus' sense of epistolary priorities seems to owe a great deal to Pliny,[13] and it is his model which seems to be most vivid to Paulinus. We are fortunate that in the Symmachan collection there has survived a letter to his son (also Symmachus), advising him on the proper composition of a letter:

Scintillare acuminibus atque sententiis epistulas tuas gaudeo; decet enim loqui exultantius iuvenalem calorem. sed volo, ut in aliis materiis aculeis orationis utaris, huic autem generi scriptionis maturum aliquid et comicum misceas; quod tibi etiam rhetorem tuum credo praecipere. nam ut in vestitu hominum ceteroque vitae cultu loco ac tempori apta sumuntur, ita ingeniorum varietas in familiaribus scriptis neglegentiam quandam debet imitari, in forensibus vero quatere arma facundiae. sed de his non ibo longius...[14]

I am delighted that your letters shimmer with pungent opinions; youthful warmth ought to speak with some exuberance. However, I wish you to use your darts of rhetoric on other matters, while for this type of writing, please mix in something considered and amusing—which I believe your teacher also advises you to do. For just as things appropriate to the place and occasion are adopted in men's attire and the rest of their way of life, a corresponding variation of character should imitate a certain insouciance in letters to friends, but brandish the weapons of eloquence in public writings. But I won't pursue this subject further...

The *Thesaurus Linguae Latinae* lists *forensis* as an antonym to *domesticus*: Symmachus is invoking the forensic eloquence fostered in his son's education, and hence the traditional division between public and private spheres of life which Christians of Paulinus' generation are to reinterpret.[15] His advice for private letters is, be witty; be versatile; be learned—but wear your learning lightly. Symmachus himself exemplifies his behest in the composition of his letter. He passes swiftly on to his next subject ('non ibo longius' ('I shan't go on about it')), for the cardinal rule of such

---

[13] See Cameron, 'Fate of Pliny's Letters'.

[14] Symmachus, *Letter* 7. 9.

[15] *TLL* 6. 1, col. 1054. This use of *forensis* also, of course, draws on its literal sense of 'quod in foro est, versatur, agitur...' (col. 1052), and thereby recalls the Roman rhetorical basis of the younger Symmachus' education.

correspondence is to be brief[16]—charmingly expressed in a letter to Paulinus' one-time tutor Ausonius:

> Petis a me litteras longiores. est hoc in nos veri amoris indicium. sed ego qui sim paupertini ingenii mei conscius, Laconicae malo studere brevitati quam multiiugis paginis infantiae meae maciem publicare.[17]

You are asking for longer letters from me. This is a mark of your true love for me. But since I am aware of my utterly impoverished talent, I prefer to strive for Laconian brevity rather than publicize my meagre burbling in manifold pages.

(This provides a telling context for a request from Augustine to Jerome for a longer letter, for from so great a man 'nullus sermo prolixus est', no speech is too long.[18])

In Christian letters of the period, the desired aim of conciseness is usually expressed as a fear of engendering *taedium* or *fatigatio* in the correspondents. So Paulinus avers at the end of a letter to his catechist Amandus, future bishop of Bordeaux, 'vellem quantum in me est adhuc prorogare sermonem, nisi et carta deficiens et *metus fatigationis tuae* cogeret verbis modum poni et epistolam terminari' ('I would like to draw out the conversation as long as I could, but the shortage of space and my fear of exhausting you compel me to put a limit to my words and conclude the letter').[19]

The idea of the *modus* of a letter as its appropriate length recurs notably in Jerome's renowned letter to Paulinus on the interpretation of scripture: 'cernis me scripturarum amore raptum excessisse *modum epistolae*...' ('you see that, in being carried away by my love of the scriptures, I have exceeded the due length of a letter').[20] (However, he proceeds undeterred to expound the 'novum breviter testamentum'!) The fear of tiring a correspondent or of going on too long is often given a peculiarly Christian twist by being characterized lightly as a *peccatum*. Paulinus poses a problem to Florentius:

---

[16] On *brevitas*-formulae (though without specific application to an epistolary context), see Ernst Robert Curtius, *European Literature and the Latin Middle Ages*, tr. Willard R. Trask (repr. Princeton, 1990), *Excursus* XIII; this also briefly treats of the theme of the *taedium* caused by lack of *brevitas*.

[17] Symmachus, *Letter* 1. 14.

[18] Augustine, *Letter* 40. 1.

[19] Paulinus, *Letter* 12. 11. For 'metus fatigationis tuae' see also *Letter* 19. 4 (to Delphinus); also 'nimium vos fatigo' in 41. 3 (to Sanctus), 'loquacius vos fatigo', in 39. 8 (to Aper and Amanda).

[20] Jerome, *Letter* 53. 9.

dum pluribus apud te verbis ago, ut pro peccatis meis vel potius adversus peccata mea promerear, cum orationes intendas, adcumulo eandem de loquacitate mea sarcinam, quam de orationibus tuis minui peto, tamquam inmemor scriptum: 'de multiloquio non effugies peccatum' [Prov. 10: 19].[21]

While I am pouring out verbiage to you, asking that I should win you over on behalf of my sins—or rather, against my sins—when you direct your prayers, I am heaping up that same burden from loquacity which I am seeking to lessen from your prayers, as if I have forgotten that it is written: 'with respect to garrulity, you shall not escape sin'.

The same passage from Proverbs resonates in the background when Paulinus justifies his lengthy remonstration with Sulpicius Severus over the latter's plans to place a portrait of Paulinus in his baptistry: 'ita te diligo, ut magis de non obtemperando tibi quam de multiloquio peccatum timerem'. ('I love you so much that I feared sin more from not checking you than from garrulity').[22] And he opens a letter to Delphinus as follows, neatly summing up the obligations of epistolary exchange: 'oportebat quidem nos sapientiae doctrinam servantes, iugum linguae nostrae et stateram verbis inponere, ut et de multiloquio nostro et de tua fatigatione *geminandum* nobis *peccatum* evaderemus' ('now, I ought to keep the counsel of wisdom and impose a yoke on my tongue and a balance on my words, so as to avoid incurring the *double sin* of my garrulity and your exhaustion').[23]

The idea of a letter as an *officium*, often expressed in Symmachus (and indeed in classical letter collections before him), remains prevalent in Christian correspondence.[24] The term itself is often used; and the idea that it represents, of the duty for measured and regular epistolary exchange, is almost invariably present. In a letter to Rufinus, who is about to leave Rome for the East, Paulinus fears not performing the *officium* of writing more than the possible wasted effort (*damnum*) if the letter fails to reach Rufinus before he leaves.[25] Similarly, the opportune presence of carriers reminds Paulinus to send the 'officium litterarum mearum', the 'affectionate obligation of my letters', to Eucherius and

---

[21] Paulinus, *Letter* 42. 5.

[22] Paulinus, *Letter* 32. 4. For the conjunction of 'multiloquium' and 'peccatum', see also 12. 2 (the letter to Amandus quoted above).

[23] Paulinus, *Letter* 20. 1.

[24] On the writing of letters as an *officium* for Symmachus, see Philippe Bruggisser, *Symmaque ou le rituel épistolaire de l'amitié littéraire* (Fribourg, 1993), 'Les *officia* de l'épistolier', 4–16.

[25] Paulinus, *Letter* 47. 1.

Galla at Lérins.[26] The first letter of Paulinus to Augustine is 'officium nostrum', and letter-writing an 'officium' in a letter to Severus.[27] Even after the disastrous encounter in letters between Augustine and Jerome, the latter feels obliged to perform the *officium* of continuing the correspondence, if in the most abbreviated form possible. He grudgingly refers to a letter as a 'promptum ... salutationis officium', a 'punctual obligatory greeting'.[28]

The frequency of the correspondence is of importance. Apologies are made for a letter that is considered belated: both Paulinus and Jerome open their letters of consolation to Pammachius on the death of his wife Paulina with an explanation of, or apology for, their delay in writing.[29] The normal expectation is of a regular reciprocated exchange, occurring about once a year. This expectation is made explicit in the case of Paulinus and Sulpicius: 'sat enim nobis erat *annuis commeatibus* emereri litteras tuas ...' ('for we were satisfied with deserving your letters *at yearly intervals* ...').[30] The expected frequency of exchange is of particular interest, given the distance that the letter-carriers were obliged to travel.[31] Deviations from the norm of annual exchange are a cause of concern: 'quid est, qui duas aestates easdemque in Africa sitire cogamur?' ('what's wrong, that we should be forced to thirst for two summers—and those in Africa?') demands Augustine of Paulinus.[32] (The emphasis is interesting in view of Augustine's recent return to Africa from a far more urbane life in Milan, at the centre of things.) Overriding the respondent's duty of reciprocation also merits apology: there is an anxious concern to explain a letter sent out of turn in Paulinus' second letter to Augustine:

et credo in manu et in gratia domini sermonem meum ad te fuisse perlatum; sed morante adhuc puero, quem ad te aliosque dilectos aeque deo salutandos ante

---

[26] Paulinus, *Letter* 51. 2.

[27] Paulinus, *Letter* 6. 1 and 17. 2.

[28] Jerome, *Letter* 103. 1. Ambrose too may refer to a letter as 'officium'—for example, 'aliquod officium sermonis mei', 8. 61 (=Maur. 89), to Alypius.

[29] Paulinus, *Letter* 13. 2 (note 'officium' again): 'si forte id ipsum culpae magis quam gratiae iudicetur, quod tardius fungar officio caritatis ...'; Jerome, *Letter* 66. 1: '... ego, serus consolator, qui inportune per biennium tacui ...'

[30] Paulinus, *Letter* 23. 2. See also the thanksgiving for the return of the carrier Cardamas after two years' absence in *Letter* 19. 1 (to Delphinus).

[31] For an estimate of the distance one could expect to travel in a day—probably 30–35 km.—see Othmar Perler, *Les Voyages de Saint Augustin* (Paris, 1969), 31–32, 'Rapidité des voyages'.

[32] Augustine, *Letter* 42.

hiemem miseramus, non potuimus ultra et officium nostrum suspendere et desi-
derium sermonis tui cupidissimum temperare.[33]

I do believe that my letter was brought to you in the Lord's hand and his grace; but
since the servant is still detained, whom I had sent before winter to greet you and
other people equally beloved of God, I could no longer postpone my obligation or
restrain my most avid desire for your conversation.[34]

Similar anxieties are expressed by Augustine: in his third letter to Jerome,
for example, he assumes (correctly!) that Jerome must be offended, since
he has had no reply to his previous sallies.[35] Indeed, the presumption of
regularity in epistolary exchange seems to be universal.[36]

However, the written text of the letter, and its forms and conventions, is
only the beginning of the historical event represented by epistolary
exchange. Other important exchanges, beyond the textual one, are taking
place. Often the text of the letter is accompanied by some sort of gift for
the addressee. This practice, once again, represents a Christian permutation of pagan aristocratic habits: it continues the ceremonial function of
gift-giving, while the symbolism of the ceremony is radically changed.[37]
Where previously Paulinus would have sent a correspondent delicacies
from his estates (despatching 'pauculas ficedulas' ('a few little fig-peckers')
to Gestidius[38]), he now sent offerings appropriate to his Christian calling.
In his early months at Nola, he favoured gifts simply of bread: Augustine
and Sulpicius Severus were both recipients, and Romanianus and Licentius were each sent five *panes* as a *buccellatum*, a military ration, for their
Christian campaigns.[39] The symbolism of these gifts does not seem

---

[33] Paulinus, *Letter* 6. 1.

[34] It seems to me no coincidence that here, as so often elsewhere, 'sermo' may equally
happily be translated 'letter' or 'conversation', according to context: q.v. the ancient idea of a
letter as a conversation between those absent, referred to above; and see Ambrose, *Letter* 7. 48
(=Maur. 66). 1 (to Romulus): 'Epistularum genus propterea repertum, ut quidem nobis cum
absentibus sermo sit, in dubium non venit.'

[35] Augustine, *Letter* 67. 2.

[36] On the expectation of regular exchange elsewhere, see for example Symmachus, *Letter*
1. 26 (to Ausonius): 'dudum parcus es litterarum'; 8. 39 (to Dynamius): 'Queri de silentio meo
non potes, qui nihil scriptorum mihi hucusque tribuisti . . . Ero deinceps ad exercendum
stilum promptior, si me fructu mutui sermonis animaveris.'

[37] Trout, *Secular Renunciation*, 274 f.; for the classical period, see Richard P. Saller,
Personal Patronage in the Early Empire (Cambridge, 1982), 122–4.

[38] Paulinus, *Poem* 1. 1. 7 of prose section. *OLD* glosses 'ficedula' *ad loc.* as 'a small bird
esteemed a delicacy in Autumn when it feeds on figs and grapes'. For further examples of
these types of 'traditional delicacies', see Trout, *Paulinus*, 92.

[39] *Panis* to Augustine: Paulinus, *Letter* 4. 5; to Sulpicius: 5. 21; *panes* as *buccellatum*,
7. 3.

primarily to be a reference to Christ's blessing of bread—the *panes* are not apparently consecrated, and no reference is made to their possible use in a liturgical context. (Such a context is far from impossible, as the idea of the eucharistic meal is well established at this period, descending from the *chabûrah* meal in Jewish custom as well as the Lord's Supper.[40]) Rather, they are intended to reinforce Christian communion in a broader sense: thus Paulinus concludes his first letter to Augustine with the words 'panem unum, quem *unanimitatis indicio* misimus caritati tuae, rogamus accipiendo benedicas' ('please bless with your acceptance the bread which we have sent to your grace *as a mark of unanimity*').[41] The gifts represent a striving for connection, and, through connection, for blessing to the giver. This is made explicit, for example, in Paulinus' presentation of *panis Campanus* to Sulpicius:

Panem Campanum de cellula nostra tibi pro eulogia misimus, tantum meritis in domino tuis freti, ut plena ad te perferendum sui gratia crederemus; tu licet uberioribus micis a domini mensa iam saturatus sis, dignare et a peccatoribus acceptum in nomine domini panem in eulogiam vertere.[42]

We have sent Campanian bread from our own little monastery to you as a blessed offering, so confident in your merits in the Lord that we trust it will be brought to you in the fulness of its grace; though you have already been filled with richer morsels from the Lord's table, please turn the bread received in the Lord's name from sinners into a blessing.

A tension between the active and passive senses of *eulogia* hovers behind this passage: the word denotes a blessing *tout court* (=*benedictio*), but also has the technical meaning of bread blessed (as opposed to consecrated) and distributed to the people. The humble loaf of Campanian bread is both a blessing bestowed by Paulinus and one bestowed upon him: there is an elegant compliment to Sulpicius in the statement that it is his spiritual merits which act as guarantor of both blessings.

Paulinus also sends to Sulpicius a 'scutella buxea', a boxwood plate, and asks that he receives this with the bread as '*apophoreta* voti spiritalis': a further *double entendre* based on the fact that *apophoretum*, while it had come to mean 'offering', had originally referred specifically to a gift given

---

[40] See Andrew McGowan, *Ascetic Eucharists: food and drink in early Christian ritual meals* (Oxford, 1999) 'dual origins', 25–7; 'a tradition of using bread and wine as the central elements of a eucharistic meal emerged at a very early stage in many Christian communities', 91.

[41] Paulinus, *Letter* 4. 5.

[42] Paulinus, *Letter* 5. 21 again.

by the host to his guests after a meal.[43] What is of importance is that the
gifts should symbolize spiritual connection, and it is as such symbols that
they are received. Instead of showing esteem with the most *outré* delicacies
possible, the lowliness of the gift becomes a material expression of both
parties' spiritual commitment. This represents, I think, a rather richer
concept than Frend's description of Paulinus as 'a clearing house for the
exchange of opinions and books'.[44]

The gifts extend the message of the written letter. Alypius' gift to
Paulinus of Augustine's five treatises 'contra Manichaeos' (which have
not been securely identified[45]) seems to have initiated Paulinus'
correspondence with the clergy of North Africa, and is described as
'prima affectus sui documenta et caritatis tuae *pignora*' ('the first intima-
tions of his [Alypius'] affection and *pledges* of your [Augustine's] love').[46]
When the gift, as here, is a book or books, they are naturally significant not
only for their symbolic value but also for their contents. Gamble notes that
the ongoing exchange of letters and dissemination of texts served to create
and reinforce a 'strong sense of translocal unity' between Christian settle-
ments.[47] So there are two ways in which Christian gifts of books are
differentiated from non-Christian: by the nature of the material shared;
and, more importantly, by their place in a greater spiritual scheme.

To illustrate this, one may compare a pagan with a Christian letter for
content and tone; both have ostensibly the same purpose, to accompany a
gift of books. The first is a cover letter from Symmachus to Ausonius for a
present of Pliny's *Natural History*:

Si te amor habet naturalis historiae, quam Plinius elaboravit, en tibi libellos,
quorum mihi praesentanea copia fuit. in quis, ut arbitror, opulentae eruditioni
tuae neglegens veritatis librarius displicebit. sed mihi fraudi non erit emendationis

---

[43] For *eulogia*, see *TLL* 5. 2. 1048; for *apophoreta*, see Blaise s.v. *apophoretum*, and *TLL*
2. 250/1 s.v. *apophoretus*, both citing this passage.

[44] Frend, 'Two Worlds', 115.

[45] Augustine wrote no 'pentateuch', as Paulinus describes it (*Letter* 4. 2), against the
Manicheans; both Lietzmann ('Entstehungsgeschichte', 273, n. 1) and Fabre (*Chronologie*,
15, n. 3) follow Buse (cit. Fabre) in suggesting that the five books were *De vera religione*, *De
Genesi contra Manichaeos libri II*, *De moribus ecclesiae catholicae*, and *De moribus Mani-
chaeorum*.

[46] Paulinus, *Letter* 4. 5. For an account of the initiation of Paulinus' correspondence with
North Africa, see Trout, *Paulinus*, 116 and 204–5; also, briefly, *Paolino di Nola: Epistole ad
Agostino* ed. Teresa Piscitelli Carpino (Naples, 1989), 28 ff.

[47] Gamble, *Books and Readers*, 142. His conclusion here is that 'both the motive and the
means for the circulation of Christian writings far exceeded those affecting the currency of
non-Christian literature'.

incuria. malui enim tibi probari mei muneris celeritate, quam alieni operis examine. vale.[48]

If you are fond of the natural history over which Pliny laboured, here are the books for you, of which I have a current abundance and in which, I think, it will displease your abundant erudition that the copyist has been careless of the true version. But I shall not have done wrong[49] by neglecting to emend it, for I preferred that you should approve me for the promptitude of my gift, rather than for my scrutiny of someone else's work. Farewell.

How different is the tone of Augustine's presentation of 'aliqua scripta nostra', ('some of my writings'), to Jerome, with a request for careful criticism buttressed by quotations from the Psalms:

Sane idem frater aliqua scripta nostra fert secum. quibus legendis si dignationem adhibueris, etiam sinceram fraternamque severitatem adhibeas quaeso. non enim aliter intellego, quod scriptum est: 'emendabit me iustus in misericordia et arguet me; oleum autem peccatoris non inpinguet caput meum' [Ps. 140: 5], nisi quia magis amat obiurgator sanans quam adulator unguens caput.[50]

The same brother is carrying some of my writings with him. If you care to read them, please apply a sincere and fraternal strictness to them. For I understand by the scriptural passage 'the just man shall correct me in mercy and chastise me; but let not the oil of the sinner enrich my head' precisely that the constructive critic displays more love than a flatterer anointing one's head.

Both writers note the need for critical emendation of the accompanying texts, but in Symmachus, the haste of the copyist proves the impetuous warmth of his friendship; in Augustine, his awareness of the deficiencies of the text denotes a humble desire for self-improvement. Further to this comparison, we may note that Augustine is sending his own work, Symmachus someone else's (and that of an author long dead). Late Roman aristocratic *mores* considered the unsolicited gift of one's own work as verging on vulgar self-advertisement.[51] But these Christian literary connections support a living, burgeoning tradition: the works exchanged are not monuments, but works in progress, and the act of their exchange—and the process of emending and commenting upon them—reinforces the

---

[48] Symmachus, *Letter* 1. 24.

[49] *TLL* 6. 1. 1268 lists 'fraudi est' as a legal term ('illicere...fallendo'), and cites this passage.

[50] Augustine, *Letter* 28. 6.

[51] For example, Symmachus, *Letter* 1. 14, exhorts Ausonius to send him a copy of his *Moselle*.

sense of community which the texts of the letters themselves create and maintain.[52]

Paulinus is a typical participant in this Christian literary community. Sulpicius sends him a work for historical emendation (which Paulinus, feeling unequal to the task, passes on to the better-qualified Rufinus); Paulinus returns some 'nugae', a *natalicium* and his panegyric on Theodosius.[53] Augustine sends Paulinus his own *De Libero Arbitrio*, and requests in return Paulinus' *Contra Paganos*[54] and some books of Ambrose 'adversus nonnullos inperitissimos et superbissimos, qui de Platonis libris dominum profecisse contendunt' ('against some exceptionally ignorant and arrogant people, who argue that the Lord profited from Plato's books').[55] The *adnotatio* of Paulinus' own letters sent by Sanctus and referred to in the introduction offers particularly interesting evidence for the creation through letters of a devotional textual tradition: drawing up an *adnotatio* involves an acknowledgement that the author whose works are listed is authoritative in some sphere; here, it is accompanied with a gift of hymns, which reinforces the suggestion that the acknowledged authority is spiritual.[56]

This burgeoning Christian tradition of textual exchange is supplemented by other, non-literary, gifts—like the *panis Campanus* above—which are more obviously symbolic in their binding together of the Christian community. For example, camel-hair *pallia* are exchanged. In one case this prompts from Paulinus an associative disquisition on the salutary

---

[52] See Mark Vessey, *Ideas of Christian Writing in Late Roman Gaul* (DPhil thesis: Oxford, 1988), on building up a Christian community of writing and response to scripture: epistolary exchange is very much part of this process. Sadly, the continuation of the correspondence between Augustine and Jerome cited here is not a luminous example of this free exchange.

[53] Paulinus, *Letter* 28. 5–6. Beyond the Christian symbolism of this particular exchange, there lies the probable political importance in the non-Christian world of the panegyric on Theodosius: see Trout, *Paulinus*, 109–13.

[54] Whatever this is: Sister Wilfrid Parsons, the translator of Augustine's correspondence, suggests here Paulinus, *Poem* 32; however, Green's analysis of the poem amounts to a dismissal of its authenticity: Green, *The Poetry of Paulinus of Nola. A study of his Latinity* (Brussels, 1971), 130–31.

[55] Augustine, *Letter* 31. 8. The books of Ambrose referred to do not apparently survive. For other instances of books sent with letters, see Augustine, *Letter* 82. 35 (a request for Jerome's *Interpretatio de Septuaginta*); Jerome, *Letter* 58. 8 (Paulinus has sent him too his panegyric on Theodosius). Sometimes, of course, the letters more or less amount to books themselves: so with Jerome, *Letter* 53 to Paulinus.

[56] Paulinus, *Letter* 41. 1. Paulinus responds with some embarrassment: 'nam vere prope omnium earum ita inmemor eram, ut meas esse non recognoscerem, nisi vestris litteris credidissem' (as cited in the Introduction). But see further below on the spiritual function of letters.

effects of the prickly hair, and on its reminder of Elijah, John the Baptist, David: the Christian community, not just at present, but historically, is thus seen as being connected by such gifts.[57] Even Jerome is not unaware of the significance of such offerings: 'palliolum textura breve, caritate latissimum senili capiti confovendo libenter accepi et munere et muneris auctore laetatus' ('I gladly received the little cloak, thin-woven but deep-napped with love, to warm an old man's head, delighted by both gift and giver').[58] And the significance of exchange for the broader Christian community is clearly seen in Paulinus' return gift to Sulpicius of a tunic, which—'addo...adhuc pretio eius et gratiae' ('I am adding to its spiritual value')—had been given to him by Melania the Elder on her recent visit. Later, he also sends to Sulpicius a 'partem particulae de ligno divinae crucis' ('a tiny little splinter from the wood of the divine cross'), from the same source.[59] To our eyes, one of the strangest of the gifts is that of an actual person: Valgius, by God's grace the survivor of the shipwreck recounted in *Letter* 49, functions in very much the same way as that 'little splinter'—Trout describes him as a 'living relic'.[60] The way in which spiritual symbolism can become more important than any personal or individual significance is clearly shown in the case of this human 'xenium spiritale'.[61]

Such gifts, then, both extend the meaning of the written letter, and prompt a shimmering of symbolic association which may be supposed to extend far beyond the purely verbal. But there is also a more important extension of the letters' meaning: 'sic hic deus in tua caritate nobis abundans non solum *litteris* tuis nos sed et *tabellariis* benedicit visitat pascit inluminat, utroque nobis aperiens thesaurum bonum cordis tui...' ('Thus God, who abounds for us in your love, blesses, visits, sustains and enlightens us not only with your *letters* but also with their *carriers*: with both, he opens to us the wholesome treasury of your heart...').[62]

The enormous role played by the carriers of the letters in the entire nexus of communication, to which the written fragments are our only

---

[57] Paulinus, *Letter* 29. 1. On Paulinus' associative patterns of thought see Chapters 4 and 5 below.

[58] Jerome, *Letter* 85. 6 (to Paulinus). Likewise, Sulpicius sends *pallia* to Paulinus, Paulinus, *Letter* 23. 3.

[59] Tunic: Paulinus, *Letter* 29. 5; splinter of the Cross: Paulinus, *Letter* 31. 1.

[60] Trout, *Paulinus*, 191.

[61] *Letter* 49. 14.

[62] Paulinus, *Letter* 23. 2 (to Sulpicius).

surviving testimony, should never be overlooked—though the fact that
two studies, those of Gorce and of Perrin, exhaust the list of modern
surveys of the subject suggests that the significance of the letter-carriers
has in fact been often passed over.[63] Gorce is more interested in the
mechanics of delivery, and in anecdotal information on the letter-carriers,
than in the implications for communication as a whole; the following
remarks serve effectively as *addenda* to the work of Perrin.

The simple fact that we often know the names of the letter-carriers gives
some indication of their importance (though Perrin shows that Paulinus is
far more assiduous in naming his carriers than any of his contemporaries[64]); further, respondents may expressly greet former carriers in subsequent letters.[65] In purely functional terms, the opportune presence of a
carrier may prompt a letter: visitors from Lérins remind Paulinus that
Eucherius and Galla are in ascetic retirement there, and provide the
occasion for an epistolary greeting.[66] (Conversely, in a letter of Symmachus, two letters received simultaneously from Ausonius prove that he
lacked a *baiulus*, not *voluntas*—a bearer, not good-will![67]) Sometimes the
opportunity to write is more forcibly created: Paulinus tells Victricius of
Rouen how God provided a long-desired occasion for writing when he met
with Paschasius, a deacon from Rouen, in Rome, and continues:

sed fatemur violentiam nostram, qua illum de urbe ad sanctitatem tuam redire
cupientem, quamvis festinationem piam iustissimi desiderii probaremus, tamen in
tuo amore conplexi Nolam perduximus . . .[68]

But I confess the violence with which I embraced him in my love for you and
inveigled him to Nola when he wished to return from Rome to your holiness, even
though I applauded the pious urgency of his extremely reasonable desire . . .

[63] Michel-Yves Perrin, '"Ad implendum caritatis ministerium"'. La place des courriers
dans la correspondance de Paulin de Nole', *MEFRA* 104 (1992), 1025–68. (This article also
contains useful appendices with a chronological table of Paulinus' letters and a prosopography of their carriers.) See also Denys Gorce, *Les voyages, l'hospitalité, et le port des lettres dans
le monde chrétien des IVe et Ve siècles* (Paris, 1925), 205–247. For comparison with the
dissemination of letters in the early Christian church, see S. R. Llewelyn, *New Documents
Illustrating Early Christianity* vol. 7 (Sydney, 1994), 1–57 (with supporting evidence from
recent papyri).
[64] See 'Courriers', 1026–7, with statistical table at 1046–7.
[65] Augustine, for example, sends greetings especially to Romanus and Agilis in *Letter* 42;
they had brought him Paulinus, *Letter* 6.
[66] Paulinus, *Letter* 51. 2.
[67] Symmachus, *Letter* 1. 42.
[68] Paulinus, *Letter* 18. 1.

A carrier may likewise hasten a letter's conclusion. A letter from Paulinus
to Augustine contains a typically self-deprecating acknowledgement of
this: the carrier, Quintus, is eager to return from the *tenebrae* of Paulinus
to the *lumen* of Augustine, and 'instantiam eius in litteris exigendis etiam
haec epistola lituris quam versibus crebrior loquitur' ('this letter bespeaks
his urgency in exacting correspondence, with more frequent erasures than
lines').[69] Carriers may also shape the narrative of letters, suggesting topics
for inclusion or reminding the writer of details. The carrier Cardamas
insists that Delphinus, the Bishop of Bordeaux who baptized Paulinus,
wishes to hear reports of things which are happening 'circa [v]os . . . in
domino'; and so Paulinus adds, giving circumstantial detail unusual for
him, 'sciat veneratio tua sanctum fratrem tuum papam urbis Anastasium
amantissimum esse humilitatis nostrae' ('your reverence should know that
your holy brother Pope Anastasius is extremely affectionate towards my
humility').[70] Similarly, Paulinus decides to include in a letter to Sulpicius
the verses inscribed in his unfinished church at Fundi, above all because
'in huius absida designatam picturam meus Victor adamavit et portare tibi
voluit . . .' ('my Victor particularly loved a picture delineated in its apse,
and wanted to bring it to you . . .').[71] It can be no coincidence that the two
carriers involved here—Cardamas and Victor, respectively—are the two
most frequently used by three of Paulinus' most frequent correspondents:
the relationship with the carrier is of crucial importance to the nature of
the letters. Sometimes an entire letter is even initiated by its carrier, as
when Victor asks Paulinus to write to former colleagues of his in the
military to urge them on in Christian conversion.[72]

But these are the least important aspects of the carriers' role in epistolary exchange. The importance attached to the choice of a carrier, and the

---

[69] Paulinus, *Letter* 45. 8. See also *Letters* 43. 1 (to Desiderius) and 50. 1 (to Augustine).
Jerome too submits to the insistence of a carrier, *Letter* 112. 1 (to Augustine); and there is an
engaging example from Augustine's correspondence with Paulinus: 'carissimus frater Celsus
cum rescripta repeteret, debitum reddere festinavi, sed *vere* festinavi . . .' (Augustine, *Letter*
80. 1; my emphasis).

[70] Paulinus, *Letter* 20. 2; this detail is particularly interesting in the light of the previous
pope Siricius' hurtful rejection of Paulinus (*Letter* 5. 14). In paragraph 3 of the same letter,
Cardamas again prompts the inclusion of circumstantial information—that Venerius, the
new bishop of Milan, has written to Paulinus.

[71] *Letter* 32. 17. It is, incidentally, of interest that 'bringing' the picture to Sulpicius must,
in the context, refer to bringing back a verbal account and the verses with which the picture is
inscribed, not a copy of the picture itself. Chapter 4 explores further the relationship between
words and images for Paulinus.

[72] Paulinus, *Letters* 25 and 25*. *Letter* 26 also seems to have been prompted by Victor.

anger ensuing when it emerges that such a choice has been made poorly, are our first hints of their wider significance. Paulinus begins his letter to Jovius by reflecting on the business of using Christian carriers to send a letter to a pagan. Paulinus does not wish to pass over the opportunity of writing: he loves writing to Jovius 'per viros religionis' ('through men of the Faith'), and feels that it would give quite the wrong impression if he did not—as if Jovius were shunned by holy men, or did not approve and study Christianity. Jovius should welcome the letter because of the carriers, not vice versa; and Paulinus concludes that the choice of carriers is particularly appropriate to his current purpose:

apte autem visa est ad id quoque huiusmodi tabellariorum persona congruere, ut aliquid de pristina illa epistola responderem tibi, quam tu ad illas mihi litteras, quibus manifestum divinae potestatis in elementis et curae circa nos beneficium praedicaveram, retulisti.[73]

Anyway, the character of carriers of this type seemed to correspond fitly to the purpose of making some response to you about that original letter which you returned to those letters of mine, in which I had proclaimed the clear beneficence of divine power in the elements and of divine care for us.

This 'beneficence of divine power' has already been proven when Paulinus' earlier letter ('argentum illud sancti commercii' ('that silver of a sacred trade')) was saved from a shipwreck and its delivery ensured. Paulinus seems to be indicating that the use of Christian carriers to take the letter to Jovius is in itself part of the proof of God's involvement in the world—and palpably extends the divine concern towards Jovius.

    In one letter, Paulinus gives explicit instructions to Sulpicius on choosing his carriers. It is important that the carriers should be drawn from among those close to him, both literally and spiritually:

Neque sat habeas occasionibus cunctis revisere, nisi et pueros tuos mittas nec solum de famulis sed et de filiis sanctis, quorum benedicta in domino prole laetaris, eligas tabellarios, quorum oculis nos videas et ore contingas.[74]

Nor should you be content to see them again on every occasion, unless you send your own people and choose letter-carriers not only from your servants but also from your holy sons—the offspring, blessed in the Lord, in which you rejoice—with whose eyes you may see us and in whose speech you may draw near to us.

The trust reposed in a carrier is so great that Sanemarius, carrying a letter to Amandus at Bordeaux, is given the duty of performing offerings in

---

[73] Paulinus, *Letter* 16. 1.   [74] *Letter* 11. 4.

memory of Paulinus' parents: this, it seems, is part of proving his suitability for ordination by Amandus:

...vobis in domo domini serviat delegatis ad parentum nostrorum memoriam obsequiis, ut per religiosam servitutem obtinere firmam libertatem sub vestra defensione mereatur.[75]

...let him help you in the house of the Lord with the funeral rites designated for the commemoration of my parents, so that through his pious service he may deserve to obtain certain freedom under your protection.

The Symmachan idea of epistolary patronage has been extended to guarantee the carrier inclusion, not in a secular, but in a spiritual community;[76] but the mission entrusted to Sanemarius also shows his importance in a context far beyond his immediate function. A certain letter of Paulinus speaks particularly, though obliquely, to the theme of trust: it is an extended meditation on desirable and undesirable characteristics in men, transparently prompted by the contrast between Marracinus *inspiritalis*, the original carrier of the letter, who has reneged on his duty of delivery, and Sorianus *spiritalis*, who has taken on the task. It is not enough that the letter should simply have arrived, by whatever means: Paulinus' sense of spiritual continuity between himself and Sulpicius has, it seems, been temporarily severed, and his lively anger at the failure of the original carrier is directly proportional to his high estimation of the spiritual responsibilities of the carrier. We see the necessity of preserving—or, in this case, re-establishing—this spiritual continuity at the close of the letter, where Paulinus requests that Sulpicius should receive Sorianus '*quasi* a te missus mihi venerit' ('*as if* he had come to me sent by you'), as if he were Sulpicius' own carrier and spiritual confrère. Thus God passed on Sulpicius' letters through him 'et ignorante te' ('even though you were unaware of it'): the spiritual continuity was broken, but the substitute carrier was still performing the work of God and striving to reconnect the correspondents.[77] It is when the relationship of absolute trust fails that we see how much is expected of a carrier.

---

[75] *Letter* 12. 12.

[76] We may recall again Matthews on Symmachus: 'his letters were primarily intended not to inform but to manipulate, to produce results'. 'Letters of Symmachus', 64.

[77] Paulinus, *Letter* 22; quotes from paragraph 3. This notion of spiritual continuity between correspondents seems to be the result of Paulinus' expansive conception of the self, which will be discussed in Chapter 6.

The most conspicuous example of a mistaken choice of carrier must be Vigilantius, whom Paulinus had sent with his second letter to Jerome.[78] After Vigilantius has delivered Paulinus' letters, Jerome pursues him with a furious letter of his own:

credidi sancti Paulini presbyteri epistulis et illius super nomine tuo non putavi errare iudicium et, licet statim accepta epistula *asunarteton* sermonem tuum intellegerem, tamen rusticitatem et simplicitatem magis in te arbitrabar quam vecordiam. nec reprehendo sanctum virum—maluit enim apud me dissimulare, quod noverat, quam portitorem clientulum suis litteris accusare . . .[79]

I believed the letters of holy Paulinus the priest, and didn't think that his judgement of your reputation could err; and though as soon as I had received the letter I recognized that your manner of speaking was incoherent, I thought it was your roughness and lack of education rather than insanity. I don't blame the holy man—he preferred to pretend to me that he didn't know what he knew, rather than to lay charges in his own letters against his letter-carrier and minor protégé . . .

This letter goes on to reveal the considerable sense of betrayal when a carrier criticizes one of those between whom he is relaying letters— because, of course, the delivery of a letter involves making one's home in the respondent's community for some time while waiting for an answer. Jerome reminds Vigilantius of a particular episode:

Recordare, quaeso, illius diei, quando me de resurrectione et veritate corporis praedicante ex latere subsaltabas et adplodebas pedem et orthodoxum conclama-bas.[80]

I ask you to remember that day, when you leapt up from my side while I was preaching about the true resurrection of the body, and stamped your feet and acclaimed[81] me as orthodox.

---

[78] See David Hunter, 'Vigilantius of Calagurris and Victricius of Rouen'; also Trout's discussion of the episode, *Paulinus*, 220–2.

[79] Jerome, *Letter* 61. 3. This is assumed to be the same Vigilantius against whom Jerome later penned his *Contra Vigilantium* (see PL 23, cols. 353–68). To Paulinus, Jerome has merely hinted, rather disingenuously, at his response to Vigilantius' sudden departure, 'qui cur tam cito profectus sit et nos reliquerit, non possum dicere, ne laedere quempiam videar . . .' Jerome, *Letter* 58. 11.

[80] *Letter* 61. 3 again. The point of the 'orthodoxy' comment is that Jerome has been engaged in heated debate with the Origenists on precisely the subject of resurrection; Bynum sees his attack on Vigilantius as related to this debate. See Caroline Walker Bynum, *The Resurrection of the Body in Western Christianity, 200–1336* (New York, 1995), 86–94, esp. 92–3.

[81] TLL 4. 70 cites this passage under the senses 'simul clamo aut valde clamo', of which either would be apt here; though 'conclamo' is intransitive, it often takes an internal object, which throws interesting light on the close relationship to it of 'orthodoxum'.

This is why the choice of carrier is so crucial: he will live and eat with the community; he will participate in its daily spiritual round; on occasion, mention is even made of the carrier nursing the writer through an illness.[82] The ongoing involvement of carrier with community is well exemplified by the case of Cardamas, whose commitment to monastic simplicity is somewhat imperfect and who consequently provokes a running joke in the letters of Paulinus to Delphinus and Amandus, who send him. His behaviour at table prompts particular comment, though Paulinus is later pleased to report that he has become so accommodating 'ut nec holuscula nec pocula nostra vitaverit' ('that he avoided neither our humble vegetables nor our minimal drinks'), as his face and figure will show—unless there is any backsliding on the way home![83] Victor, on the contrary, who brings the letters from Sulpicius, cooks meals so very meagre as to excite playfully despairing comments: 'panes illos tribulationis imitatus est' ('he imitated bread—the bread of tribulation')![84] But he also nurses Paulinus, and prompts him to exclaim: 'servivit ergo mihi, servivit, inquam, et vae mihi misero, passus sum . . . ' ('so he served me, I repeat, he served me, and—wretched me!—I allowed him to . . . ').[85] Victor it is who swiftly becomes the trusted inmate of both Paulinus' and Sulpicius' houses, and who both effects and guarantees the spiritual continuity of their correspondence. It is significant that we can discover little about him personally from the letters: he seems to have been a monk; but in general his deeds or words are recorded either because they are spiritually exemplary or prompt spiritual reflection, or because they enhance the communication between Paulinus and Sulpicius.

Enough has been said to indicate how intimately a carrier would have become involved in the daily life of his respondents. Moreover, his involvement with the community might extend over several months: for example, Paulinus apologizes to Sulpicius for keeping Victor with him for the entire spring and summer one year.[86] Indeed, a trusted, frequently-used

---

[82] Examples: *Letter* 23. 6: Victor teaches Paulinus to eat more simply and sparingly; *Letter* 18. 2: Paschasius nurses Paulinus; *Letter* 23. 5: Victor anoints Paulinus with oil.

[83] Reports on Cardamas are contained in Paulinus, *Letters* 14, 15, 19, and 21; the quotation is from *Letter* 19. 4. Though 'pocula' is not technically a diminutive, it seems to me that, by pairing it here with 'holuscula', Paulinus is emphasizing their similarity and playing with the notion of abstemiousness: hence my choice of translation.

[84] Paulinus, *Letter* 23. 6. Paulinus also comments on the 'olida caligo', the 'stinking smoke', issuing from the kitchen (*Letter* 23. 7)!

[85] *Letter* 23. 4.

[86] Paulinus, *Letter* 28. 3.

carrier like Victor will end up splitting his time more or less equally between the two respondents. The carrier's message therefore ends up consisting partly in his entire comportment while he stays with the correspondent. He represents the one who has sent him, and much may be inferred from his actions. Thus Victor adds to the blessings of letters and gifts from Sulpicius with 'contubernio spiritali' and 'corporeo famulatu' ('spiritual fellowship and bodily service'); Paschasius is the 'speculum spiritale', the 'spiritual mirror' of Victricius' virtue.[87] The case of Paschasius further illuminates that of Marracinus and Sorianus discussed above: it appears that it is of particular importance to address a correspondent through a carrier in close contact with him, and Paulinus begins his letter to Victricius by rejoicing that after so long God had granted 'occasio nobis ad venerandam sanctitatem tuam scribendi per domesticum fidei et eum potissimum fratrem, qui in domino tuus pariter et noster esset' ('an opportunity for me to write to your reverend holiness through a servant of the faith, and especially through that brother, who is equally yours and mine in the Lord').[88] The most pungent example of a carrier as spiritually exemplary must be that of Theridius.[89] The seventh *Natalicium* tells of a terrible injury sustained to his eye from a hook on a hanging lamp, while he is at Nola to take part in the festival of Saint Felix.[90] Theridius' own spiritual interpretation of his partial blinding,[91] his prayer to Felix as 'his' patron, and the final miraculous withdrawal of the hook by Felix, all attest to his status as a vector of spiritual symbolism, as well as simply to his active participation in the community at Nola.

Of course, the effect of all this on the nexus of communication is immense. For the carrier does not just speak for his sender by behaviour, but in words, sometimes again in conversations lasting over weeks or months.[92] There are often references to the verbal accounts of the carrier supplementing the written text of the letter.[93] In at least one instance, the

---

[87] Victor: *Letter* 23. 3; Paschasius: *Letter* 18. 2.

[88] *Letter* 18. 1.

[89] Mentioned, paired with Postumianus, at *Letters* 16.1 and 27. 1.

[90] See *Poem* 23. 106 ff.

[91] Theridius laments that he is 'caecus iustis, oculatus iniquis', and avers that 'peccatorem luscum... *decet* esse': *Poem* 23. 237–38 (my emphasis).

[92] 'En véritables lieu-tenants de leur père en ascèse, [les porteurs de lettres] peuvent représenter, *au sens le plus fort du terme*, leur mandat auprès du destinataire de la lettre.' Perrin, 'Courriers', 1034; my emphasis. Perrin goes on to discuss the implications of this 'representation', drawing some similar conclusions to mine on the self in Chapter 6.

[93] For example, Paulinus, *Letter* 31. 1: 'frater Victor, inter alias operum tuorum et votorum narrationes...'

material letter is declared to be redundant, as God has provided as carrier Ianuarius 'per quem, etiamsi non scriberemus, omnia, quae circa nos sunt, posset sinceritas tua tamquam per viventem atque intellegentem epistulam noscere' ('through whom, even if we didn't write, your truthfulness could come to know everything which is happening here as if through a live and comprehending letter').[94] Indeed, the carrier is often described as a 'second letter'. Augustine again provides a good example: 'sanctos fratres Romanum et Agilem, aliam epistulam vestram audientem voces atque reddentem et suavissimam partem vestrae praesentiae... suscepimus' ('we have received the holy brothers Romanus and Agilis, your other letter which hears voices and answers, and the sweetest part of your presence').[95]

The carrier thus performs an extraordinarily liminal role. He is an independent agent, and comments are passed on him as such; but he is also representative of something beyond himself. At the most literal level, he represents his sender and his community. But the relationship goes further than representation, and this is revealed in the language consistently used to describe it. Thus Paulinus can say that carriers 'non ... a me alieni forent tecum manentes' ('could not be remote from me while they are staying with you [Sulpicius]').[96] Carriers are commended to Augustine 'ut nos alios' ('like other selves'): 'per hos, si quo me gratiae quae tibi data est dono remunerari voles, tuto facies. sunt enim, velim credas, unum cor et una in domino anima nobiscum' ('through them, you may safely accomplish the repayment to me of any gift of the grace which is bestowed on you. For please be assured that they are of one heart and spirit with us in the Lord').[97]

Victor first comes to Paulinus from Sulpicius 'in nomine dei tuaque persona' ('in the name of God—and representing you'). Occasionally the carrier even participates in another *persona*: Victor again is described as the 'formula' of saints Martin and Clarus, and Paulinus protests later in the same letter that he has allowed himself to be served by him 'ut minimam saltem guttulam de sacris Martini actibus delibarem' ('so that I may taste

---

[94] Augustine, *Letter* 186. 1.

[95] Augustine, *Letter* 31. 2 (to Paulinus and Therasia); this passage is discussed further in Chapter 6. For a similar idea see Jerome, *Letter* 53. 11 (to Paulinus): 'habes hic amantissimum tui fratrem Eusebium, *qui litterarum tuarum mihi gratiam duplicavit* referens honestatem morum tuorum...'

[96] Paulinus, *Letter* 27. 2.

[97] Paulinus, *Letter* 6. 3.

just the tiniest drop from the sacred deeds of Martin').[98] There is something more powerful than representation here: the carrier is patently
assigned great vicarious significance. The patterns of thought beginning
to emerge from the letters of Paulinus apparently delight in overthrowing
the obvious boundaries set by embodiment in favour of a spirituality of
integration and paradox: such patterns are particularly thrown into relief
by the liminality of the carriers. This will be explored further in Chapter 6;
for the time being, it suffices to observe that a carrier is very far from being
a mere mechanism, or a transparent relayer of others' words.

[98] Both *persona* instances are from Paulinus, *Letter* 23. 3; 'tiniest drop' quote from *Letter*
23. 4.

Sacramenta epistularia: letters as sacraments

Given the role of the carriers—their omnipresence in delivering and supplementing the written text of the letter—Paulinus' letters could never, whatever their subject matter, be described as 'private' letters in the modern sense.[1] The written text is open-ended; it is constantly ⇐ supplemented by the carrier's words and behaviour. Therefore, as one might expect, the audience is open-ended too: certainly, letters are not written only for their explicit addressees. The audience will extend beyond the immediate community, and its composition will be largely beyond the control of either the writer or the recipient of the letter.

At times, there are references to others' reception of the letters. Paulinus fears lest the 'filii prudentes' standing around may laugh when his foolish questions to Augustine are read out.[2] Certainly, Augustine has given him reason to expect that his letters will be read in his community as a whole: his first letter to Paulinus asserts,

legi...litteras tuas fluentes lac et mel, praeferentes simplicitatem cordis tui... Legerunt fratres et gaudent infatigabiliter et ineffabiliter tam uberibus et tam excellentibus donis dei, bonis tuis.

I have read your letters which flow with milk and honey and portray your heart's simplicity...The brothers have read them, and they rejoice tirelessly and inexpressibly at your virtues, such rich and exceptional gifts of God.

and closes:

---

[1] So, for the Middle Ages, Constable, *Letters and Letter-Collections* 11: 'In view of the way in which letters were written and sent, and also of the standards of literacy in the Middle Ages, it is doubtful whether there were any private letters in the modern sense of the term.'

[2] Paulinus, *Letter* 50. 1: '...nemo prudentium filiorum, qui forte de nostris in hora lectiunculae huius circa te steterint, de insipientia mea rideat...'

fratres non solum qui nobiscum habitant et qui habitantes ubi libet deo pariter serviunt, sed prope omnes, qui nos in Christo libenter noverunt, salutant, venerantur, desiderant germanitatem, beatitatem, humanitatem tuam.[3]

Not only the brothers who live with us, and those who live elsewhere and serve God in the same way, but almost everyone who has joyfully come to know us in Christ greets, reveres, and longs for your brotherhood, sanctity, and humanity.

'Greets, reveres, and longs for you': the envisaged audience, already exceeding Augustine's own community, seems to expand with every fresh verb. It should, however, be made clear that the open-endedness of the audience does not eliminate altogether the significance of the specific addressee. Hence, on one occasion Paulinus feels impelled to explain (in this instance, to Amandus) why he is not sending a letter to the *fratres*—which implies that one would have been expected, even though the *fratres* would have formed part of the audience for Amandus' letter itself.[4] This illustrates neatly that despite the general urge to collectivity, individuation is not rendered obsolete: a *caveat* that bears, once again, on Paulinus' conception of the self.

So the audience of a letter will almost definitely extend to the recipient's community; this is no surprise in any genuinely communal form of life, and an audience which is open-ended in this sense continues into the modern era.[5] However, we have many hints in Paulinus' correspondence, and (as seen above) that of his contemporaries, that the audience will be far greater. It is clearly expected that a letter will be to some degree an open document, and that its circulation will extend far beyond the original addressee. This must be the context of Augustine's explanation of Alypius' reticence on his life history: he fears lest an ignorant person should read it and infer that his gifts were not divinely given, but his own—'non

---

[3] Augustine, *Letter* 27. 2 and 6 respectively. Of the valedictory passage, we may note that this is an elaboration of what seems to be a peculiarly African formula: 'Omnes nostri qui nobiscum sunt te amant et salutant et videre desiderant.' See A. A. R. Bastiaensen, 'Le cérémonial épistolaire des chrétiens latins', *Graecitas et Latinitas Christianorum Primaeva* Suppl. 11 (Nijmegen, 1964), 7–45 (index 89–90). Compare too Augustine, *Letter* 31. 9: 'fratres quoque omnes nobiscum domino servientes tam id faciunt, quam vos desiderant, tam vos desiderant, quam vos diligunt, et tam diligunt, quam estis boni.'

[4] Paulinus, *Letter* 15. 3. The passage will have been as much for the *fratres* as for Amandus. Have other such letters to the *fratres* been lost?

[5] There is a telling aside, for example, in a letter from Jane Austen to her sister Cassandra (October 1813): 'Your Letter gave pleasure to all of us, we had all the reading of it of course, I *three times*—as I undertook to the great relief [*sic*] of Lizzy, to read it to Sackree, & afterwards to Louisa' (Austen's emphasis). *Jane Austen's Letters*, ed. Deirdre le Faye (Oxford/New York, 1995), 233.

enim abs te solo illa legerentur' ('for [the letter] would not be read only by you').[6] Later, Augustine quotes an extended section of a letter of Paulinus back to him, insisting that no apology is necessary:

cur enim non etiam isdem verbis uteremur? agnoscitis enim, credo, haec esse ex epistula vestra. sed cur potius haec vestra sint verba quam mea, quae utique quam vera sunt, tam nobis ab eiusdem capitis communione proveniunt?[7]

For why should we not also use the same words? For I think you recognize that these are from your letter. But why should they be your words rather than mine, since, inasmuch as they are true, they come to us from our sharing the same head?

Augustine also quotes *verbatim*, again to Paulinus, a passage from a letter sent *by* Paulinus *to* Sulpicius[8]—fascinating evidence for wide further dissemination, as well as for readers beyond the addressee, since this text has made its way from South Italy to central France to North Africa. This bespeaks an expected lack of ownership of the text once disseminated, which corresponds with the idea of an open-ended audience: as Augustine writes, 'Why should they be your words rather than mine?' Clearly, the writer cannot control either the process of reception or the attribution of the text once it has been sent out; and nor should he need to, given the desire to enact the dictum that Christ 'est caput corporis Ecclesiae' ('is the head of the Church's body') (Col. 1: 18), of which all are limbs. If all share the same head, the notion that anyone should exclusively own the Christian message which he has passed on must be nonsense.

In this context, Jerome's obsession with the apparent misdirection of Augustine's early letters to him becomes particularly out of place: at one stage he concludes rudely, 'et hoc a me rogatus observa, ut, quicquid mihi scripseris, ad me primum facias pervenire' ('and take note of this request, that you should make sure that whatever you have written to me gets to me first')[9]—a demand both impossible to fulfil and simply irrelevant to the conventions accepted by Augustine and Paulinus. This must be explained by Jerome's equally obsessive, and anachronistic, concern for individual authorship—a concern which is obviously redundant in the context of

---

[6] Augustine, *Letter* 27. 5; the fear of inference that gifts were Alypius' own is presumably due to his concern about Pelagianism.

[7] Augustine, *Letter* 31. 3. This passage neatly foreshadows my two subsequent major themes: the communion of friendship and of the self.

[8] Augustine, *Letter* 186. 40.

[9] Jerome, *Letter* 105. 5. The same letter has begun testily, after stating the unreliability of the carriers, 'quae cum ita sint, satis mirari nequeo, quomodo ipsa epistula et Romae et in Italia haberi a plerisque dicatur et *ad me solum* non pervenerit, *cui soli* missa est . . .' *Letter* 105. 1 (my emphasis).

such open-ended *mores* of communication. Writers such as Paulinus appear to be attempting to dissolve the classical sense of authorship and its cohesion with textual authority, while Jerome is reinstating such a sense with a vengeance, adding to the notion of authority not just personal authorship, or ownership, of a text, but authenticity in the form of orthodoxy.[10] Such dissolution of the notions of ownership has, once again, important implications for ideas of the self.[11]

The idea of a letter being implicitly directed to a far wider circle than its immediate addressee is unsurprising, given the copious internal evidence that the letters were sustaining and reinforcing a widespread Christian network. Despite the lack of detail in Paulinus' accounts of events which is so bitterly lamented by social historians, the names of other members of the Christian community are repeatedly mentioned to give a distinct, if unelaborated, image of extensive contacts. Paulinus, writing to Romanianus, tells the news, just learnt in letters from Aurelius, Alypius, Augustine, Profuturus, and Severus, that they are now all bishops. (In this case he does give a few more details, of Augustine's irregular election as co-bishop with Valerius.)[12] The letter cited earlier, from Ambrose to Sabinus, Bishop of Placentia (modern Piacenza), is primarily designed to tell the dramatic tale of Paulinus' and Therasia's conversion and renunciation of wealth, and goes on to muse on the effect of this spectacular gesture on the 'proceres viri' of the empire.[13] When Paulinus writes his *consolatio* to Pammachius for the death of his wife, he specifies that he has gathered 'tui maeroris indicium' ('the news of your grief'), from the writings of Olympus.[14] Sometimes, for all the geographical dispersion of the correspondents, the

[10] This point was first suggested to me by a passage in Mark Vessey, 'Erasmus' Jerome: The Publishing of a Christian Author', *Erasmus of Rotterdam Society Yearbook* 14 (1994), 62–99; relevant passage, 77. This refers to Michel Foucault, who traces the modern idea of the exclusivity and superiority of authorship back to Jerome's processes of categorization in *De Viris Illustribus*: 'It seems...that the manner in which literary criticism once defined the author...is directly derived from the manner in which Christian tradition authenticated (or rejected) the texts at its disposal.' 'What Is an Author?' in Josué V. Harari (ed.) *Textual Strategies: perspectives in post-structuralist criticism* (Ithaca, 1979), 141–60; quote from 150. See also on this issue Vessey, 'The Forging of Orthodoxy in Latin Christian Literature: A Case Study', *JECS* 4 (1996), 495–513.

[11] See Chapter 6.

[12] Paulinus, *Letter* 7. 1. It is perhaps no coincidence that this unusually factual letter is preserved in the Augustinian corpus, not the Paulinian (see Introduction, esp. text to nn. 71 and 76).

[13] Ambrose, *Letter* 6. 27. 1–3 ('proceres viri' from 3: 'haec ubi audierint proceres viri, quae loquentur!').

[14] Paulinus, *Letter* 13. 1.

effect borders on the claustrophobic. Jerome hears from Domnio about a monk at Rome attacking his *Adversus Jovinianum* (and counter-attacks him in a letter to Paulinus): this is the same Domnio who has the copy of Eusebius which Alypius requests from Paulinus at the beginning of their correspondence.[15] The literary network mentioned earlier is, of course, extended through letters; and epistolary contacts are also set up to further the network, as when Paulinus intimates to Venerius, the new bishop of Milan, that there is an opportunity to write to Delphinus. From numerous further examples we may single out an instance from Jerome, in which ostensible reinforcement of the Christian network takes a somewhat back-handed form. A letter to Augustine and Alypius, dated to around 419, ends 'sancti filii communes Albina, Pinianus et Melania plurimum vos salutant' ('the holy son and daughters whom we share, Albina, Pinian, and Melania send especial greetings to you'). It was only about two years earlier that a spate of anxious letters from Augustine to this very trio had tried to explain away the débâcle in which his congregation at Hippo had tried to empress Pinian into the priesthood.[16]

At times, it is the choice of contents for the letters which makes it clear that they are intended for an audience greater than the specific addressee. Part of the *consolatio* to Pammachius on the death of his wife Paulina takes the form of an extended description of a feast for the poor given in her memory at the basilica of Saint Peter's.[17] Paulinus assures Pammachius that 'tua virtus tristitiam tegit' ('your virtue has buried grief'), and that he knows this rather than guesses it because 'opera tua hoc de te contestantur et me conperta loqui cogunt' ('your deeds bear witness to this fact about you and, once discovered, compel me to speak out'). Paulinus goes on to describe the scene in Saint Peter's—'videre enim mihi videor' ('for I seem to see it')—notwithstanding the fact that for him, this is merely hearsay. Something more complex is involved here than merely describing to Pammachius an episode for which Paulinus' correspondent was not only present, but the instigator. Part of the consolatory message is clearly to rehearse the virtue of Pammachius' actions, placing them in a public context through approving reportage and thereby both ratifying them and ensuring their wider dissemination. That a wider dissemination is visualized, even for a letter with so 'private' a theme, is intimated by an apostrophe following Paulinus' reflection on the divine rewards for

[15] Some details in Trout, *Secular Renunciation*, 68. Jerome, *Letter* 53. 7 counter-attacks the monk; Paulinus, *Letter* 3 responds to Alypius' request for a copy of Domnio's Eusebius.

[16] Jerome, *Letter* 143. 2; Augustine, *Letters* 124–6.

[17] Paulinus, *Letter* 13. 11 ff.

Pammachius of his almsgiving: 'Poteras, Roma, illas intentas in apocalypsi minas non timere, si talia semper ederent munera senatores tui' ('O Rome, you wouldn't have to fear those threats laid out in the Apocalypse, if your senators always produced such gifts').[18] Apparently, this is not just a *consolatio* for Pammachius; it serves also as a hortatory letter for those of his own senatorial class who might chance to read it.

A similar extension from 'private' to 'public' material is seen in the first letter of Paulinus to Victricius of Rouen.[19] Once again, the letter revolves around an account of the addressee's own actions. This letter rehearses at some length the circumstances of Victricius' conversion, of his triumphs at Rouen, and so on, in part retelling the story of Victricius' own *De Laude Sanctorum*. The expectation must have been that Victricius would circulate this to a wider audience as a quasi-hagiographical endorsement by Paulinus of his activities. The first three paragraphs of the letter might be labelled 'personal', with their tale of empressing the letter-carrier Paschasius from Rome to Nola, and of his subsequent care for Paulinus when sick; but the closing paragraphs tie in this episode to the glorificatory themes of the letter: Victricius, the 'martyr vivus', is the 'formula omnibus perfectae virtutis et fidei; sicut et frater Paschasius ostendit, in cuius gratia et humanitate quasi quasdam virtutum gratiarumque tuarum lineas velut speculo reddente collegimus' ('pattern for all of perfect virtue and faith; just as brother Paschasius showed: in his grace and humanity we inferred something like outlines of your virtues and graces, as if in a mirror's reflection').[20] Clearly the letter was intended for circulation as a whole, unified by the notion of Victricius, and by extension Paschasius, as a 'pattern for all', and thus once again challenges our expectation of the division between the private and the public.[21]

There are two further extended hagiographical *narrationes* in the letters of Paulinus, both addressed to Sulpicius Severus. One provides context for Paulinus' gift to Sulpicius of a fragment of the true cross, and tells the tale of its discovery by Helena, mother of the emperor Constantine.[22] But its purpose in the letter is also to serve as a basis for spiritual reflection: Sulpicius is invited to mediate on the faith of the *latro* crucified alongside Christ, who believed in Christ's resurrection even before it happened. The other *narratio* is essentially a *Vita* of Melania the Elder. Paulinus is sending to Sulpicius a tunic given to him by Melania during her recent

---

[18] Ibid., 15.   [19] Paulinus, *Letter* 18.   [20] *Letter* 18. 10; 'martyr vivus' at *Letter* 18. 9.
[21] Fabre reaches a similar conclusion: *Saint Paulin de Nole*, 233–5.
[22] Paulinus, *Letter* 31. 3–6.

stay (as mentioned above), and he observes flatteringly that 'te dignior visa est, cuius fides illi magis quam noster sanguis propinquat' ('it seemed more worthy of you, whose faith brings you closer to her than my kinship does').[23] Victor, bringing letters and gifts from Sulpicius, has coincided with Melania at Nola. At this point the flow of the letter breaks off for a dramatic exclamation and an extended simile in the epic style, which is sufficiently unusual to bear quotation at some length:

at quam tandem feminam, si feminam dici licet, tam viriliter Christianam! quid hoc loco faciam? vetat fastidii intolerabilis metus voluminibus adhuc addere; sed personae dignitas, immo dei gratia postulare videtur, ut commemorationem tantae animae praegressus non raptim omittam et paulisper ad eam tibi narrandam, velut navigantes si aliquem in litore locum spectabilem videant, non praetervehuntur, sed contractis paululum velis aut remigio pendente pascunt oculos intuendi mora, ita sermonis mei cursum detorqueam, quo etiam inlustri illi materia et eloquentia libro tuo vicem aliquam videar reddere, si feminam inferiorem sexu virtutibus Martini Christo militantem prosequar, quae consulibus avis nobilis nobiliorem se contemptu corporeae nobilitatis dedit.[24]

But what a woman she is—if she may be called a woman, when she is so manfully Christian! What should I do here? Fear of intolerable boredom forbids me to add to these rolls; but the dignity of her person, or more precisely the grace of God seems to demand that, having advanced to commemoration of so great a spirit, I should not cursorily pass over it, and should twist aside the course of my narrative for a little to tell you about her, just as people sailing don't pass on by if they see some beautiful spot on the shoreline, but reef the sails a little or ship their oars and feast their eyes in a contemplative pause; and in this way I may make some return for that book of yours, illustrious in subject-matter and style—if I may describe a woman, inferior in sex, as fighting for Christ with the virtues of Martin, a woman ennobled by her consular forebears[25] who made herself yet nobler with her contempt for worldly nobility.

This paragraph performs several functions. The exclamation serves to introduce, with appropriate pomp, Melania herself at the beginning of her *Vita*, and to reflect on her unusual—even unnatural—holiness. The rhetorical deliberation acts as a half-serious *apologia* for the forthcoming exercise in hagiography, while at the same time drawing particular attention to it, both through ostentatiously contravening the traditional *modus*

---

[23] Paulinus, *Letter* 29. 5; the Melania *narratio* runs from chs. 5 to 14 (the end of the letter).

[24] Paulinus, *Letter* 29. 6.

[25] Melania's grandfather, Antonius Marcellinus, was consul in 341; if *PLRE* is correct that she married Valerius Maximus, then her father-in-law was also a consul (in 327). See *PLRE* I, 592–3 and *stemmata* 20 and 30.

of a letter and through introducing the grandiose simile. The culmination
of the paragraph compares this exercise explicitly with Sulpicius' own
hagiographical *Vita Martini*; and the two tales are clearly linked once again
at the end of the letter:

Non tuli, frater, ut te ista nesciret. ut gratiam in te dei plenius nosceret, tuo te illi
magis quam meo sermone patefeci. Martinum enim nostrum illi studiosissimae
talium historiarum ipse recitavi.[26]

Brother, I couldn't bear that she shouldn't know you. For her to come to know the
grace of God in you more fully, I laid you open to her in your own words rather
than mine. For I myself read aloud to her our 'Martin', since she is extremely keen
on stories of that type.

It is apparent once again that Paulinus is not writing only for Sulpicius,
any more than Sulpicius wrote 'Martinum nostrum' only for Paulinus: a
wider audience is certainly envisaged. Here is further proof that a letter,
though it may contain 'personal' material, far from necessarily corresponds in any respect with a modern definition of the 'private'. Through
its blending of levels which modern readers tend to separate, this letter
and those discussed above also challenge categories of genre. The tales of
Melania and Victricius are not hagiography *tout court*, any more than they
are private messages: generic labels are clumsy in this epistolary form
which represents not so much a conscious combining of genres as an
habitual subversion of categories.

This is not to say that these correspondents do not have a notion of the
private and public, but merely that their content is different, and that the
two are differently constructed in relation to each other.[27] We may recall
the 'forensis'/'domesticus' distinction of Symmachus:[28] sometimes, Paulinus seems to echo this distinction. When he speaks of the 'domestica
munera' of Saint Felix, it is certainly the miraculous gifts to Paulinus' own
household and family that are meant.[29] And the 'public' may, as was

---

[26] Paulinus, *Letter* 29. 14. The emphasis of 'ipse recitavi' is interesting: it must imply that
normally such readings would be performed by another member of the community (and
hence bears further witness to an essentially communitarian way of life).

[27] Compare a similar questioning of the boundaries between sacred and secular in Trout,
Paulinus, 149: 'we may . . . sense the inadequacy of such categories for capturing the essence of
the cultural moment'. Trout draws on R. A. Markus' remarks about 'desecularization': see
Markus, *The End of Ancient Christianity* (Cambridge, 1990), 16. Since the dissolution of the
public/private boundary is linked to the spiritualization of both spheres, these are closely
related phenomena.

[28] See text to Chapter 1, n. 15.

[29] *Poem* 21. 49–50.

traditional, be represented by a life of service to the state: thus he describes to Sulpicius his withdrawal from public life at Rome to Aquitania as the pursuit of 'otium ruris'.[30] But this is probably an ironic description: as Fontaine has observed, 'The word *otium*, in Paulinus, has an almost exclusively negative value: it is idleness, not leisure.'[31] Paulinus better describes his practice in his longer verse letter to Ausonius: 'vacare vanis, *otio aut negotio,/* et fabulosis litteris/ vetat . . . ' ('[God] forbids one to give time to useless things, *either in leisure or business,* and mythical writings').[32] 'Otium' and 'negotium', the private and the public, are here dissolved and dismissed together. Paulinus seems consciously to be attempting to make the distinction between public and private irrelevant; inasmuch as he does invoke the private, he tries, as it were, to eradicate its privacy, to make it something generally available and relevant and shared.[33]

This is seen particularly clearly not in the letters but in the *Natalicia*. Here it is an intrinsic part of the ongoing sanctification of St Felix and his activities that the private should be made public. There is a revealing phrase in the ninth *Natalicium*: Felix's feast day has given birth to a mighty eternal patron for Paulinus 'privato specialius astro' ('more especially [for me] than a private star').[34] This seems to hint at something more specific to the individual person than the 'private' can be; and it seems to be through the dual channels of Felix's divine influence and Paulinus' publication of it that the 'specialis' is achieved. Paulinus quite literally emerges from his domestic quarters to reveal the happenings within them to the worshippers at Felix's shrine: he makes public the 'domestica munera' of the saint, be they the apprehension of a thief, the healing of a letter-carrier, or the restoration of Nola's water-supply.[35] On one notable occasion, this technique of bestowing spiritual significance on private

---

[30] Paulinus, *Letter* 5. 4: ' . . . nec rebus publicis occupatus et a fori strepitu remotus ruris otium et ecclesiae cultum placita in secretis domesticis tranquillitate celebravi . . . '

[31] 'Le mot d'*otium* a presque exclusivement, chez Paulin, une valeur négative: il est oisiveté, et non loisir.' See Jacques Fontaine, 'Valeurs antiques et valeurs chrétiennes dans la spiritualité des grands propriétaires terriens à la fin du IVe siècle occidental', in *Epektasis: mélanges patristiques offerts au Cardinal Jean Daniélou* (Paris, 1972), 571–95; reprinted in idem, *Études sur la poésie latine tardive d'Ausone à Prudence* (Paris 1980), 241–65; quote from 255.

[32] *Poem* 10. 33–5.

[33] This notion is further discussed in Chapter 6.

[34] *Poem* 27. 146. Walsh, however, sees this simply as a derogatory comment about astrology: Walsh, *Poems*, 406.

[35] The healing of the letter-carrier Theridius (*Poem* 23, *Nat.* 7) has already been discussed, Chapter 1, text to nn. 89–91. Apprehension of a thief: *Poem* 19 (*Nat.* 11). 378–603; restoration of Nola's water supply: *Poem* 21 (*Nat.* 13). 650–858.

events by publicly expounding them and linking them with the saint results in the nearest that Paulinus has left us to an autobiography. Each episode of his life is reinterpreted in a way that shows the presence of Felix's guiding hand.[36]

The *Natalicia* are, of course, expressly written for public performance, and are thus particularly likely sites for the crossing of boundaries between public and private. Both their metre and their vocabulary appear to be chosen, as it were, for popular consumption: unfamiliar language is avoided, and their episodic tales told at a leisurely pace.[37] The one occasion on which Paulinus allows himself considerably more latitude in choice of metre, and even a relatively wide range of classical allusion, is that on which he has an audience to appreciate it, when Melania the Younger, Pinian her husband, and their entourage are all visiting Nola.[38]

Audience appears also to be an important factor for Paulinus in deciding whether to compose his letters metrically or in prose. In the *Natalicia* he essays the largely novel project of writing in de-classicized verse, using uncompromisingly Christian language and content; but when writing for those who would be alert to classical resonances, he displays some sensitivity to the non-Christian implications. In this he was typical of his time. Caelius Sedulius, in the letter to Macedonius that forms a preface to his *Carmen Paschale*, provides us in the second quarter of the fifth century[39] with a remarkably full *apologia* (in prose) for the use of metre as well as prose, which reveals that metrical composition was still associated with the pagan world:

... multi sunt quos studiorum saecularium disciplina per poeticas magis delicias et carminum voluptates oblectat. hi quicquid rhetoricae facundiae perlegunt, neglegentius adsequuntur, quoniam illud haud diligunt: quod autem versuum viderint

---

[36] *Poem* 21 (*Nat.* 13). Trout's comparison with Paulinus' earlier account of himself to Sulpicius produces a fascinating commentary on the way in which Paulinus has come to reconfigure his life as one directed by divine influence: *Paulinus*, 15–22.

[37] On the choice of language, see R. P. H. Green, 'Paulinus of Nola and the Diction of Christian Latin Poetry', *Latomus* 32 (1973), 79–85.

[38] *Poem* 21 (*Nat.* 13). The poem, while framed in Paulinus' customary dactylic hexameters, also uses iambic trimeters and elegiac couplets. Green, 'Diction', does not remark on the exceptional nature of this *Natalicium*, presumably because his diagnostic matrix uses a relatively small number of words.

[39] Sedulius' dates are doubtful; but there is a secure *terminus ante quem* in that he is quoted by Peter Chrysologus of Ravenna, who died in 450. For a convenient review of the scant details of Sedulius' life, and of the sources for them, see Michael Roberts, *Biblical Epic and Rhetorical Paraphrase in Late Antiquity* (Liverpool, 1985), 77–8.

blandimento mellitum, tanta cordis aviditate suscipiunt, ut in alta memoria saepius haec iterando constituant et reponant.[40]

... there are many people whose secular training causes them to be more diverted by poetic delights and the pleasures of verse. These people pursue with indifference whatever they read of rhetorical eloquence [i.e. prose], for they have no love for it; but when they read something sweetened with the allure of poetry, they take it to heart so eagerly that by frequent repetition they store it deep in their memory.

For Paulinus, immersed as he would formerly have been in the pagan classics and techniques of metrical composition,[41] we may infer that the tension between prose as a Christian medium and verse as a pre-Christian one was particularly powerful. He observes in his letter to Licentius (quoted below) that 'a quo studio ego aevi quondam tui non abhorrui' ('I didn't shrink from the study [of verse] when I was your age')—but the implication is that now Paulinus has grown beyond such frivolity.[42] Having previously been a master of the verse epistolary form, Paulinus responded after his ascetic conversion with an almost complete rejection of metrical form for letters. R. P. H. Green observes, 'We can detect no hesitation in Paulinus' mind about the propriety of continuing to write poetry';[43] but it is clear from his change of practice that Paulinus does reconsider his ideas about the proper application for poetry. It is not his medium of choice for Christian communication. In any case, Green's observation is not entirely accurate. We may call to witness the renowned exchange of verse letters with Ausonius.[44] Paulinus observes sadly to his former mentor that vicious jokes of the sort which Ausonius has indulged in his previous letter 'saepe poetarum, numquam decet esse parentum' ('often befit poets, but never parents').[45] The tension between classical, Muse-inspired poetry and a Christian world-view has already been much in play in the letter. Paulinus insists that he cannot be summoned back to Gaul with the Muses: 'non his numinibus tibi me patriaeque reduces' ('you won't bring me back to you and my homeland with these divinities').[46] In

---

[40] Sedulius, *Epistola ad Macedonium*, 5 in the edition of Huemer, CSEL 10.

[41] For Paulinus' education, see Introduction, n. 12, and Chapter 1, n. 6.

[42] Paulinus, *Letter* 8. 3.

[43] Green, *Poetry*, 16.

[44] The most recent edition of this exchange is that in Green, *Ausonius*, 708–19 for Paulinus' letters (= Poems 10 and 11 in Hartel's edition), 215–31 for those of Ausonius. I discuss the exchange more fully in Chapter 6.

[45] Paulinus, *Poem* 10. 264. The accusation is, ironically, buttressed by a borrowing in the previous line from Persius *Sat.* v. 86, 'mordaci lotus aceto'.

[46] Paulinus, *Poem* 10. 113.

this context, the distinction between the behaviour appropriate to *poeta* and to *parens*, so unfavourable to the former, implies first, hurtfully, that Ausonius is not the *parens* to Paulinus which he claims to be, and second, that poetry is unsuited to the universal Christian *parens*, God.[47] From then on, Paulinus almost never again uses verse for epistolary purposes—which reflects the fact that for Paulinus the significance of poetry has been unalterably changed.

When Paulinus does write in verse, a rationale is required, and his choice, like that of Sedulius, tends to be connected with a project of suasion. In his letter to the luke-warm Licentius in the late 390s, Paulinus felt compelled to explain his decision to write in metrical form: he fears to disgust or bore Licentius with the 'asperitate temerarii sermonis' (the 'harshness of importunate language'—the letter has been solicited by Augustine); but, noticing that his correspondent is familiar with metrical forms ('musicis modis'), he will write in verse, 'ut te ad dominum harmoniae omniformis artificem modulamine carminis evocarem' ('to call you to God, the maker of multifarious harmonies, with melodious song').[48] It is notable that the only other letters written in verse subsequent to Paulinus' withdrawal are also planned to persuade those much involved in the secular world of the merits of Christianity;[49] he also attempts the versification of some psalms, and of the life of John the Baptist, further projects which suggest the communication of a Christian message to those of refined classical tastes.[50] It is no coincidence that the *Natalicia*, Paulinus' project of Christian suasion *par excellence*, occupy the greatest part of Paulinus' surviving poetic corpus: these, it seems, were instrumental in popularizing the cult of an obscure saint and dubious martyr. But, despite his attempts to Christianize the genre, Paulinus clearly had misgivings about turning his talent for prosody even to these. In a *Natalicium* written a decade after he had established himself at Nola (406), he still finds it necessary to include the apologia, 'Non adficta canam, licet arte poematis utar' ('I shall not sing lies, even though I am using the poetic art'), and goes

---

[47] Paulinus has emphasized this dual application of *parens* in the course of the letter: see, again, the discussion in Chapter 6.

[48] Paulinus, *Letter* 8. 3. *Taedium*, unfortunately, is not avoided in the rather plodding result.

[49] These are *Poem* 22, to Jovius (the pagan dabbling in philosophy to whom *Letter* 16 is also addressed), and *Poem* 24, to Cytherius. It seems that the latter, from a noble Aquitanian family, was much involved in public life, although he had placed his son in Sulpicius' monastery.

[50] Life of John the Baptist: *Poem* 6; versifications of the Psalms: *Poems* 7–9.

on, 'at nobis ars una fides et musica Christus' ('my only art is faith, and my metre is Christ'):[51] this bespeaks a continuing uneasiness at the association of the 'poetic art' with the pre-Christian.

Poetry, in fact, becomes Paulinus' primary didactic mode, which perhaps accounts for the fact that the verse written after his conversion tends to be far more pedestrian than his prose letters. Green points out that Paulinus attempted, after his conversion, to 'please the cultured and teach the uneducated' in his poetry (but, unfortunately, does not really develop this point).[52] In fact, these divisions seem to apply to two separate poetic modes, to the letters of suasion or celebratory poems[53] addressed to cultivated Christians on the one hand, and to expository works—above all, the *Natalicia*—directed to a faithful but not particularly educated audience on the other. Meanwhile, Paulinus' adoption of prose for his epistolary endeavours does not necessarily imply a smaller expected audience; but it does, for the most part, suggest a readership which has already attained some level of commitment to Christianity. Indeed, his desire to shape his thoughts in prose seems to form an essential part of his deeper Christian commitment; it is perhaps connected not just with the avoidance of pagan taint but also with the desire to respond creatively to types of writing that were being formulated as distinctively Christian. At Cassiciacum and afterwards, in the mid-380s, Augustine had explored, and ultimately rejected, the potential of dialogue form as a Christian medium; Jerome, meanwhile, was exhorting Paulinus to write biblical commentary.[54] Perhaps the prose epistolary form appealed to Paulinus by being a less dogmatic, more fluid means of communicating his Christian thoughts; perhaps this impression is a mere accident of survival. Certainly, it circumvents the invitation to pagan content and vocabulary in metrical composition, while comfortably accommodating Biblical allusion, echo, and direct quotation.

Paulinus' apparent preference for prose over metrical letters bears witness to the way in which Christian writers were beginning to forge a

---

[51] *Poem* 20. 28 and 32.

[52] Green, *Poetry of Paulinus*, 129.

[53] Such as the epithalamium for Julian of Eclanum, or the propemptikon for Nicetas (*Poems* 25 and 17 respectively).

[54] Jerome, *Letter* 58; see further Chapter 5, text to nn. 51–2. On the creation and formalization of ideas of Christian reading and writing at this period, see Vessey, *Ideas of Christian Writing*, especially 41–57 on the exchange between Paulinus and Jerome. Note Jerome's insistence on the need for exemplars—notably, himself! (56). I am indebted to Mark Vessey for suggesting to me the significance of Paulinus' choice of prose over metrical form for his letters.

new role for their letters, to create something very different from those of their pagan contemporaries—though they were perhaps as yet unsure precisely what that role was to be. We have already explored the wider role played by the letters and their carriers in creating and sustaining a continuous sense of Christian community; interwoven with this is the spiritual import of the letters, their ongoing literary commentary—explicit or otherwise—on the growth of the textually-orientated faith. Hence the difficulty of schematically separating treatises—or, for that matter, hagiography—from letters: the epistolary 'genre' is not a separate genre at all, but is seamlessly interpenetrated by other Christian ways of writing. Augustine, for example, defies the distinction, with the instruction: '. . . rescribe, ut *vel epistulis vel libris*, si adiuverit deus, ad omnia respondere curemus' ('write back, so that if God assists me I may carefully respond to everything, *either in letters or treatises*').[55] It is in collections of letters like those of Paulinus that we see the role of the Christian epistolary medium evolving.

If letters, then, are not a clearly distinct genre according to modern categories, this begs the question of what their own writers saw as distinctive about them. To put it another way, what was the particular purpose of their letters? To use the case of Symmachus once again for contrast, Bruggisser gives a succinct formulation. Epistolary contacts functioned on three levels: 'to create the relationship between friends, to make it work, and to make it bear fruit' (through the process of *commendatio*).[56] But this, though true also for Christian epistolographers of the time, is very far from being a complete account. The role of letters historically in the church—from the letters of the New Testament to the issuing of canons in epistolary form—had been too important for them now to be reduced to the status of mere 'visiting cards'.[57]

The process of the composition and circulation of letters—indeed, the entire nexus of communication around a letter—apparently becomes for Christian writers a sacramental activity. This phenomenon was briefly, but aptly, remarked upon by Gorce: 'For those converted to the ascetic ideal, *everything is conceived*—as follows from its very nature—*as a function of the inner life*, and human affairs only have value to the degree that

---

[55] Augustine, *Letter* 138. 20 (to Marcellinus). In general, literary forms in late antiquity do not respond well to genre distinctions.

[56] 'Faire exister la relation [entre amis]', 'faire fonctionner la relation', and 'faire fructifier la relation'. Bruggisser, *Symmaque*, 8.

[57] Term from Matthews, 'Letters of Symmachus', 62.

they relate to it in some way.'[58] In the *City of God*, Augustine explains the notion of a sacramental activity in the context of his account of *sacrificium* not as something physically and literally performed, but as a constant dedication of one's life to God: 'Sacrificium ergo visibile invisibilis sacrificii sacramentum, id est sacrum signum est' ('so a visible sacrifice is the sacrament, that is, the sacred sign, of an invisible sacrifice').[59] For Paulinus, the letters are an outward and visible sign of the invisible connection in Christ between those who write and those who receive and read them. The letter as 'historical event' becomes a sign of spiritual dedication.

In its sacramental function, the text of the letter is not just a bearer of information or of spiritual advice: it is itself a spiritual offering and a basis for general meditation and reflection. The carrier, too, becomes part of that offering: hence the outrage when the carrier proves inadequate. On the most elementary level, this is shown by the fact that requests for prayers from the correspondent (and often his or her wider circle) become a regular component of the letters. Sometimes this will be more or less the unique function of the letter: in one letter to Paulinus, Augustine makes the request for prayer his priority after an explanation of the brevity of the letter: 'nunc ergo, quod soleo, rogo, ut, quod soletis, faciatis: oretis pro nobis' ('so now I ask what I usually do, that you should do what you usually do: please pray for us').[60] It is the sacramental aspect of the letters which makes explicable the composition of so brief a note, and its despatch all the way from Hippo to Nola: if the primary purpose of the letter is to serve as a tangible sign of an invisible communion between writer and recipient, the length of the letter will be insignificant—and a request for prayers will form the most appropriate possible contents.

Certain aspects of the letters illuminate the assertion that their function is sacramental. First, the nature of the writing and reading of the letters: one needs peace to do justice to reading a letter, just as one needs *otium* to compose it. Paulinus writes to Augustine:

---

[58] 'Pour les gens conquis à l'idéal ascétique, *tout est conçu*—cela va de soi—*en fonction de la vie intérieure*, et les contingences humaines n'ont de valeur que dans la mesure où elles s'y rapportent de quelque manière.' Gorce, *Les Voyages*, 199 (my emphasis).

[59] *City of God* 10. 5. J. de Ghellinck comments that *sacramentum* in post-Nicene writers—especially Augustine—has two meanings: (1) a sacred rite; (2) 'celle de signe ou de figure, comportant un élément secret ou mystérieux qui requiert explication': *Pour l'histoire du mot 'sacramentum'* Vol. 1: *Les Anténicéens* (Louvain/Paris, 1924), 14–15. The latter meaning is obviously relevant to my observations here, though there is little of 'explication' in Paulinus, who seems to take the sacramental function of letters for granted.

[60] Augustine, *Letter* 80. 1.

fateor tamen venerandae unanimitati tuae non potuisse me volumen ipsum, statim ut acceperam, Romae legere. tantae enim illic turbae erant, ut non possem munus tuum diligenter inspicere et eo, ut cupiebam, perfrui, scilicet ut perlegerem iugiter, si legere coepissem.[61]

But I confess to your reverend unanimity that I couldn't read that package at Rome, as soon as I had received it. For the crowds there were so huge that I couldn't peruse your gift with care and enjoy it as I wished—that is, to read it through without interruption, if I had begun to read.

The verb which Paulinus chooses for his encounter with the letter, 'perfrui', is an intensified form of that famously used by Augustine to encapsulate human experience of the divine.[62] Elsewhere, Paulinus makes explicit why this repose is necessary for the reception of letters:

Accepimus litteras sanctae affectionis tuae, quibus iubes nos in epistolis, quas ad te facimus, aliquem praeter officium[63] de scripturis adicere sermonem, qui tibi thesaurum nostri cordis revelet.[64]

I have received the letters of your affectionate holiness, in which you command me to supplement the obligatory content in the letters I'm writing to you with some discussion of the scriptures, to reveal to you the treasury of my heart.

The 'officium' alone will fulfil the sacramental function; but some commentary on the scriptures (or words resonating with them, to describe something closer to Paulinus' actual practice) to further the spiritual closeness of the correspondents will reinforce the invisible offering. Reflecting on the necessity of peace of mind for detecting the hidden divinity in things, Paulinus tells Sulpicius that truth only manifests itself to one in a state of *vacatio*, rest (a word used of God's repose after the effort of creation[65]); God, because he is God, is available to be seen by all, but 'deum in Christo vel Christum in deo esse non videt occupatus et curarum terrestrium nube circumdatus' ('someone who is preoccupied and sur-

---

[61] Paulinus, *Letter* 45. 1.

[62] The renowned *fruor/utor* distinction used in *De Doctrina Christiana*: see, for example, 1. 3: 'Res ergo aliae sunt, quibus fruendum est, aliae quibus utendum, aliae quae fruuntur et utuntur. Illae quibus fruendum est, nos beatos faciunt. Istis quibus utendum est, tendentes ad beatitudinem adiuvamur . . .'

[63] Hartel prints 'officii' here: it is hard to determine on what grounds, as the far more natural 'officium' is securely attested in the manuscript tradition (LM). On these manuscripts, see Appendix, esp. text to n. 16; 'officii' is, needless to say, the reading of O.

[64] Paulinus, *Letter* 10. 1 (to Delphinus).

[65] See Blaise *ad loc.* for references.

rounded with a cloud of earthly cares does not see that God is in Christ or Christ in God').[66]

The writing and reading of these letters is itself a spiritual activity. ⟵ There are passages which suggest the practice of meditating on the letters:

ita ego hanc epistulam in tui sermonis retractatione contexam et voluptatem meam referam, nihil tibi largiens, nec votum erga te meum potius quam de te experimentum loquar. expresserunt enim mihi faciem cordis tui litterae tuae, illae litterae spei bonae, litterae fidei non fictae, litterae purae caritatis.[67]

So let me weave this letter in memory of your words, and recount my pleasure, while bestowing nothing on you; I shall not speak of my prayer for you, but of my experience of you. For your letters expressed to me the appearance of your heart— those letters of good hope, letters of unfeigned faith, letters of pure love.

As we see here, the language of the letters, in particular, bespeaks their spiritual function. The power of language is vividly felt: 'sermo... viri mentis est speculum' ('words are the mirror of a man's mind').[68] Phrases describing the reception of letters in the language of spiritual refreshment abound. The passage from Paulinus' letter to Augustine quoted above continues with the statement that he reined in his mental hunger for the letters, certain that when devoured they would bring satiety, until he was completely at liberty 'ut in deliciis epistulae tuae spiritalibus ab omne faece curarum et suffocatione turbarum liber epularer' ('to feast on the spiritual delights of your letter, free from every sordid worry and the stifling crowds').[69] Similar examples are widespread, often expressed in the same extravagantly imagistic language: the writer may have his thirst refreshed by his correspondent's words; his 'bones are fattened'; the words are a light to his feet.[70] Once again, the letter to Augustine contains a particularly vivid image:

---

[66] Paulinus, *Letter* 24. 19; note the closeness in sense, in the passage quoted, of 'seeing' to 'knowing (that)'.

[67] Paulinus, *Letter* 44. 2 (to Aper and Amanda). Note the use of the tricolon (*spes, fides, caritas*) from 1 Cor. 13. Augustine, *Letter* 130 to Proba, is explicitly a text for meditation.

[68] Paulinus, *Letter* 11. 11.

[69] Paulinus, *Letter* 45. 1. The expression which I have paraphrased as 'mental hunger' is 'avidae... mentis esuriem'.

[70] Examples: 'rain from God', Paulinus, *Letter* 19. 3 (from Ps. 68: 9); 'bones are fattened', *Letter* 14. 1 (from Prov. 15: 30 or Ecclus. 26: 16—not 26: 13 as in Hartel); 'light to feet', *Letter* 45. 1 (from Ps. 118: 105). References are to Biblia Vulgata.

... quotienscumque litteras beatissimae sanctitatis tuae accipio, tenebras insipientiae meae discuti sentio et quasi collyrio declarationis infuso oculis mentis meae purius video ignorantiae nocte depulsa et caligine dubitationis abstersa.[71]

Whenever I receive letters from your most blessed holiness, I feel the darkness of my foolishness struck aside, and, as if the salve of revelation[72] had been poured into the eyes of my mind, the night-time of my ignorance is driven away and the shadow of doubt wiped off, and I see more clearly.

All these images are firmly lodged in biblical reference—including that of the eye-salve, which is rooted in Revelation (Rev. 3: 18). The significance of this active integration of biblical imagery into epistolary language will be explored in my fourth and fifth chapters; for now, it suffices to note the way in which it constantly reasserts and reinforces the sacramental nature of the letters.

The composition of letters in which the sacramental function is paramount is practised more consistently by Paulinus than by any other writer of Latin letters in late antiquity. This may reflect the tradition of cultivated aristocratic *otium* from which Paulinus *par excellence* derives,[73] with a spiritualization of the aristocratic habit of forming and maintaining connections by letter; it may be an accident of preservation—though clearly Paulinus was renowned for the writing of such letters in his own lifetime. But other writers participate at times in the sacramental nature of epistolography, even if they may also use letters for more prosaic purposes. (As remarked in the Introduction, the great range of form and function in the surviving letters of Augustine—from those dealing with the minutiae of church administration to extended treatments, expressly for meditation, of religious themes—is a case in point.) Bruggisser observes of the letters of Symmachus that 'the technical perfection of the message ... is in itself a message'.[74] For Paulinus, however, one may substitute for the initial phrase 'the spiritual perfection'; and this is the most important part, indeed, the point, of the letter's message.

These two chapters have explored the 'nexus of communication' that surrounded the letters which are our textual remnants of that nexus. The idea of epistolary exchange has been expanded to embrace the whole

---

[71] Paulinus, *Letter* 45. 1.

[72] *TLL* 5. 1. 182 s.v. 'declaratio' lists this passage under the sense 'manifestatio', but also gives the sense 'explicatio': whereas I have translated in accordance with the former, the sense here may well hinge on the availability of both interpretations, given that the context embraces both text and illumination.

[73] See again Fontaine, 'Valeurs antiques et valeurs chrétiennes'.

[74] 'La perfection technique du message est ... elle aussi message'. Bruggisser, *Symmaque*, 3.

network of writers, bearers, and recipients of letters, of the words and gifts exchanged both literally and spiritually, of written and oral and non-verbal communication. Most importantly, a sacramental function has been pro-posed for the letters: their composition, delivery, and perusal became a sign of inner spiritual dedication. In the next chapter, I wish to show how this entire nexus of communication is instrumental in the development, reinforcement, and extension of the Christian community in late anti-quity. Above all, I shall explore the way in which ideas about Christian friendship are introduced and enacted in the letters of Paulinus.

3

Amicitia and *caritas Christi*: friendship and the love of Christ

Abripui vel potius subripui et quodam modo furatus sum memet ipsum multis occupationibus meis, ut tibi scriberem antiquissimo amico, quem tamen non habebam, quam diu in Christo non tenebam. nosti quippe, ut definierit amicitiam 'Romani', ut ait quidam, 'maximus auctor Tullius eloquii'[1]. dixit enim et verissime dixit: 'Amicitia est rerum humanarum et divinarum cum benivolentia et caritate consensio'[2] . . . ita fit, ut, inter quos amicos non est rerum consensio divinarum, nec humanarum esse plena possit ac vera. necesse est enim, ut aliter, quam oportet, humana aestimet, qui divina contemnit, nec hominem recte diligere noverit, quisquis eum non diligit, qui hominem fecit. proinde non dico: 'Nunc mihi plenius amicus es, qui eras ex parte', sed, quantum ratio indicat, nec ex parte eras, quando nec in rebus humanis mecum amicitiam veram tenebas.[3]

I have torn myself away—or rather, sneaked off and in some way stolen myself away from my many preoccupations—in order to write to you, my oldest friend, whom I still did not have as a friend as long as I did not hold you in Christ. You surely know how the man someone called 'Tully, the greatest originator of Roman eloquence' defined friendship. For he said, and with absolute truth: 'Friendship is a benevolent and loving accord in matters human and divine'. . . . So it is the case that there could not be full and true accord in human matters between friends who have none in the divine. For one who despises the divine would necessarily rate human things differently from how he should; and whoever does not love Him who made man could not know how to love man rightly. So I do not say: 'Now you are more fully a friend to me, who were so formerly only in part', but, as the reasoning

---

[1] Lucan, *Pharsalia* 7. 62–63.

[2] Based on Cicero, *Laelius* 6 (20).

[3] Augustine, *Letter* 258. 1 and 2. He expresses a similar opinion in the *Confessions*, describing with hindsight a youthful friendship: 'Sed nondum erat sic amicus, quamquam ne tunc quidem sic, uti est vera amicitia, quia non est vera, nisi cum eam tu agglutinas inter haerentes tibi caritate diffusa "in cordibus nostris per spiritum sanctum" . . .' *Conf.* 4. 4. 7. From his earliest work, however, Augustine is insistent on the importance of friendship: in the midst of directives for combining Philosophy and the 'lex Dei' in life, he says: 'in omni autem vita loco tempore amicos aut habeant aut habere instent'. *De Ordine* 2. 8 (25). James

points out, you used to be not even partly a friend, when you didn't even have a true friendship with me in human matters.

The exact date of this letter of Augustine, and the identity of the Marcianus to whom it is addressed, are not known, though the letter may be guessed to have been written quite early in Augustine's bishopric.[4] However, the letter is significant for its succinct exploration of the main concerns of Christian friendship in the late fourth and early fifth centuries. Augustine takes as his starting point the famous definition of *amicitia* from the *Laelius* of Cicero—'est enim amicitia nihil aliud nisi omnium divinarum humanarumque rerum cum benivolentia et caritate consensio' ('for friendship is nothing other than a benevolent and loving accord in all things, divine and human')[5]—only to offer a critique of its central elements: how, he asks, can there be *consensio* in human affairs if there is no corresponding *consensio* concerning the divine? For Christ is all-permeating: one cannot think rightly about earthly matters unless this is acknowledged, and hence there is no true division between 'res divinae' and 'res humanae'. A friendship in the secular realm which does not acknowledge the pervasiveness of Christ is not a part-friendship, but no true friendship at all.

Paulinus too expresses the emptiness of human friendship without Christ:

dudum enim, ut procul dubio recognoscis, Sancte frater, diligere coepi te; et dilexi iugiter, quamquam non ista dilectione quae Christi est, sed illa familiaritatis humanae amicitia, quae blandimenta in labiis habet et radicem in cordibus non habet, quia non est fundata super petram quae non aedificatur in Christo [Matt. 7: 25; 16: 18].[6]

McEvoy comments on Augustine, *Letter* 258 in '*Anima una et cor unum*: Friendship and Spiritual Unity in Augustine', *Recherches de théologie ancienne et médiévale* 53 (1986), 76–80.

[4] Marcianus may be Marcianus 14 in *PLRE* I. 555–6, who was proconsul of Africa in 393/4. As the authors admit, the evidence seems tenuous; but the proconsul did receive five letters from Symmachus, so could conceivably have come into contact with Augustine via Ambrose, also a correspondent of Symmachus, during Augustine's time in Milan. 'Early in Augustine's bishopric' would refer to 395 or shortly thereafter.

[5] Cicero, *Laelius* 6 (20). Note the slight differences from the version in Augustine, who is, we may conclude, as usual quoting from memory. For Augustine's use of Cicero's ideas on friendship, see Tarsicius J. van Bavel, 'The Influence of Cicero's Ideal of Friendship on Augustine', in *Augustiniana Traiectina* (Paris, 1987), 59–72; this contains useful further bibliography on the subject. Van Bavel argues for more continuity of thought between Augustine and Cicero than I shall allow here; interestingly, however, he remarks on Augustine's consistent inversion of the Ciceronian 'divinarum humanarumque' in using the extract here.

[6] Paulinus, *Letter* 40. 2 (to Sanctus and Amandus). Note here the use of the prosaic term 'familiaritas': Paulinus elects to use it or its cognates several times elsewhere in his corre-

For, brother Sanctus, I began to love you a long time ago, as you undoubtedly realize; and I have loved you continually—though not with that love which relates to Christ, but with that friendship of human acquaintance, which has charm on the lips and no root in the heart, because what is not built in Christ is not based on a rock.

Paulinus and his associates saw themselves as participating in an entirely new notion of friendship, reinterpreted through their faith. But to explore the significance of the Christian reinvention of ideas of friendship, we must first look at their classical antecedents to get a sense of the extent of the change.

The tradition of philosophical discourse on friendship was strong in classical antiquity, a natural product of philosophical schools concerned with the question of what it might mean to lead a good life in the fullest sense, a *beata vita*.[7] (We may note in passing that one of Augustine's earliest works was entitled *De Beata Vita*.) For Western writers in the fourth century, this tradition was encapsulated above all by Cicero's *Laelius*, which is referred to directly or indirectly with remarkable frequency. Ausonius, for example, recalls to Paulinus the renowned friendship between Laelius and Scipio as analogous to their own.[8] The tone of the *Laelius* is an idiosyncratic mixture of the ideal and the pragmatic. The work starts from the common-sense assumption that *amicitia* consists in a bond of advanced sympathy between two or more—but not many—people. Early on in the dialogue, Laelius claims of his friendship with Scipio:

spondence, for example at *Letters* 4. 2 ('familiariter'), 6. 1 ('alloquio... familiari'). This is of particular interest in the light of the debate about the terminology of Christian friendship, discussed below.

  [7] For an excellent recent discussion of the Greek tradition on friendship, see A. W. Price, *Love and Friendship in Plato and Aristotle* (Oxford, 1989). I do not discuss the Greek antecedents of Roman thought on friendship here, as they were not generally available to the Latin writers of the fourth century; for a glimpse at what would have been known of the Greek tradition, see the polemical summary of Greek positions on friendship in *Laelius* 13 (45) to 16 (59); and the contents of the *Laelius* are themselves, of course, more generally informed by Greek tradition. On Paulinus' knowledge of Greek, Courcelle is scathing: 'Tout au plus lui arrive-t-il de se reporter très rarement à la Septante et de citer des étymologies ou des mots grecs très courants.... Il est l'ennemi de la culture grecque, parce qu'il la connaît bien mal.' Pierre Courcelle, *Les lettres grecques en occident de Macrobe à Cassiodore* (Paris, 1943), 133.

  [8] Ausonius, *Letter* 24. 36–7: 'nos documenta magis felicia, qualia magnus/Scipio longaevique dedit sapientia Laeli'. For other reminiscences of the *Laelius*, see Augustine, *Letter* 73. 4 (to Jerome)—enemies may serve us better than friends: compare Laelius 24 (90)—and Symmachus, *Letter* 1. 37 (to Ausonius), on *fides*.

quocum mihi coniuncta cura de publica re et de privata fuit, quocum et domus fuit et militia communis, et id in quo est omnis vis amicitiae, *voluntatum studiorum sententiarum summa consensio.*[9] With him I held a common concern for public and private affairs, with him I shared both household and military service, and that in which the full force of friendship resides, *the most perfect accord of wills, enthusiasms, and opinions.*

He moves swiftly on to decide that *amicitia* can only exist between *boni*— though, he argues, we should not be too high-falutin about our definition of the *bonus*,[10] but take it to mean a characteristic combination of moral virtue and social position (like the English 'gentleman'). As the dialogue progresses, it is precisely the moral qualities of the friends that emerge as most important: a number of practical challenges to friendship are tested against the ideal, and in each case the solution is found in the *virtus* of the parties. So pronounced is this ethical bias that Cicero begins his conclusion—effectively a peroration in the mouth of Laelius—with the words, 'virtus, virtus inquam . . . et conciliat amicitias et conservat' ('vir-tue—virtue, I repeat—both brings together friendships and preserves them').[11]

Once again, it is Augustine who offers an explicit refutation in Christian terms of Cicero's ideas.[12] His *Letter* 155 to Macedonius opens with the statement, reminiscent of his letter to Marcianus, that true *amicitia* cannot exist unless one is first an *amicus veritatis*, a friend of the truth. Thus, although philosophers have said much about friendship in their search for the *beata vita*, how can they say anything worthwhile if they think that they have gained it through their own virtues, and 'non ab illo fonte virtutum' ('not from the actual wellspring of virtues')?[13] Again, the ethical aspects of friendship are central, but their application redrawn, as Christian notions of the *beata vita* supplant the Ciceronian. Similarly with the

---

[9] Cicero *Laelius* 4 (15). J. G. F. Powell's concern to play down the idea of sharing households (he translates here 'I was associated with him . . . at home') seems to me to be misplaced. See his Commentary (Warminster, 1990), 84.

[10] Cicero is here reacting against the Stoic tradition that only the truly *sapiens* can be *bonus*—which, he argues, ends up eliminating everybody.

[11] Friendship can only exist between *boni*: *Laelius* 5 (18), reiterated at 18 (65). Conflict with the interests of the *res publica*: 12 (40). Friendship arises from love of the *virtus* displayed in its object: 8 (28). Peroration: 27 (100).

[12] For Augustine's use of and relationship with Cicero, see Harald Hagendahl, *Augustine and the Latin Classics* (Göteborg, 1967), 35–168 for *testimonia* and 479–588 for discussion.

[13] Augustine, *Letter* 155. 1 and 2. The Ciceronian work explicitly referred to is the *Tusculan Disputations*: paragraph 3 contains extensive echoes of *Tusc.* 5. 110–17. For

question of the *res publica*: Augustine plays on the ambiguity of application
when he says 'Quoniam vero te rei publicae scimus amatorem . . .' ('since,
indeed, I know that you are a lover of the republic'), but he settles firmly
for the sense of the *res publica caelestis* at the end of the letter.[14] (This was a
particularly relevant sphere of reflection for Macedonius, who at the time
of the letter (*c.* 414) held the post of *vicarius Africae*; it ought, however, to
have been redundant, as the exchange of letters took place round the gift of
the first three books of the *City of God!*) Augustine summarizes his
inversion of the Ciceronian position by stating that we should pray for
virtus in this life and the *beata vita* in the next; and 'in hac vita virtus non
est nisi diligere quod diligendum est' ('there is no virtue in this life except
for loving what ought to be loved').[15] So he proceeds to a discussion of the
first two commandments, which, as we shall see, are crucial to Christian
thought about friendship and its importance.[16]

I have spent so long with Augustine's redrawing of Cicero on friendship
because it seems to me that a similar reassessment is present in the thought
of Paulinus, though it is never so explicitly discussed. A further preliminary question seems to be begged by this discussion: namely, if the boundaries of friendship are so radically reconceived, what becomes of the
classical terminology of friendship?

Caritas, used more or less interchangeably with the more classical
dilectio, was from early on adopted as an appropriate translation of the
New Testament *agape*, and remained the primary term for Christian love
at this period. Pétré says aptly of *caritas*, '*Caritas* is no longer simply a
human emotion—it is a virtue, the highest of virtues, the one which relates
man to God.'[17] However, her study treats *caritas Christi* only as an
objective phrase, as 'love of Christ', not as the blend of the objective and

---

full details of the citations in this letter, see Hagendahl, *Augustine, testimonia* 300, 302,
and 328.

[14] 'rei publicae . . . amatorem', *Letter* 155. 7; the heavenly republic, 17. Augustine exploits
similar ambiguity in the word *civitas*: does it refer to Carthage or to the 'civitas Dei'? 'hoc
nobis velimus, hoc civitati, cuius cives sumus; non enim aliunde beata civitas, aliunde homo,
cum aliud civitas non sit quam concors hominum multitudo'. *Letter* 155. 9.

[15] Summary: *Letter* 155. 9; quotation from 13.

[16] The 'first two commandments', for Augustine as for Paulinus, are not the first of the ten
in Exod. 20, but those revealed by Christ as most important in Mark 12: 30–31: '. . . diliges
Dominum Deum tuum ex toto corde tuo, et ex tota anima tua, et ex tota mente tua, et ex tota
virtute tua. Hoc est primum mandatum. Secundum autem simile est illi: Diliges proximum
tuum tanquam teipsum. *Maius horum aliud mandatum non est.*'

[17] 'La *caritas* n'est plus un sentiment simplement humain, c'est une vertu, la plus haute
des vertus, celle qui configure l'homme à Dieu.' For a study of *caritas*, its evolution and uses,

the subjective phrase, 'Christ's love', that her comment implies.[18] (In fact, the diminution or dissolution of boundaries of subjectivity and objectivity are of crucial importance in early Christian thought, as will be discussed below.)

While *caritas*, then, was particularly associated with Christ, the phrase *amicitia* *amicitia Christi* was not, to my knowledge, ever used at this period: it is certainly not present in the letters of Paulinus. The received wisdom has long been that the terms *amicus* and *amicitia* were blighted by political connotations—although P. A. Brunt, in a renowned article, strove to counter the idea that *amicitia* and *factio* were equivalent, insisting that *amicitiae* could be both political and personal, and that insofar as they were political, they were not factional but fluid. However, the terms of the article as a whole imply that the political was more pervasive than he allows, since it is clear that *amicitia* could only exist among the gentlemanly élite of politically active citizens.[19] Yet the term *amicitia* itself is far from being eliminated from Christian usage. We have seen above its conscious reworking by Augustine; and Paulinus uses it in parallel with *caritas* in his own second letter to Augustine: 'dominus enim testis est . . . ut nobis non novam aliquam amicitiam sumere, sed quasi veterem caritatem resumere videremur' ('for the Lord bears witness . . . that we are apparently not just taking some new friendship upon ourselves, but, as it were, resuming a time-honoured affection').[20] Fabre claims that Paulinus always uses *amicitia* and its cognates in the sense of human, not divine, bonds, and systematically seeks to explain away the counter-examples; but this smacks of special pleading.[21] Both Fabre's discussion and that of Konstan, who has recently supported his conclusions,[22] seem to me to have the wrong emphasis: what is remarkable is that Christian writers continue to use the words *amicus* and *amicitia* at all, given the availability

see Hélène Pétré, *Caritas: étude sur la vocabulaire latin de la charité chrétienne* (Louvain, 1948): this quote from 354.

[18] Indeed, this blend of objective and subjective love is clearly envisaged in the Gospels: see John 15: 12: 'hoc est praeceptum meum, ut diligatis invicem, sicut dilexi vos'. The passage is very important for ideas of friendship, which it goes on to discuss directly: note especially, 'vos autem dixi *amicos*, quia omnia quaecumque audivi a Patre meo, nota feci vobis', John 15: 16.

[19] See Brunt, '*Amicitia* in the Late Roman Republic', *PCPS* 191 NS 11 (1965), 1–20.

[20] Paulinus, *Letter* 6. 2.

[21] Fabre's discussion of the vocabulary of friendship: *Saint Paulin de Nole*, 142 ff. Counter-examples to his claim that *amicitia* is always used in the sense of human, not divine, bonds: 150–52.

[22] David Konstan, 'Problems in the History of Christian Friendship', *JECS* 4 (1996), 97; idem, *Friendship in the Classical World* (Cambridge, 1997), 157–8.

of other options—particularly the more obviously Christian *frater* and its cognates. It seems more accurate to say that *amicitia* is used where there is primary emphasis on the human bond; on the few occasions when it is used uniquely of human connections it tends to be qualified by *humana*.[23] There is a clear example in a letter to Eucherius and Galla, where it is contrasted with divine grace: 'non enim humana amicitia sed divina gratia invicem nobis innotuimus et conexi sumus per viscera caritatis Christi'. ('For we have come to know each other not through human friendship but through divine grace, and we have been bound together through the vitals of Christ's love.')[24] Again, primarily human bonds are contrasted with the divine by using *amicitia* and *amor* in one of the *Natalicia*, where Nicetas is described as 'victus amicitia, victus Felicis amore' ('overcome by friendship, and by the love of Felix').[25]

A letter to Sulpicius quite clearly uses *amicitia* twice within the same paragraph of friendships both before and after the commitment of the friends to Christ: 'ubi amicitia vetus?' ('where is our old friendship?'), is answered with 'pro parentibus et fratribus et amicis tu nobis factus a domino es...tota non fictae amicitiae fide sedulus' ('you have been made by the Lord into a substitute for us of parents, brothers and friends, assiduous in the total trust of an unfeigned friendship'). The same letter also uses the still more prosaic *necessitudo* with an explicitly spiritual application: 'a familiaritate carnali...in aeternam necessitudinem affectu potiore mutavit' ('[Christ] has changed [our bond] from fleshly association into an eternal intimacy with more powerful affection').[26] As we shall see, for Paulinus and his correspondents there came to be no such thing as a friendship without divine involvement; and the sense of *amicitia* was stretched accordingly.

---

[23] Carolinne White reaches a similar, though less specific, conclusion at the end of her discussion of Fabre's terminology: '...Paulinus did not feel that the use of the word *amicitia* was anathema in Christian circles: while *caritas* is applied exclusively to the love in Christian relationships, *amicitia* can be used of either secular or Christian friendships'. White, *Christian Friendship in the Fourth Century* (Cambridge, 1992), 159. Luigi Franco Pizzolato is on similar ground when he echoes, then modifies, Fabre's conclusion: the adjective *humana* brings a negative connotation to *amicitia* which, in Paulinus, it does not otherwise possess. Pizzolato, *L'idea di amicizia nel mondo antico classico e cristiano* (Turin, 1993), 290.

[24] Paulinus, *Letter* 51. 3. See also *Letter* 40 to Sanctus and Amandus, quoted in text to n. 6 above.

[25] Paulinus *Poem* 27. 343 (*Nat.* 9).

[26] *Amicitia*: Paulinus, *Letter* 11. 3; *necessitudo*, *Letter* 11. 2; it is also used at paragraphs 3 (with the qualifier 'corporalis') and 4. We may note that there is no entry for *necessitudo* in Blaise.

Christian writers, then, are aware of the classical tradition of thought on friendship, yet seek self-consciously to revise it; the most significant locus of revision comes in the relationship between personal friendships and the divine.[27] This is especially clearly seen in the letters of Paulinus, which repeatedly engage in the assertion and negotiation of the bonds between friends and their relationship with Christ.[28]

The whole process of the formulation and enactment of Christian friendship is intimately bound up with the manner in which epistolary relations were sustained. We have already discussed the 'sacramental' nature of the letters, and remarked on the ceremonial of delivery, of the contact between correspondents and letter-carriers, of the sending of gifts. We have also discussed more practical aspects of the composition and delivery of letters, and seen the way in which this process is characteristically creative and continuous. Now we begin to turn towards the metaphysical implications of that process.

We have seen, in Chapter 2, that Christian writers were consciously forging a new role for their letters; inextricably involved with this is the forging of a new notion of friendship. The very fact that epistolary relations are fundamental—rather than an adjunct—to Christian friendship shows how far we have come from the classical tradition. Letters are no longer merely a substitute for the presence of the friend; they become a crucial constitutive part of the expression of friendship. By this, I mean that contact through letters—ideally, at any rate—comes to be considered as superior to the enjoyment of the physical presence of the friend. This leap is certainly never made in the classical tradition of thought on friendship, which tends to be caught in the tension between the obvious quotidian good of close friendships as a contributing factor in the *summum bonum* and the philosophical ideal of self-sufficiency and contemplation.[29] Paulinus simply steps aside from this problem to posit a notion of friendship that, while continuing to value the human bond, is actually better sustained in the friend's absence. The spiritual connection through letters actually supplants the literal connection of friends, expressed in classical

---

[27] The most 'self-conscious' revision comes in Paulinus' letter-exchange with Ausonius, which is discussed in Chapter 6.

[28] The letters of Paulinus form 'the most complete expression of the Christian ideal of friendship': Brian Patrick McGuire, *Friendship and Community: the Monastic Experience 350–1250* (Kalamazoo, 1988), 66.

[29] The *locus classicus* for this tension is Aristotle's *Nicomachean Ethics*: the image of the solitary striving for *theoria* put forward in Book 10 is directly at odds with that of *philia* as a good in Book 8; and the tension remains unresolved.

authors by the desire to share a house and every aspect of public and private life.[30] It seems that, for Paulinus, this solution may have developed out of a combination of the deepening of his Christian sympathies and a very real sense of being rejected by many of his former associates. Letter 11 to Sulpicius, in which he discusses the changing nature of their *amicitia*, contains the following passage:

amici mei et proximi quondam mei nunc a longe steterunt; et sicut fluvius decurrens et ut fluctus pertransiens, sic transeunt me et in me forsitan confunduntur et erubescunt, ut scriptum est, venire ad me; facti sunt mihi qui prope longe et qui longe prope.[31]

My friends, and those who were once closest to me, have now taken up positions far off; and like a river running through and a wave washing over, they pass me by and are, perhaps, confused at me and are embarrassed, as has been written, to come to me; those who are close to me have become far away, and those who are far away, close.

The first line quotes Psalm 37: 12; but this passage resonates most strongly with Ephesians: 'Nunc autem in Christo Iesu vos, qui aliquando eratis longe, facti estis prope in sanguine Christi' ('But now in Christ Jesus you, who were once far off, have been made close in the blood of Christ') (2: 13). It is interesting that Paulinus elaborates the passage with its antithesis: for him, association with Christ has driven some away as well as bringing others closer. He seems to draw once again on his experience in reassuring Aper in a similar situation: Aper has earned this grace from the Lord, 'ut te ... oderint omnes, quod non fieret, nisi verus imitator Christi esse coepisses' ('that everyone hates you, which would not happen if you hadn't begun to be a true imitator of Christ').[32] The world hates what it sees is alienated from itself. Paulinus seems in his earlier letters to be striving to bring meaning to his own initial sense of alienation.[33] It is by taking seriously the sense of 'in Christo Iesu' and the notion of the 'imitator Christi' that he succeeds in doing so.

Once again, spiritual symbolism prevails. Indeed, paradoxically, the very fact of absence becomes significant, for it enables the spiritual and the

---

[30] As in the quote from *Laelius* 4 (15) above.

[31] Paulinus, *Letter* 11. 3. Pizzolato sees here 'il confronto, velato di sottile nostalgia, con altri rapporti antichi...': *L'Idea*, 289.

[32] Paulinus, *Letter* 38. 2.

[33] Trout's emphasis on the shocking and provocative nature of Paulinus' secular renunciation should be borne in mind here.

physical to be seen in their true relationship.[34] Paulinus writes to Sebastianus that the bridging of the distance between them is a gift of God: 'ipse dominus deus noster donavit nobis licet longo intervallo distantibus appropinquare tibi in dilectione...' ('Our Lord God himself has granted that we might approach you in love, even though we are a long distance apart...').[35] The process of spanning a separating distance through love alone is here configured as a gift of God. So too in the consolatory letter to Pammachius:

cucurri igitur in siti desideriorum ad te, mi frater in Christo unanime atque venerabilis, et si me vicissim intueris animo, tecum esse me totum videbis et senties. nam si verum illud est sensu nos potius videre et audire, certe adsum tibi et potiore mei parte, qui animo ad te venerim, quo nisi adsimus, ubi et corpore intersumus, praesentiam non probamus, vacua nostri imagine mentis absentia. quamobrem signatum amicitiae munus inpendi aptumque nostra fide feci, ut te spiritali aditu visitarem.[36]

And so in the thirst of my desires I have run to you, my concordant and revered brother in Christ; if you in turn look upon me with your spirit, you will see and feel that I am entirely with you. For if the claim is true that we see and hear more powerfully with that sense[37], I am certainly present to you, and in my more effective part, when I have come to you in spirit. After all, if we were not present in spirit when we are together in body, we would not declare it truly 'presence', in the empty absence of our mind's image. Hence I have laid out the sealed gift of friendship, and by our faith made it fit for me to visit you by a spiritual approach.

The disadvantage of physical separation becomes, once again, a spiritual advantage, as Paulinus can be present to Pammachius in his better part ('potiore...parte'): the 'imago mentis' becomes the guarantor of the friend's presence—and is no less accessible from afar. Moreover, the

---

[34] There is a resonant twentieth-century parallel in Rose Macaulay's *Letters to a Friend*, ed. Constance Babington Smith (2 vols.: London, 1961 and 1962), in which the voyage of spiritual discovery is clearly enabled by physical separation.

[35] *Letter* 26. 1.

[36] *Letter* 13. 2.

[37] I note that 'animo quam sensu' has been conjectured here (by Sacchinus in his Antwerp edition of 1622) as a replacement for the rather awkward 'sensu' *tout court*. However, in support of the reading of the MSS., see Augustine *Reconsiderations* 3. 2–3 (on *De Ordine*): 'Verum et his libris displicet mihi...quod non addebam: corporis, quando sensus corporis nominavi.' This clearly implies that, to a developed Christian sensibility, *sensus* may be physical or spiritual—hence my addition of 'that' to the translation.

'signatum amicitiae munus' ('sealed gift of friendship'), suggests an ana-
logy with the sealing of a letter, and reinforces the conception of the letters
as the vectors of spiritual friendship. It may also be noted in passing that
there is here another instance of the explicit adaptation of the word
amicitia to a more spiritual sense; and this is to a correspondent who,
being still very much involved in public affairs at Rome, would have been
vividly aware of its Ciceronian sense.[38]

Linked with this spiritual interpretation of separation is a strong sense
of the ritual of connection as it is played out in the letters. The adjective
unanimis, seen at the beginning of the extract above, is frequent in
Paulinus' letters, especially in passages reflecting on his friendship with
the recipient; and its cognate noun *unanimitas* is often used as an honor-
ific—naturally so in examples like the letter to the Christian Pammachius,
but also in the letter to the pagan Jovius: this is particularly interesting
in view of the fact that, as Bastiaensen has pointed out, 'unanimitas tua'
was formerly an 'appellation mutuelle confraternelle des évêques',
and suggests, as with *amicitia* (only in reverse), the extension of an
accepted range of meaning to embrace both Christian and non-Christian
spheres.[39]

The implications of the idea behind *unanimitas* are taken very seriously.
Two phrases from the epistles of St Paul are repeatedly quoted or drawn
upon (often in combination) to express the simultaneous connectedness
and unity of the Christian community: 'quoniam sumus invicem membra',
and 'ita multi unum corpus sumus in Christo, singuli autem alter alterius

---

[38] There is a further instance of this adaptation a little later in the same letter: 'in veritate,
qua stamus in Christo, expressum his tibi litteris animum meum suscipe, *nec volo amicitiam
nostram tempore metiaris.*' Chris McDonough has pointed out to me that the refusal here to
measure the friendship in temporal terms strengthens the negative invocation of the classical
tradition, in which the length of standing of a friendship was considered of great importance.
On Pammachius and Roman tradition: he was a 'leading Roman senator' and proconsul,
though where is not attested (certainly, though *PLRE* suggests Africa, there is little space left
for him in the list provided by T.D. Barnes, 'Proconsuls of Africa, 337–392', *Phoenix* 39
(1985), 152–3); it will be remembered that his response to the death of his wife Paulina was a
vast almsgiving ceremony at St Peter's—very much the response of a wealthy public figure
drawing on traditions of euergetism. For a fuller prosopography, see *PLRE* 1. 663; for
traditions of euergetism, see Paul Veyne, *Bread and Circuses*, abridged Oswyn Murray;
translated Brian Pearce (Harmondsworth, 1990).

[39] Jovius as 'unanimitas tua': *Letter* 16. 1. On the rise of such abstract nouns as terms of
address in the fourth century, see Bastiaensen, 'Cérémonial épistolaire', 43–4, from which the
quote is taken. See also the discussion of Perrin, 'Courriers', 1039–41, who rightly dwells
upon the significance of the word *unanimitas* in Paulinus.

membra'.[40] We are all members of one body; and it is through Christ, or ∠—
often expressly through the *caritas Christi*, that we are connected.[41] Exam-
ples of this conjunction of thoughts are superabundant in the letters of
Paulinus: I select here only a few of the most densely expressed versions.
First, a continuation of the above-quoted train of thought in the letter to
Pammachius:

Hac igitur te caritate conplexus ita veneror ut membrum Christi, ita diligo ut
commune membrum meum. quomodo enim non una mens, quibus una fides?
quomodo non unus animus, quibus unus deus? ac per hoc quomodo diversum
pectus sit in affectione tolerandi, quibus corpus unum est in compage credendi?[42]

So having embraced you with this love, I revere you as a member of Christ, and I
love you as my own limb.[43] For how could we not have one mind, when we have
one faith? How could we not have one spirit, when we have one God? And
accordingly, how could our hearts be divided in feeling what must be borne [the
pain of Paulina's death], when we have one body in the union of belief?

Second, an instance in which Paulinus is justifying the sending of an
unsolicited letter to Victricius, for which purpose he has diverted Victricius' deacon from Rome to Nola. The sense of oneness in the Christian
community is powerfully invoked, again in explicit connection with spatial
displacement:

nam etsi regionum intervallis corporaliter disparemur, spiritu tamen domini, in
quo vivimus et manemus, ubique effuso coniuncti sumus, ut unius corporis
membra et cor unum et unam animam habentes in uno deo.[44]

---

[40] These citations are from Eph. 4: 25 and Rom. 12: 5 respectively. 1 Cor. 12: 12 should
also be remembered: 'Sicut enim corpus unum est, et membra habet multa, omnia autem
membra corporis cum sint multa, unum tamen corpus sunt: ita et Christus.' Similar in import
is the passage from John's gospel quoted earlier (n. 18), especially 'ego sum vitis, vos palmites'
(John 15: 5).

[41] See Wayne A. Meeks, *The First Urban Christians. The Social World of the Apostle Paul*
(New Haven, 1983), 89–90, on the use of the 'body of Christ' metaphor by the early Christian
communities. Meeks attributes Paul's emphasis on love (particularly in the well-known
excursus of 1 Cor. 13) to a desire 'to reinforce the cohesion of the group'. Augustine radically
revised Paul's notion of community, changing a socially specific idea into a more general,
symbolic one: to explore this revision lies beyond the scope of this study, but we surely see a
parallel process in Paulinus' rereading of Paul.

[42] *Letter* 13. 3.

[43] Literally, I think, 'a common limb of mine', which strengthens still further the case for
unity in Christ.

[44] *Letter* 18. 1. This resonates startlingly with Victricius' own comments on the power of
relics in his *De Laude Sanctorum*—as does, for example, *Poem* 19 (*Nat.* 11) on the 'cineres
quasi semina vitae' (358), the scattered relics of the saints. The passage immediately

For even if we are physically disunited by the intervening lands, yet we are joined by the spirit of the Lord which suffuses everything and in which we live and stay, and as members of one body we have one heart and one soul in the one God.

Finally, an example may be drawn from the correspondence of Paulinus and Sulpicius, in which Paulinus tactfully emphasizes not the unity of the body but the diversity of the limbs:

Itaque de ipsius domini verbis nostras pariter ac tuas pende rationes, ne vel tibi ut inpedito diffidas vel nobis ut iam liberis congratuleris, divisiones esse gratiarum [1 Cor. 12: 4][45] et mensuras donationum, quas ut in corporis sui membris unus atque idem dispensator operatur deus, diversa in suo corpore distinguens placitis membra muneribus, sed corpus unum ex diversitate membrorum struens, ut hinc quoque gratia sacri corporis augeatur . . . [46]

And so, ponder my behaviour[47] and yours with respect to those words of our Lord himself, that graces are divided up and gifts measured out, so that you may not be diffident about yourself as encumbered [with worldly possessions] or congratulate me for now being unencumbered, since one and the same God disposes these gifts among the members of his body, marking out different members in his body for appropriate gifts, but constructing a single body from the diverse group of limbs, so that from this too the grace of the sacred body might be increased . . .

This emphasis on the differences between the limbs is, however, very much an *ad hominem* adaptation. In general, Paulinus' use of the 'invicem membra' motif revolves around similarity and community. It is notable that the honorifics most commonly used by Paulinus emphasize friendship, sanctity, and unanimity. The *superscriptiones*, textually unreliable though they may be, are good *ad hoc* indicators: 'dilectissimus', 'beatissimus', and 'venerabilis' are with 'unanimus' by far the most frequent adjectives applied to the addressees. Paulinus almost never uses words directly indicating title or status: the one exception as printed, 'Augustino episcopo' in *Letter* 45, is extremely ill attested in the manuscripts; and he never uses 'episcopus' of himself.[48]

preceding this, which elaborates in considerably greater detail the metaphysical implications of this thoroughgoing notion of community, will be discussed in Chapter 6.

[45] Note that this leads up to the crucial passage quoted in n. 40 above.

[46] *Letter* 24. 2. Walsh solves the awkward displacement of the quotation by inserting an introductory imperative: 'Remember that . . .' Walsh, *Letters* 2. 52.

[47] Blaise supplies 'manière d'agir' s.v. *ratio* 5, which seems apt here.

[48] This point alone is not conclusive, as almost all the surviving letters have been dated as preceding Paulinus' elevation to the bishopric.

The logical progression from the idea that 'we are all members one of another' led to the facet of Christian friendship that modern commentators have often found most surprising: it was considered capable of arising instantaneously. Paulinus makes this connection explicit at the beginning of what was to be a lifelong correspondence with Augustine:

nec mirum, si et absentes adsumus nobis *et ignoti nosmet novimus*, cum unius corporis membra simus, unum habeamus caput, una perfundamur gratia, uno pane vivamus, una incedamus via, eadem habitemus domo.[49]

Nor is it any wonder if, even when we are absent, we are present to each other *and know each other though unknown*, since we are members of one body, we have one head, we are suffused with one grace, we live by one bread, we tread one way, we inhabit the same house.[50]

It is not irrelevant that the initiation of the correspondence has been explicitly attributed to *caritas Christi*: 'Caritas Christi, quae urget nos et absentes licet per unitatem fidei adligat, ipsa fiduciam ad te scribendi pudore depulso praestitit . . .' ('The love of Christ, which stimulates us and binds us together through the unity of faith even though we are apart, that very love has driven away diffidence and offered the confidence to write to you . . .').[51] The friendship between Paulinus and Augustine was not apparently considered by either of them to be vitiated by the fact that they never actually met.[52] This was, as stated above, in striking contrast to the *mores* of classical *amicitia*.[53] We may note that Augustine was already beginning to revise these *mores* by 386, when he chose, instead of a party of the like-minded, an extraordinarily disparate group of people to withdraw to Cassiciacum for discussion and meditation upon Christian themes.[54] This seems to have been an attempt simply to overlay Christian directives (here, the inclusive implications of such tenets as 'sumus invicem membra') on classical *mores* of friendship; and its failure involved his acknowledgement that this could not be done, and

---

[49] *Letter* 6. 2.

[50] This last idea seems to be a pleasing expansion of the classical *desideratum* that friends should live together: Augustine and Paulinus live together in the house of the Lord.

[51] The first words of *Letter* 4. 1. Paulinus continues (4. 2): 'Vides, frater unanime admirabilis in Christo domino et suspiciende, *quam familiariter te agnoverim . . .*'

[52] Casati comments, 'il tono delle lettere di Agostino e di Paolino era quello che si usa tra amici . . .' Giuseppe Casati, 'S. Agostino e S. Paolino di Nola', *Augustinianum* 8 (1968), 40–57.

[53] See *Laelius* 4 (15).

[54] Augustine describes this attempt himself in *Confessions* 9; see also the account of Peter Brown, *Augustine*, 115–27, and of Wills, *Augustine*, 48–55.

that instead the idea of friendship had to be completely rethought.[55] A similar intellectual move, if in a less well-documented form, seems to have been made by Paulinus. Such was the transformation wrought by Christianity.

As members of one spiritual body, one must spiritually be aware of other parts of that body: Paulinus refers to the faith 'qua *accorporamur* in Christo Iesu domino nostro' ('through which *we are bodily assimilated to Jesus Christ our Lord*').[56] Hence to strike up a new friendship is only to give outward expression to a pre-existing relationship: in his first letter to Alypius, Paulinus writes, 'accepimus... litteras tantam nobis sanctitatis tuae lucem adferentes, ut nobis caritatem tuam non agnoscere, sed recognoscere videremur' ('we have received letters that impart to us so great a light of your holiness that we seemed not to make the acquaintance of your love, but to renew our knowledge of it').[57] In some sense, too, the spiritual friendship, as opposed to *amicitia humana*, will not be subject to the normal patterns of development over time, for it stands as a permanent spiritual symbol. Paulinus expresses this in a letter to a new correspondent, Florentius:

Laetamur in domino visitatos nos litteris sanctitatis tuae et provocatos, ut qui neque notitiae tuae prius gratiam gesseramus nunc repentino dei munere *plenam tuae tamquam veteris amicitiae fiduciam sumeremus.* 'vinum', inquit, 'est amicus: veterescet, et cum suavitate bibes eum' [Ecclus. 9: 15][58]. ecce istam prophetae sententiam superavit sanctitas tua, quae tam perfecto diligere nos coepit affectu, ut inveteratae nobis dilectionis suavitatem in prima huius foederis novitate reddiderit...[59]

I rejoice in the Lord to have been visited by the letters from your Holiness, and summoned forth, so that, having previously not even had the favour of your acquaintance, now by the sudden gift of God *I have taken on the full pledge of what seems like an old friendship with you.* 'A friend,' he says, 'is wine: he matures, and you shall drink of him with delight.' Behold, that dictum of the prophet has

---

[55] I gave a paper, 'Did Women Have a Beata Vita?', which discussed this development in Augustine's thought, at the 1997 International Medieval Congress at Leeds.

[56] *Letter* 4. 1 again.

[57] Paulinus, *Letter* 3. 1. Compare *Letter* 6. 2 (to Augustine), quoted above: '... ut nobis non novam aliquam amicitiam sumere, sed quasi veterem caritatem resumere videremur'.

[58] I have here emended Hartel, who reads, 'vinum... et amicus veterescet, et cum suavitate bibes eum'. The substitution of 'est' for 'et', and the repunctuation, avoids the problem of two nouns governing the singular 'veterescet' and the double referent for 'eum', while moving closer to the sense of the passage in Ecclesiasticus. The confusion of 'est' and 'et' could have been easily made in the manuscripts, though Hartel reports no variant.

[59] *Letter* 42. 1. Note another 'Christian' use of *amicitia*.

been surpassed by your Holiness, who have begun to love me with so perfect a sentiment that you have given me the delight of a well-aged love in the first youth of this bond . . .

The preceding verse in Ecclesiasticus illuminates Paulinus' revisionism: 'Ne derelinquas amicum antiquum; novus enim non erit similis illi' ('Do not desert an old friend; for a new one will not be like him'). Paulinus, on the contrary, is arguing that a new friend is not *like* an old friend, he *is*, miraculously, an old friend. Just as a friendship may begin instantaneously, so it no longer needs to develop and mature.

We see in situations like this how critical to Christian friendship is every aspect of epistolary exchange. Above all, the sense of continuous participation in a matrix of Christian communication, which is created and sustained by the letters and their carriers, feeds into the notion of being members of one body; so does the tendency to symbolic thought which confounds recipient as friend with recipient as both member of the church and *membrum Christi*, and creates the 'sacramental' properties of letters. Moreover, there is the growing attachment of spiritual significance to spatial separation, with the sense that it is by the grace of God that its disadvantages are transcended. The delivery of letters becomes the ritual through which spatial separation is negotiated.

At first sight, the *desiderata* for friendship are less demanding than those of the classical tradition, if a friendship may be instantaneously generated and thereafter conducted only in letters; but they are the logical concomitants of a belief that communion in the spiritual sphere is superior to that in the physical. In practice, this principle is sometimes assented to rather grudgingly (as we shall see further in the chapter on the self), but the idea remains and is frequently adverted to.

In the case of friendship, the primacy of the spiritual sphere is particularly emphasized by the imperative to love supplied by the first two commandments as reported in Mark.[60] As we have seen, Augustine discusses the first two commandments explicitly in the context of friendship in his letter to Macedonius;[61] and he reverts to them in the letter to Marcianus with which I began this chapter: 'haec duo si mecum firmissime teneas, amicitia nostra vera ac sempiterna erit et non solum invicem nos sed etiam ipsi domino sociabit' ('If you keep these two in firmest faith

---

[60] See Mark 12: 30–31 and n. 16 above.

[61] Augustine *Letter* 155. 14 ff. Amusingly, this quotation is supported with the tag from Terence ('homo sum, humani nihil a me alienum puto') that was later to become the mantra of secular humanism.

with me, our friendship will be true and everlasting, and will unite us not only with each other but also with our Lord himself ').[62] The imperative to love, and its connection with the spiritual sphere, is, of course, famously endorsed by Paul in 1 Corinthians: 'Sectamini caritatem, aemulamini spiritalia' ('Follow love, imitate spiritual things').[63] But it is Christ himself who sets the pattern for expansive love. All *amicitia* relates to Christ: this, of course, is the central element in Christian friendship which has so far been skirted around. This point has, to remarkable degree, been passed over or minimized in previous discussions—even that of Fabre, who acknowledges the omission in his closing words: '...this affection ult- imately sustained and nourished his thought, just as it sustained and nourished—more exalted than any human affection, *and beyond the scope of our current analysis*—his love of his God.'[64] Yet Christ is—or should be—inseparable from Christian friendship: specifically Christ, not the triune God. Cassian expressly invokes him as a pattern for *vera amicitia*.[65] Augustine's definitions, as we have seen, all add Christ as the crucial element; and Paulinus, though as usual avoiding the dogmatic, writes to Sulpicius of their love for each other:

sed tamen in hanc, qua modo interventu dei nectimur, copulam per consuetudi- nem illius familiaritatis inolevimus, ut diligendo nos et in infideli via fideliter diligere etiam spiritaliter disceremus, quia tam religiose nos semper uterque dileximus, *ut ad nostram inter nos dilectionem nulla adici posset affectio nisi caritas Christi*, quae sola omnem sensum affectumque supereminet.[66]

---

[62] Augustine, *Letter* 258. 4. This passage is immediately preceded by direct quotation of the relevant two commandments, followed by their connection with the Ciceronian definition of *amicitia*: 'in illo primo rerum divinarum, in hoc secundo rerum humanarum est cum benivolentia et caritate consensio'.

[63] 1 Cor. 14: 1. This immediately follows the well-known passage on 'fides, spes, caritas', which concludes: 'maior autem horum est caritas'.

[64] '...cette affection [for his friends]...a finalement soutenu et nourri sa pensée, comme elle a soutenu et nourri, plus haut que toute affection humaine, et hors de portée, cette fois, de nos analyses, son amour pour son Dieu'. Fabre, *Saint Paulin de Nole*, 393. Both McGuire in *Friendship and Community* and White in *Christian Friendship in the Fourth Century* also fail to discuss this crucial aspect of Christian friendship. Konstan (*Friendship*, 170) does discuss it, aptly if briefly, but—like Fabre—does not appear to differentiate between God and Christ.

[65] Cassian, *Conference* 16, 6. I do not make further reference to Cassian in this discussion of Christian friendship, largely because I think that McGuire is correct to observe that Cassian's *De Amicitia*, which treats mainly of the resolution of disputes and the control of anger in a monastic context, would be better entitled *De Concordia in Claustro*: hence it concerns only a small subdivision of my theme here. See *Friendship and Community*, 79.

[66] Paulinus, *Letter* 11. 5. Contrast Augustine's more rigorous treatment of pre-conversion love which opens this chapter.

But we have grown into this bond, by which we are now joined with God's mediation, through the habit of that intimacy, so that by loving each other we might learn, even on the path of faithlessness, to love faithfully and even spiritually: for we have always loved each other so devotedly *that no affection could be added to the love between us except for the love of Christ*, which alone surpasses every affection one can feel.

The statement that 'nulla adici posset affectio nisi caritas Christi' would be quite extraordinary in its claims for affection prior to conversion, were it not for a passage later in the same letter: 'nihil habemus nisi Christum, et vide, si nihil habeamus qui omnia habentem habemus' ('we have nothing except Christ; and consider whether we, who have the one who contains everything, really have nothing').[67] In the light of this addition, it appears that the claim that only 'caritas Christi' could be added to the relationship between Paulinus and Sulpicius is paradoxical, and perhaps even ironic: there can be nothing to connect them *except* 'caritas Christi'. There could be no more forceful expression of the complete centrality of Christ for Paulinus.[68]

Christ is utterly pervasive in the letters of Paulinus; yet his relationship to other themes is expressed in such an imprecisely associative manner that it is hard to pick out salient passages through which to discuss the nature of his centrality. But a few claims may be securely supported. Even at the stage of his dispute with Ausonius, Paulinus' theology was already strongly Christocentric.[69] We have already discussed the issue of members of the Church being configured as limbs of Christ's body. It becomes clear that this is far from an idle metaphor. In accordance with the metaphor, the members of Christ's Church must work together in unity:

quia scissura ... in corpore esse non potest [1 Cor. 12: 25], cui caput Christus est, quem communem sibi apicem una membrorum suorum compago comitatur. quae quoniam sibi discrepare non possunt, curramus pariter, ut adprehendamus omnes sine aemulatione invidiae cum aequalitate victoriae, ut sicut in contentione

[67] *Letter* 11. 14.

[68] For a systematic exposition of the theological centrality of Christ for Paulinus, see Matthias Skeb, *Christo vivere: Studien zum literarischen Christusbild des Paulinus von Nola* (Bonn, 1997).

[69] See *Poems* 10 and 11, especially 10, 278–end. Michael Roberts suggests that Paulinus is fashioning in Poem 11 a 'Tityrus Christianus': 'Paulinus Poem 11, Virgil's first *Eclogue*, and the limits of *amicitia*', *TAPhA* 115 (1985), 271–82; but his argument is based on an interpretation of only a small part of the poem.

currendi labor Christi sumus, ita in perveniendi fine Christi triumphus esse possimus et benedicat nos in corona anni benignitatis suae.[70]

For there cannot be division in the body whose head is Christ, the shared summit which accompanies a single conjunction of his own limbs. Since these cannot be at odds among themselves, let us run together, so that we may all understand, without the rivalry of envy and with an equal victory, that just as in the effort of running we are the work of Christ, so in the goal of arrival we shall be able to be the triumph of Christ and he shall bless us at the crown of the year of his loving-kindness.

The image of running is derived from 1 Corinthians,[71] but Paulinus has made one significant alteration: according to Paul, only one man receives the prize, and the passage forms part of an exhortation to be that one man; in Paulinus' interpretation, we shall all gain the prize, in community in Christ and through our membership in his body. As both 'labor Christi' and 'triumphus Christi' we work through him and he through us; our goal is Christ and we are his. The idea is that it is *in action* that Christians become the 'labor Christi'. The conception is utterly processual: in the process of running, one becomes a process, the *labor*; in arrival, one does not receive the prize of Christ but simply *is* that prize.

This paradox of divine/human reciprocity through process is achieved by 'imitatio Christi', the imitation of Christ that is at the core of Paulinus' theology and of his interpretation of how to conduct himself in this life and achieve a 'beata vita' in the next.[72] 'Quomodo aliter', he demands of Sulpicius, 'putas Christum sequendum nisi lege qua docuit et forma quam praetulit?' ('How else do you think that Christ is to be followed except by the law with which he taught and the template which he proffered?').[73] (Though Paulinus also offers in the same letter an unusual permutation of this precept: 'imitando enim imitatorem Christi perveniemus ad imitationem dei' ('for by imitating the imitator of Christ we shall attain the imitation of God'). The 'imitatorem Christi' here appears to be Paul, which is of particular interest in view of the revision of Paul documented above.)[74] It is in a letter to Augustine that Paulinus clarifies

---

[70] Paulinus, *Letter* 24. 15. The whole letter is unusually specific about Paulinus' views of Christ and Christ's role in the life of a Christian.

[71] 1 Cor. 9: 24 ff.: 'Nescitis quod ii qui in stadio currunt, omnes quidem currunt, sed unus accipit bravium?'

[72] Examples of *imitatio Christi*: *Letters* 12. 8 and 24. 9.

[73] Paulinus, *Letter* 11. 12.

[74] *Letter* 11. 7. The 'imitatio Pauli' is perhaps less surprising given that the passage cited here, 1 Cor. 15: 49, resonates closely with Paulinus' general concerns: ' . . . sicut portavimus imaginem terreni, portemus et imaginem caelestis'.

what is implicit elsewhere in his correspondence: how the *imitatio Christi* is above all to be achieved.

Quae autem virtus hanc in nobis efficit mortem nisi caritas, quae 'fortis est ut mors' [S. of S. 8: 6]? sic enim oblitterat nobis et perimit hoc saeculum, ut inpleat mortis effectum per affectum Christi, in quem conversi avertimur ab hoc mundo et cui viventes morimur ab elementis huius mundi.[75]

What virtue brings about this death in us other than love, which 'is strong as death'? For thus it erases for us and destroys this world, so as to fulfil the effect of death through the affection of Christ:[76] converted to him, we are turned away from this world, and living for him, we die to the elements of this world.[77]

Paulinus makes of humans and their human life a palimpsest on which the love of Christ is written: it is love through which the salvific death to the world is to be effected, love of Christ and of others in Christ. Thus we return to the first two commandments, but with an entirely Christocentric twist. Paradoxically, the re-enactment of the Law of the Old Testament through Christ becomes the quintessential expression of the Spirit of the New.[78] Loving friendship towards other Christians is not *a* way to achieve assimilation with Christ: it is *the* way. The active practice of Christian friendship is a crucial part of living a virtuous Christian life: Augustine observes epigrammatically that only good *amores* make good *mores* (as opposed to good habits of life creating virtuous desires: a sort of inverted Aristotelianism).[79] Hence the enormous importance both of Christian friendship itself and of its maintenance through letters. Hence the spiritual significance attached to the writing and reception of letters themselves. It can now be seen how truly they contribute to the 'development, reinforcement and extension of the Christian community'.

This reveals another characteristic of Christian friendship: whereas classical notions of friendship centred on exclusivity—one could sustain

[75] Paulinus, *Letter* 45. 5.

[76] The use of the phrase 'affectum Christi' here encapsulates precisely the blending of the subjective and objective genitives which I discussed above: it refers both to our affection for Christ, and to Christ's for us.

[77] An echo of the ideas in Col. 2: 20: 'Si ergo mortui estis cum Christo ab elementis huius mundi, quid adhuc tanquam viventes in mundo decernitis?' Compare too Acts 14: 14.

[78] The spiritual 'circumcisio in corde' as opposed to the literal 'circumcisio' of the Old Testament is originally stated in Paul—'circumcisio cordis in spiritu, non littera' (Rom. 2: 29)—and is frequently adverted to in the letters of both Paulinus and Augustine. See for example in Paulinus, *Letter* 50. 3 (to Augustine); *Letter* 20. 1 (to Delphinus), which is discussed in Chapter 6, text to n. 17.

[79] Augustine, *Letter* 155. 13.

⫗7

a true *amicitia* with two or three friends at most—the Christian ideal bespeaks a functional inclusivity.[80] Paul's dictum 'quoniam sumus invicem membra', combined with the first and second commandments and taken as a design for friendship, implies that *amicitia* should ideally embrace every individual member of the Church of Christ.[81] The realization of this is crucially bound up with the manner of delivery of the letters. We have already seen how letters were written for the eyes not just of those expressly addressed, but of the communities in which they lived and of anyone in the wider Christian community into whose hands the letter might fall. This extended implicit audience naturally both created and was created by an inclusive notion of *amicitia*. It is not that personal bonds of friendship (in a more traditional, exclusive and individuated style) cease to be important, but that *potential* bonds of friendship with the broader Christian community come to be considered as equally important.[82]

women

The ideal participants in Christian *amicitia* are, then, the whole community of the Christian Church. The question now arises: can *amicitia* include women as well as men? Certainly, several women were playing prominent roles in the Church at this period[83] (and we may note that the 'sexus minor' is given equal billing in the iconographic programme for Paulinus' new portico![84]). Paulinus' own attested circle includes, besides

---

[80] I choose the qualifier 'functional' because the Christian notion of inclusivity seems to me to be sharply different, in practice, from attempts in the Hellenistic period to develop a theory of universal *philia* in the face of Aristotelian partialism. See Julia Annas, 'Aristotelian political theory in the Hellenistic period' in André Laks and Malcolm Schofield (eds.), *Justice and Generosity: Studies in Hellenistic Social and Political Philosophy*, Proceedings of the Sixth Symposium Hellenisticum (Cambridge, 1995), 74–94, esp. 84–5.

[81] Van Bavel discusses Augustine's arrival at this conclusion in 'The Double Face of Love in St. Augustine. The Daring Inversion: Love is God', in *Congresso Internazionale su S. Agostino nel XVI centenario della conversione* (Rome, 1987) III. 81–102.

[82] It may be fruitful to compare with this observation Catherine Osborne's recent discussion of the way in which love characterizes trinitarian bonds in the thought of Augustine: *Eros Unveiled: Plato and the God of Love* (Oxford, 1994), ch. 9, esp. 214–16. 'For Augustine, I am suggesting, it is possible to describe as love *some kind of tendency that causes us to enter into loving relationships*' (215; my emphasis).

[83] The bibliography on the subject of women in the early church is extensive and increasing. Those working in the area today are perhaps particularly indebted to the pioneering work of Elizabeth Clark and Kari Børresen; some of the evidence has been recently reviewed by Gillian Cloke, *This Female Man of God: Women and Spiritual Power in the Patristic Age*, AD 350–450 (London/New York, 1995).

[84] See *Poem* 28. 20–27; 'sexus minor', 26. The treatment of the martyrs is particularly interesting: 'martyribus mediam pictis pia nomina signant,/quos *par in vario* redimivit *gloria sexu*', 20–21.

his wife Therasia, Melania the Elder, Paulina the wife of Pammachius (and daughter of Jerome's follower Paula), Amanda the wife of Aper, and Galla the wife of Eucherius, who lived with him close to the monastery at Lérins.[85] Equally certainly, classical theories of *amicitia* tacitly agree that the superior form of friendship can only exist between men (who alone can be *boni*). It seems that, once again, a certain gulf exists between theory and practice, a certain tension between conditioned assumptions and Christian logic. There seems to be no inherent or stated reason why women should not be included—indeed, James McEvoy observes, in his useful survey of the topic of friendship (and argument for its centrality), 'the ancient ideal [of friendship] had been devised by men for a male world; Augustine's rule had little in it that could not be put into the feminine form'.[86] It is just that in practice they very seldom are.[87]

There is little direct discussion of the subject; but, in the cases where friendship is offered to women, the offer tends to be made on male terms. This is the conclusion of Elizabeth Clark in her study of the issue: women become acceptable as friends to the degree that they deny their femaleness through ascetic suppression of their sexual characteristics.[88] Melania the Elder—who is the only woman without a male consort who is alluded to in the letters of Paulinus[89]—is a case in point. She is typically referred to by Paulinus as 'Melanius'; in one instance he emphasizes this transsexual

[85] *Letters* 38, 39, and 44 are addressed to Aper and Amanda; *Letter* 51 to Eucherius and Galla. Melania's story is told in *Letter* 29; *Letter* 13 is the *consolatio* to Pammachius on the death of Paulina.

[86] '"Philia" and "Amicitia": the Philosophy of Friendship from Plato to Aristotle', *Sewanee Mediaeval Colloquium Occasional Papers* (1985), 1–24; quote from 16. George Lawless surveys the opinions on whether Augustine's Rule was written originally for men or women: *Augustine of Hippo and his Monastic Rule* (Oxford, 1987), 135–54.

[87] I note with some amusement that this is precisely the opposite conclusion to that formulated a century ago by Gaston Boissier: '*En théorie*, l'Église traite assez mal les femmes; elle se défie de leur légèreté, elle accuse leur faiblesse. ... *Dans la pratique*, on tient grand compte d'elles ... et, pour tout ce qui tient à la science de salut, on leur reconnaît des droits égaux.' *La Fin du Paganisme: étude sur les dernières luttes religieuses en occident au quatrième siècle* (2 vols.: Paris, 1894), II. 80.

[88] See 'Friendship between the Sexes: Classical Theory and Christian Practice', in *Jerome, Chrysostom and Friends: Essays and Translations*, Studies in Women and Religion II (New York/Toronto, 1979), 35–106. Augustine seems to me to be the exception to this rule, at any rate in his correspondence, and I present this argument in 'Spaces Between Letters', forthcoming in Kathryn Kerby-Fulton and Linda Olson (eds.) *Reading Women: New Approaches to Female Literacy in Late Antiquity and the Middle Ages*.

[89] The only contemporary woman, that is; there is an extended account of the discovery of the true cross by Helena, mother of the emperor Constantine, in *Letter* 31. 4 f.

attribution with 'benedict*a* Melani*us*'. He also praises her with the words 'sexum evacuat fides' ('her faith cancels out her sex').[90] A rather confused passage on the status of women in general looks forward to the ultimate dissolution of masculinity and femininity in Christ, 'in quo nec masculus nec femina sumus [Gal. 3: 28]' ('in whom we are neither male nor female'), but concludes that in the present world the hierarchy of gender should be maintained.[91] We may compare with a rare comment of Paulinus' on the nature of God: the divinity must be sexless and incorporeal, and 'dea numquam/esse potest mater nec femina' ('neither mother nor wife can ever be divine').[92] The only God must be simply 'deus unus', one—masculine-gendered—God.[93]

The only extensive comment on a specific woman in the letters of Paulinus is made of Amanda, wife of Aper:

illic et coniunx, non dux ad mollitudinem vel avaritiam viro suo, sed ad continentiam et fortitudinem redux in ossa viri sui, magna illa divini cum ecclesia coniugii aemulatione mirabilis est, quam in tuam unitatem reductam ac redditam spiritalibus tibi tanto firmioribus quanto castioribus nexibus caritas Christi copulat, in cuius corpus transistis a vestro.[94]

There too is your wife, who does not bring her husband to indulgence or greed, but brings back restraint and strength into his bones; that great woman is miraculous for her imitation of the divine marriage with the church, and the love of Christ, into whose body you have been transformed, joins her to you, led back and received into your unity, with spiritual bonds as firm as they are chaste.

Paulinus goes on to praise Amanda for taking care of Aper's secular affairs so that he can devote himself more fully to a spiritual life. Two observations may be made about this. First, Amanda is praised not for her own spiritual achievement, but for furthering her husband's—that is, for taking an appropriately subordinate position to the endeavour of true value. Second, this passage of praise is almost identical to that addressed to Therasia by Augustine some years earlier.[95] As we have already

---

[90] For 'benedicta Melanius' and 'sexum evacuat fides', see Paulinus, *Letter* 31. 1 (to Sulpicius). 'Melanius' again: *Letter* 45. 2 and 3 (to Augustine).

[91] Paulinus, *Letter* 23. 24.

[92] Paulinus *Poem* 19 (*Nat.* 11). 132–3.

[93] I am reminded of a recent quote from the Church of England's *Church Times*: God is 'a relatively genderless male deity'. Cited in Grace Jantzen, *Becoming Divine: Towards a Feminist Philosophy of Religion* (Manchester, 1998), 65.

[94] Paulinus, *Letter* 44. 3.

[95] Augustine, *Letter* 27. 2. Despite the similarities, a comparison of the two passages in fact yields fascinating results concerning the different emphases of the two men. The passage in

observed, this would not have been considered as invalidating the sentiments of admiration; on the contrary, to echo another's words takes the logic of 'invicem membra' to its ultimate extent. But it is of material importance in considering whether the relationship within a celibate marriage might amount to *amicitia*.[96] Much has been made of Augustine's praise of Therasia; but, as the index to CSEL says, 'praeterea non memoratur nisi in inscriptionibus' ('otherwise she is not mentioned except in the superscriptions [to the letters]').[97] Moreover, Augustine's very praise takes the form of justifying the collapse of Therasia's identity into that of Paulinus: 'in te uno resalutamus' ('in return, we salute her in you alone . . . '). Christian reasoning might seem to demand a far more expansive notion of marriage; but it seems that the role of women, even in such marriages as that of Paulinus and Therasia, remained essentially subordinate, and praised inasfar as it was so. This may be illustrated specifically from Paulinus' letters: he makes Therasia his cosignatory in eleven out of forty-five possible instances in the letters; however, the only passage in the prose works in which she is referred to by name is in a prayer to Clarus composed for inscription in Sulpicius' basilica.[98] Although the relationship between husband and wife was occasionally referred to as *amicitia*, it was fundamentally unequal and, except on certain pastoral issues, generally ignored.[99] The call of Saint Paul for wives to be subject to their husbands, as the husbands to Christ (as at Eph. 5: 22–23), was always

Augustine reads: 'videtur a legentibus ibi coniunx non dux ad mollitiem viro suo, sed ad fortitudinem redux in ossa viri sui, quam in tuam unitatem redactam et redditam et spiritalibus tibi tanto firmioribus, quanto castioribus nexibus copulatam officiis vestrae sanctitati debitis in te uno resalutamus.' Paulinus has expanded the 'dux/redux' antithesis with, respectively, a vice and virtue specific to Aper and Amanda's situation. More importantly, (1) Paulinus adds the typological comparison to the marriage of Christ and *ecclesia*; (2) he shifts the syntax of the latter half of the sentence to make the *caritas Christi*, instead of himself, the subject; (3) he expands the *caritas Christi* reference with an allusion to Aper's assimilation into Christ's body. His manipulation of Augustine's original thus corresponds exactly with the issues I discuss in this chapter and the following one; it also suggests that Paulinus is quoting from memory and unconsciously altering Augustine to reflect his own concerns.

[96] This issue has recently been raised by White, *Christian Friendship*, 159–61; she appears to feel that a celibate marriage may amount to *amicitia* (161).

[97] CSEL 58, 325.

[98] *Letter* 32. 6. However, she is also clearly referred to at *Letter* 5. 19, to Sulpicius: 'conserva in domino mea fraternitatem tuam quo veneratur affectu salutat'.

[99] See Gillian Clark, ' "The bright frontier of friendship": Augustine and the Christian body as frontier', in Ralph W. Mathisen and Hagith S. Sivan (eds.) *Shifting Frontiers in Late Antiquity* (Brookfield, VT, 1996), 217–29; and compare Paul Veyne on late Roman marriage

more to the forefront than the Christ in whom male and female was to be dissolved.

Paulinus acknowledges freely the presence of women in the Christian community; he propounds a rationale of all-embracing friendship which logically should include those women. But it is for his male friends that a lavish rhetoric of friendship is reserved. Most lavish of all is the rhetoric bestowed upon Sulpicius by Paulinus.

Quid extorques, ut te plus amemus? crescere summa non recipit. si potest mare superfluere obices suos et quaecumque naturalem plenitudinem servant incrementum temporale sentire, potest et caritas in te nostra cumulari, quam suo fine conplemus, cum te sicut nosmet ipsos diligamus. itaque ut cubitum ad staturam nostram adicere, sic amoris tui cumulum facere non possumus; desideriis tamen modum nullum ponimus.[100]

Why do you extort that I should love you more? Plentitude does not admit of increase. If the sea can overflow its bounds and whatever has a natural fullness can experience growth over time, then there can also be increase in my love for you, which [at present] I fill to its brim, since I love you as myself. And so, just as I cannot add a cubit to my height [Matt. 6: 27], neither can I increase my love for you; yet I place no boundary on my desires.

It is no coincidence that the motif of impossibilities or *adynata*, reflecting the extremes of the writer's love, is to be found also in Latin love poetry[101]—although Paulinus, typically, elaborates it with a biblical allusion. Paulinus' language to Sulpicius of loving friendship is often strikingly passionate. The combination of this with the fact that more letters are preserved from Paulinus to Sulpicius than to any other single recipient has led to considerable exploration of the psychological trajectory of their relationship, most notably by Fabre.[102] Fabre portrays an originally close friendship marred by Sulpicius' failure to visit Paulinus, first in Barcelona, then at Nola; after the explosive demand quoted above, the friendship cools, and remains more detached until their deaths. This scenario has

---

as friendship between superior and inferior partners, *A History of Private Life* (Cambridge, MA/London, 1992), 1. 37 and 45.

[100] Paulinus, *Letter* 23. 1. This sort of language may be readily compared with even the most affectionate of Cicero's letters to show how far we have come from the classical tradition. See, for example, Cicero's letter to his dying freedman Tiro, *Ad Familiares* 16. 5.

[101] The *locus classicus* is Virgil *Eclogue* 8. 53 ff., though the force is there reversed to 'anything is possible now I have been betrayed in love'. The *Eclogues* were certainly familiar to Paulinus; however, Hartel's identification of an allusion to *Eclogue* 1. 11 at *Letter* 17. 4 seems far-fetched. For *adynata* more generally, see Curtius, *European Literature*, 94–8.

[102] Fabre, *Saint Paulin de Nole*, 282–337.

proved extremely compelling, and has been repeatedly rehearsed.[103] Here, as a 'case study' of Christian friendship, we shall consider a rather different reading of their interactions. This will be based on my observations about Christian friendship in the preceding pages.

The critical issue in the friendship between Paulinus and Sulpicius is the one with which we opened the chapter, that of the nature of friendship before and after conversion. This correspondence is extraordinarily instructive in supplying a view both of the new rhetoric of friendship and of the tensions it entailed in practice. The two had been intimates in what they both now regarded as a former life (from which unfortunately no letters or similar documents now survive[104]): in the first surviving letter from Paulinus to Sulpicius, written from Barcelona in early 395,[105] Paulinus says 'abscidatur ut inutilis dextera a corpore tuo, qui tibi in Christi corpore non cohaeret' ('let the man who does not join with you in Christ's body be cut off from your own body like a useless right hand').[106] There is more in the same vein; and the letter ends with a plea to Sulpicius to come to him. The next letter complains of Sulpicius' absence, but seeks consolation in terms which will by now be familiar:

Et excusandum putasti, frater dilectissime, quod ad nos non ipse venisses secundum sponsionem tuam expectationemque nostram? tu vero *potiore tui parte* quam qua manseris, solo corpore domi residens, voluntate ad nos et spiritu et sermone venisti; quamquam ne corporaliter quidem penitus afueris, quando *in pueris tuis* sancta in domino tibi servitute conexis corporis ad nos tui membra venerunt.[107]

And do you think that you ought to be excused, my most beloved brother, for not having come to us yourself as you had promised and we had hoped? It's true that you did come to us *with a more effective part of you* than that which remained, since

---

[103] McGuire goes so far as to entitle his section on Paulinus 'Paulinus of Nola: Friendship as Disappointment'; *Friendship and Community*, 66. Even White, who wishes to emphasize the love of Paulinus for Sulpicius, echoes this opinion: *Christian Friendship*, 152. The interpretation seems to have been long-lived: in a fifteenth-century manuscript of Paulinus' letters (Hartel's U), Ausonius' reproachful poem 'Quarta tibi haec . . .' (*Letter* 21) is attributed to Sulpicius.

[104] There are only the allusions in Sulpicius Severus' *Vita Martini* to Paulinus being cured by Saint Martin of a disease of the eyes at Vienne, and later being held up by the saint as exemplary for his renunciation: *Vita Martini* 19. 3 and 25. 4–5 respectively.

[105] That is, between his ordination on Christmas Day 394 and his departure for Nola in April 395.

[106] Paulinus, *Letter* 1. 5. See Matt. 18: 8 for the origins of this figure, and compare also Mark 9: 44. See also the text to Chapter 6, n. 72.

[107] Paulinus, *Letter* 5. 1. For the distinctive phrase 'potiore . . . parte', compare 'potiore mei parte' in *Letter* 13. 1, discussed above.

you stayed at home only in body, while you came in volition and spirit and conversation; although indeed you were not even entirely absent physically, since the members of your body came to us *in your servants*, joined to you in the Lord with holy service.

First, Sulpicius was spiritually present, through his letters and the volition which they represented; second, he was even partially present physically, through the presence of his letter-carriers. The latter claim we shall explore further in the chapter on the self. As for the first, it is clear that once again we are confronted with the tension between the physical and the spiritual, the symbolic and literal forms of communication. (This tension is vividly felt also by Augustine at the beginning of his correspondence with Paulinus: he demands ironically, 'Vellem tamen scire, utrum hanc absentiam corporalem vos patientius quam nos facilius toleretis' ('so I would like to know whether you can bear this physical absence with a patience corresponding to my ease')[108]). It is the negotiation of this tension that gradually effects the change of tone in the letters of Paulinus to Sulpicius. The difficulty, but the necessity, in Christian friendship is to progress from the literal, intuitive models of friendship to those which recognize spiritual communion as supreme.[109] This progression is, surely, particularly difficult to realize when one has established a prior friendship with one's counterpart. Hence Paulinus' celebrated requests for Sulpicius to visit, including the renowned outburst, 'Et invitando te et expectando defessi sumus' ('I am fed up with inviting you and waiting for you').[110] But these requests are interspersed with passages of extravagant tribute to the friendship of Sulpicius:

> In domino deo Iesu Christo sentio et in te potissimum munere et verbo dei laetus experior, quia 'amico fideli nulla est conparatio' [Ecclus. 6: 15]... 'quid retribuemus domino nostro praeter omnia quae retribuit nobis' [Ps. 115: 12], pro hac etiam gratia, qua te nobis et in saeculari prius amicitia dilectissimum, in suis quoque rebus, quod inconparabilis pretii ducimus, individuum comitem atque consortem spiritali germanitate conexuit?[111]

---

[108] Augustine, *Letter* 31. 4.

[109] Fabre does note this change, summarizing in his index 'efforts vers une amitié plus désincarnée et plus purement spirituelle'; but he sees this as an effect, not a cause, of Paulinus' frustration at stages in the correspondence.

[110] Paulinus, *Letter* 17. 1.

[111] Paulinus, *Letter* 11. 1. Several paragraphs expressing similar sentiments culminate in the passage quoted above: only the *caritas Christi* could be added to their love for each other.

In the Lord God Jesus Christ I am aware of the gift and word of God, and in you especially I experience them with joy, because 'there is no comparison to a faithful friend'... 'What shall we return to our Lord for all that he has bestowed upon us', and particularly for this grace, through which he has bound you to me, both formerly, when you were most beloved to me even in secular friendship, and now too in his own affairs, which we think precious beyond compare, when you are an exceptional companion and comrade in spiritual brotherhood?

Paulinus attempts to capture the symbolic value of his friendship for Sulpicius later in the same letter:

... illud in te speciale nobis donum est, quod praedestinatos nos invicem nobis in caritate Christi iunctissima prioris quoque vitae amicitia signavit, adhuc eorum, quae nunc per Christum avertimur, amatores.[112]

That [property] in you is a particular gift to me, that an exceptionally close friendship in our former life as well marked us out as predestined for each other in the love of Christ, and we still love those things towards which we are now directed through Christ.

Their friendship prior to conversion is here configured as a foreshadowing of their true love in Christ—just as the Old Testament foreshadows the New; indeed, as the Old Testament is redirected in the new light of Christ. This symbolic reading of friendship seems to me to gain its final statement, and resolution, at the end of the letter with whose initial rhetorical demand ('Why do you extort that I should love you more?') we began this section:

diligitur autem et in nobismet ipsis, quia ipse dixit *hoc signum fore* discipulorum suorum, si diligerent invicem dilectione qua ipse dilexit nos, id est ut cor unum et unam animam habeamus in Christo et id quisque proximo suo faciat, quod sibi fieri cupit.[113]

But he is loved even between ourselves, because he himself said that *this would be a sign* of his disciples, if they felt for each other the love with which he loved us,[114] that is, that we should have one heart and one soul in Christ, and that each one should treat his neighbour as he wishes to be treated himself.

The secular friendship of Paulinus and Sulpicius has been reinvented as a symbol of Christ's love, and of their status as his disciples; their Christian

---

[112] *Letter* 11. 5.

[113] Paulinus, *Letter* 23. 47.

[114] Note that this echoes the passage at John 15: 12, cited at n. 18 above, which emphasizes the blend of subjective and objective love.

friendship is the revealed fulfilment of its original promise.[115] *Amicitia* in classical terms had been a pragmatic mixture of reciprocal obligation and affective state; Christian *amicitia* interpreted affective states in terms of spiritual symbolism, and used the logic of spirituality to presuppose affective states. The symbolic level was all-pervasive.

Thus the development of the friendship between Paulinus and Sulpicius represents a progression from the literal to the abstract. Such a progression was facilitated by the counter-intuitive[116] nature of much of Christian thought. It was also far from unique: the interpretative progress documented in Augustine's *Confessions* moves, likewise, from the literal to the abstract. In the next chapter, we shall explore some of the configurations of doctrine that make this progression necessary, and some of the patterns of thought that make it possible, as evinced in the letters of Paulinus.

First, however, a brief coda on the so-called 'friendship' of Paulinus with Felix. There has been an extraordinarily persistent perception that Paulinus, disillusioned with human friendships, turned instead to an ideal friendship with his patron saint.[117] Fabre bases this perception particularly on the way in which Paulinus refers to Felix in the first two *Natalicia* (*Poems* 12 and 13), the annual poems which he wrote for the saint's feast day; White prefers to emphasize *Natalicium* 13 (*Poem* 21). In theory, of course, Paulinus' relationship with Felix should exemplify *par excellence* exactly the type of triangular formation for Christian friendship which I have been suggesting: the *amici* in constant enriching interrelationship in and through the third member, Christ. However, in the first two *Natalicia* the language of friendship is simply not present: Felix is invoked with 'o pater, o domine', and referred to as 'praesul'—language appropriate to a hierarchical relationship.[118] This tone continues throughout the *Natalicia*; nor do we find the elaborate reflection on the love of Paulinus for Felix that we have come to expect from the letters. Where the language of

---

[115] Paulinus may have partially effected this move by a translation into the human sphere of the idea that he is spiritually close to Felix even when he is not at Nola: already in the first *Natalicium* (of 395, written while he was still in Spain) he is writing that he has lived for many years far from the *sedes* of the saint 'quamvis non mente remoti' (*Poem* 12. 17).

[116] This notion is explored further in Chapter 4.

[117] This notion first aired, to my knowledge, by Fabre, *Saint Paulin de Nole* 339–389; pursued by White, *Christian Friendship*, 161–3: 'Paulinus . . . portrays their relationship not as one-sided devotion to the memory of the dead but as the Christian friendship *par excellence*.'

[118] 'o pater, o domine': *Poem* 12. 10 and 13. 5; 'praesul': *Poem* 13. 26. Further examples: 'servitium nostrum', *Poem* 14. 122; Felix as 'patronus', *Poem* 18. 5.

friendship does intrude—and it does so only occasionally—it is used of the relationship of Felix with Christ: he is the 'sodalis' of Christ, he is 'Christo carissime',[119] and when the possessive pronoun is attached to Felix's name, it is Christ, not Paulinus, who is the possessor.[120] Christ is the 'amicus' of Felix while Paulinus is his 'famulus' and 'alumnus'.[121] In fact, the terms *amicitia* and *amicus* are nowhere used of Paulinus' relationship to Felix. Certainly, we continue to see the pervasiveness of Christ; but as we have observed, Paulinus' theology is entirely Christocentric. The relevance of Christ is adumbrated in *Poem* 15:[122] 'nonne unus in omni/Christus adest sancto?' ('Surely the one Christ is present in every saint?'). Christ remains all-penetrating for Paulinus; but there is a hierarchy of the earthly and celestial, where he and Felix naturally stand in different places. Hence the language of patronage remains appropriate,[123] despite the fact that he and Felix can both be said to be suffused with Christ.

There is a further objection to Fabre's thesis in the dating of the *Natalicia*, for the early poems, which he considers as containing protestations of friendship to Felix, pre-date the supposed rift with Sulpicius: the first was written for the feast day of St Felix in January 395 (following the dating of Trout and Fabre himself), around the same time as the first surviving letter to Sulpicius and before the removal of Paulinus to Nola; the second, presumably, a year later. How, then, could one consider the relationship with Felix the perfect friendship to which Paulinus turned for consolation?

The nearest parallel to the relationship with Felix is Paulinus' former friendship with Ausonius. Paulinus invokes Felix in an early *Natalicium*: 'tu pater et patria et domus et substantia nobis' ('you are my father, my country, my home and my fortune'), which quite closely recalls the 'patrone praeceptor pater' ('patron, teacher, father'), addressed to Ausonius.[124] If the relationship with Felix is replacing any previous relationship in Paulinus' life, it is that with Ausonius—which, of course, is not one of committed Christianity.

---

[119] *Poem* 21. 195 and 345. In the latter instance, we may note that the full invocation is: 'nunc ad te, venerande parens, aeterne patrone,/susceptor meus et Christo carissime Felix...' Once again, therefore, the language used of Felix is entirely hierarchical.

[120] For example, Paulinus, *Poem* 15. 51, 'Felicem tuum'.

[121] *Poem* 21. 355–6.

[122] *Poem* 15. 257–8 (*Natalicium* 4).

[123] On the saint as *patronus*, see Peter Brown, *Cult*, ch. 3, esp. (on Felix) 59–60.

[124] Paulinus, *Poem* 15. 15; *Poem* 10. 96. See also the discussion of Paulinus' conscious shifting of the sense of 'pater' and 'patria' in Chapter 6.

These comments do, however, help finally to emphasize what was a crucial aspect of Christian friendship for Paulinus: that he considered it as subsisting between those who were equals in God's eyes. It is not surprising that the closest echoes of the language used of Felix are with Paulinus' most conspicuous pre-conversion friendship. After his renunciation, and the development of his ideas about Christian friendship, he never uses hierarchical language in addressing those whom he considers to be his friends: it runs entirely counter to every precept of friendship he espouses.[125] Fabre's reading of the Felix/Paulinus relationship, however, explains why he is so insistent that Paulinus made friends only with those in whom he acknowledged some superiority; for this makes the anomaly of the relationship with Felix less glaring.[126] Konstan has just revived this idea, arguing that adopting a stance of humility instead of equality towards a friend was one of the principal things which distinguished Christian from classical modes of friendship.[127] This, while essentially more sympathetic, still fails to take into account the consistency with which Paulinus claims equality in attachment if nothing else. The problem seems partly to be that Konstan does not attach sufficient weight to the notion of *caritas Christi*. The fact that it is, in Christian eyes, unearned, does not make it an empty or invalid concept.

The only hierarchy which Paulinus consistently acknowledges, on renouncing classical modes of thought, is that of the spiritual to the temporal. Felix, as saint and heavenly mediator, could not be treated on the same plane as Paulinus' living friends.[128] It is to the realization of the interrelationship of spiritual and temporal in the expression of Paulinus that we now turn.

---

[125] See my observations on the language of the *superscriptiones*, text to note 48 above.

[126] We do not really have the evidence to support even Fabre's milder conclusion: 'à la base de toutes ses amitiés, il y a un sentiment d'admiration'. *Saint Paulin de Nole*, 387.

[127] See Konstan 'Problems', 100; *Friendship*, 159–60.

[128] Trout does make the excellent point that 'friendship and the promotion of the cult of the saints were intertwined' (*Paulinus*, 238), with especial reference to Primuliacum and Nola; but this does not mean that Paulinus' relationship with Felix, or Sulpicius' with St Martin, were analogous to their friendship with each other.

4

Imago terrena and *imago caelestis*: the earthly and the heavenly image

As we have seen, an overarching theme is emerging in treating of the letters of Paulinus of Nola and of his circle of correspondents: the question of the relationship between the spiritual and the temporal realms, and hence between symbolism and literalism. The friendship expressed in the letters is literally an emotional connection between two or more human beings; but it is also, and more importantly, a connection which symbolizes God's love for humans in the love they bear each other and Christ himself. The letters themselves are not merely written artifacts; they are part of an entire system of communication which is once again laden with symbolic value. Even the physical displacement of the correspondents and the process of travelling between them is coming to be assigned symbolic value. The texts of the letters and the process of delivery are exalted by an ongoing spiritual extrapolation from the literal circumstances.

How are the ideas expressed by which the spiritual becomes superior to the physical, while the physical is taken as capable of implying the spiritual? How, indeed, is the idea realized that the 'letter' (as segment of correspondence or as semiotic unit) is never sufficient, but always merely a small part of a greater 'nexus of communication'? These connections are made possible essentially through the figural use of language and figural modes of thought, through techniques of imagery and visualization. The first stage of my enquiry into Paulinus' use of figuralism will be to investigate the way in which he describes or alludes to material, as opposed to imaginary, objects. (By 'imaginary', I mean those represented in the imagination rather than in material reality.) In the next chapter we shall explore more specifically the role which figuralism and imagistic thought play in Paulinus' correspondence, and begin to suggest how they might be effective in uniting the temporal and spiritual realms.

The investigation into Paulinus' treatment of material objects gives us an obvious starting point, for Paulinus' descriptions of his building projects at Nola have long been a celebrated source for art historians of the period.[1] A letter to Sulpicius contains an extended discussion of the new basilica which he is constructing to interconnect with the old basilica of Felix at Nola, along with a brief allusion to further construction at Fundi.[2] This letter may be supplemented with passages from *Poems* 27 and 28, the ninth and tenth *Natalicia* respectively;[3] the three works all date from the same period, 403–404, and describe the same improvements.

The first notable aspect of these descriptions is that Paulinus displays relatively little interest in describing material objects as such. We gather that he has built a new basilica interconnecting with the old one; that he has paved over a sterile kitchen garden to make a marble courtyard adorned with fountains; and that he has built a new baptistry (which *Poem* 28 is written to dedicate); but he gives us very few hints of their exact construction or their topological relationship to each other. We have, for example, few allusions to building materials or to details of design;[4] when Paulinus does occasionally focus on a sustained and specific description, it seems to be more for symbolic purposes than for conveying any precise architectural content.[5] The description of the courtyard within the cloisters is a case in point. The fact that it connects the three buildings (the old and new basilicas and the martyrium) is so emphatically dwelt upon that an allusion to the Trinity must surely be intended;[6] the precise dynamics of the connection, however, remain obscure.[7] Note too the trinitarian significance—'alta/lege sacramenti' ('by the profound law of

---

[1] See Rudolf Carel Goldschmidt, *Paulinus' Churches at Nola: Texts, Translations and Commentary* (Amsterdam, 1940); Helena Junod-Ammerbauer, 'Les constructions de Nole et l'esthétique de Saint Paulin', *RÉAug* 24 (1978), 22–57: she, however, dismisses *Poem* 28 as merely representing Christian epigram (as opposed to architectural description). The argument below leads to the conclusion that this is probably a false distinction.

[2] Description of building at Nola: *Letter* 32. 9–16; it abuts on the old basilica of Felix, 13. The building at Fundi: *Letter* 32. 17 (introduced with 'Egrediamur iam Nolana hac basilica et in Fundanam transeamus').

[3] The descriptive passages are hard to isolate with precision, as they tend to be interspersed with moral extraction and commentary; but *Poem* 27. 345–595 and the whole of *Poem* 28 seem to be broadly relevant.

[4] Building materials: *Poem* 27. 385 refers to 'biiuges laqueari et marmore fabri'; *Poem* 28. 14 to decorations in 'marmore pictura laquearibus atque columnis'. The ceiling is made to look like ivory, *Poem* 27. 389.

[5] Trout speaks, in a particularly happy phrase, of Paulinus' 'symbolic exegesis of space' at Primuliacum and Nola: *Paulinus*, 243.

[6] *Poem* 28. 28–52.

[7] This is not to say that there was not a tripartite relationship between the buildings: the work on the archaeological site of Tomas Lehmann and, subsequently, Annewies van den

the mystery')—drawn from the three entrances of the martyrium, and, once again, the symbolism of one body with Christ as the head in the multifarious but united constructions on the site: 'etsi culmina plura/sint domibus structis, sanctae tamen unica pacis/est domus' ('though the buildings may have many gables, yet there is a single domain of sacred peace').[8] Elsewhere—in the eleventh *Natalicium*—the description of the cross stolen from Nola (and later miraculously restored) is so laden with symbolic significance, especially a paradoxically multiplicitous trinitarianism, that its exact form is lost in cumbersome detail.[9] Besides, Paulinus specifies that the cross displays its double form ('effigiem . . . utramque') 'ut modo, si libeat spectari comminus ipsam,/prompta fides oculis' ('to impart immediate faith to the eyes that gaze closely upon it'). The double image is constructed 'modis . . . miris' ('in miraculous fashion').[10] It is the faith, not the form, that is of paramount importance.

Paulinus seems particularly reticent when his accounts are compared with the exuberant description by his contemporary Prudentius of the—purely imaginary—Temple of Wisdom, which vibrates with colour and form.[11] There is no colour in Paulinus' accounts.[12] He does, however, evince a consistent concern with light: words such as 'splendor' and 'nitor' and their cognates are abundant; so too 'illustrare', 'lucidus', and 'lumen': 'aperta per arcus/lucida frons bifores perfunderet intima largo/ lumine . . . ' ('the gleaming façade, which is revealed through the arches with their double doors, suffuses the interior with a flood of light').[13]

Hoek has shown that there was; but their work has augmented, rather than merely confirmed, Paulinus' symbol-laden account. Tomas Lehmann, 'Lo sviluppo del complesso archeologico a Cimitile/Nola', *Boreas* 13 (1990), 75–93; Annewies van den Hoek, 'Paulinus of Nola, Courtyards and Canthari', unpublished paper given at the International Medieval Congress, Kalamazoo (May 1999).

[8] *Poem* 27. 455–62; quotes from 455–6 and 459–61.

[9] *Poem* 19. 608–76. Notwithstanding the obscurities here, Wiman attempted to reconstruct the appearance of this cross: see 'Till Paulinus Nolanus' Carmina', *Eranos* 32 (1934), 118, fig. 2.

[10] Quotes from *Poem* 19. 660, 661–2, and 659.

[11] Prudentius, *Psychomachia*, 804–87. A typical extract from his description: 'Ingens chrysolitus nativo interlitus auro/hinc sibi sappirum sociaverat inde beryllum,/distantesque nitor medius variabat honores.' (854–6).

[12] Not even when, as it were, there *is*: note his description of dawn, *Poem* 18. 405–8. The dim light reddens ('rubescebant'), but then 'noctis et extremae fuga . . . /coeperat ambiguos rerum reserare colores'. Is it precisely the 'ambiguus' nature of colours that is the problem for Paulinus?

[13] *Poem* 27. 373–5. See also especially lines 377–9, 387–8, and 496–7; and elsewhere, note that after the death of Felix 'positis ex ossibus emicuit lux' (*Poem* 18. 157).

Although we do not know the exact construction of the church, we do know how it was lit:

> in ligno mentitur ebur, tectoque superne
> pendentes lychni spiris retinentur aënis
> et medio in vacuo laxis vaga lumina nutant
> funibus, undantes flammas levis aura fatigat.[14]

Wood simulates ivory, and lamps, hanging high above from the roof, are held by bronze cables; in the middle of the space, lights nod to and fro on free-swinging ropes, and a light breeze agitates the wavering flames.

The elaborate cross discussed above is, literally as well as metaphorically, a source of light in the basilica; and its own exegesis is preceded by a detailed description of the other beautiful lanterns available to—but passed over by—the thief.[15] Moreover, the somewhat reprehensible episode in which the hovel of a *colonus* in the compound is burned down, and attributed as a miracle to Felix, all revolves around light for the basilica:

> ...namque patentis
> ianua basilicae tuguri brevis interiectu
> obscurata foris in cassum clausa patebat.[16]

...for when the basilica was open, its door stood vainly open as if closed, darkened from the outside by the little hovel in the way.

We shall see that this emphasis on illumination aptly reflects a more general concern of Paulinus with sight—and, correspondingly, with blindness[17]—and a desire to see things in a fitting manner.[18]

---

[14] *Poem* 27. 389–92.

[15] Cross as source of light: *Poem* 19. 460–4; other lanterns in the basilica: 405–24.

[16] *Poem* 28. 66–8. Textually, this is an extremely vexed passage. I have preferred 'foris' (attested in the MSS.) to Hartel's incomprehensible 'fores'. This, however, involves the new problem of artificial lengthening before the caesura. There is, unfortunately, no comment on this practice in Green's treatment of Paulinus' hexametric caesurae: see Green, *Poetry*, 114–15. I have also strained the sense of the participle 'clausa': Paulinus presumably liked the paradoxical juxtaposition of 'clausa patebat', but to try to reproduce this in the English is to make the passage even more confused.

[17] Note, for example, that in *Poem* 28 he describes the huts as 'foedo/obice prospectum *caecantia*' (65–6).

[18] For a practical instance of the symbolic value attached to sight in the fourth century, see Margaret Miles on the issue of inclusion in the Mass. Catechumens withdrew to side rooms for the communion itself: 'Visual participation made the difference between outsider and member'. *Image as Insight. Visual Understanding in Western Christianity and Secular Culture* (Boston, 1985), 51.

A second aspect of Paulinus' descriptions is particularly noteworthy. He alludes, famously, to the pictorial cycle in his basilica, and explains why he has chosen to have it painted:

> forte requiratur quanam ratione gerendi
> sederit haec nobis sententia, pingere sanctas
> raro more domos animantibus adsimulatis.
> accipite et paucis temptabo exponere causas.
> quos agat huc sancti Felicis gloria coetus,
> obscurum nulli; sed turba frequentior hic est
> rusticitas non cassa fide neque docta legendi.[19]

Perhaps you may ask on what rationale this decision possessed me, to paint the holy dwellings in an unusual manner[20] with the pretence of living creatures. Listen, and I will try briefly to explain the reasons. Everyone knows what crowds the glorious reputation of Saint Felix gathers here; but the greater part of the throng here are peasants, of earnest faith but not trained to read.

Paulinus has already observed that these pictures should nourish the mind for reflection: 'qui videt haec vacuis agnoscens vera figuris/non vacua fidam sibi pascit imagine mentem' ('the person who sees these things and recognizes the truth in the bare figures, feeds his own faithful mind on no empty image').[21] But in spite of his concern that the unlettered should be reminded by pictures of the sacred purpose of their visit, Paulinus goes on to specify that these pictures should be appropriately explained with *tituli*, captions probably of verse couplets or quatrains, 'ut littera monstret/quod manus explicuit' ('so that the letter may show what the hand has set forth').[22] The peasants, it seems, may point out these *tituli* and read

---

[19] *Poem* 27. 542–8.

[20] A canon of the Council of Elvira (early fourth century) forbade representational art in churches (for full references, see Trout, *Paulinus*, 182, n. 135). As the fifth century progressed, however, this type of project became less of a 'mos rarus': in the early 420s, the nave of Sta Maria Maggiore in Rome was decorated with Old Testament scenes on one side and New Testament on the other. (For a description, see Emile Mâle, *The Early Churches of Rome*, tr. David Buxton (London, 1960), 65–6.) Paulinus preferred to decorate his old basilica from the New Testament and his new one from the Old: 'est etenim pariter decus utile nobis/in veteri novitas atque in novitate vetustas...' (*Poem* 28, 174–5.)

[21] *Poem* 27. 514–15. I take 'vacuus' to mean 'available [to the viewer] for interpretation'— being, until interpreted, of open reference—not 'empty' *tout court*, hence my choice of translation for the 'vacuus'/'non vacuus' contrast.

[22] *Poem* 27. 584–5. *Tituli* are raised to a literary mode in the contemporaneous *Dittochaeon* of Prudentius, which displays in compressed form the characteristics of imagistic typological allusion which will be discussed later in the chapter. We may perhaps infer that the *tituli* in

them aloud to each other.[23] Perhaps Paulinus was—consciously or other-wise—inspired by the influence of the Epigrams of Pope Damasus, which marked and celebrated the shrines of saints and martyrs at Rome;[24] yet it is very striking that even when the depictions are expressly directed at the unlettered, Paulinus cannot envisage material images without an explanatory or illustrative text.[25]

This textual orientation becomes even more apparent in the prose letter (*Letter* 32) which describes Paulinus' building projects to Sulpicius. Paulinus barely comments on the constructions as such; instead, his descriptions serve primarily to situate the extensive verses placed at strategic points around the basilica, which he then proceeds to quote in full. These verses, dogmatic as well as descriptive, are clearly intended to direct the reader both on his literal progress round the church and on his spiritual progress through Christian doctrine. It seems that in some way for Paulinus these inscriptions *are* the church; they are certainly, as he describes it to Sulpicius, its most prominent feature.

Another feature of the basilica hints at a use for these texts.

cubicula intra porticus quaterna longis basilicae lateribus inserta secretis orantium vel 'in lege domini meditantium' [Ps. 1: 2], praeterea memoriis religiosorum ac familiarum accomodatos ad pacis aeternae requiem locos praebent. omne cubiculum binis per liminum frontes versibus praenotatur . . .[26]

Four chapels have been placed within the colonnades on each[27] of the long sides of the basilica as a retreat for those praying or 'meditating on the law of the Lord':

Paulinus' basilica were of similar nature. On the *Dittochaeon*, see Renate Pillinger, *Die Tituli Historiarum oder das sogenannte Dittochaeon des Prudentius* (Vienna, 1980).

[23] The end of *Poem* 27 may provide further evidence for architectural inscriptions at Nola, when Paulinus invites Nicetas and the assembled throng to join with him in a prayer: '. . . gratantes dicite mecum:/haec tibi, Christe deus, tenui fragilique paratu/pro nobis facimus . . .' (*Poem* 27. 638–40). These would have been characteristically self-deprecating but apt lines with which to adorn his building project: are we to envisage Paulinus' audience reading along with him from an inscription?

[24] A suggestion made by Trout, *Paulinus*, 43. Damasus preceded the disdainful Siricius as Pope, presiding from 366–84. The Damasan epigrams are edited by Antonio Ferrua, *Epigrammata Damasiana* (Rome, 1945).

[25] The importance of the written text for Paulinus is well expressed in a sidelong remark: 'sed de hac absida aut abside num magis dicere debuerim, tu videris; ego nescire me fateor, quia hoc verbi genus nec legisse reminiscor'. Having never *read*—not heard—that case of the word 'apse', he is uncertain how it should be correctly constructed. *Letter* 32. 17.

[26] *Letter* 32. 12.

[27] Goldschmidt, *Churches*, translates 'quaterna' simply as 'four'; but its specific distributive sense seems to me more likely, not least because 'binis' later in the passage is undoubtedly

they provide places particularly suited to remembrance[28] of the saints or family members so that they may rest in eternal peace. Each chapel is marked out with two verses on the front of the lintel . . .

Paulinus does not give us these verses; but we may infer that they would have formed suggestive starting points for the prayer or meditation in these little oratories.

These examples of Paulinus' extensive textual supplementation of material objects[29] bespeak a theory of reading in which the creative emphasis lies on the active response of the reader. The architectural structures or pictures fade into the background when set alongside the textual commentary upon them, which is in turn intended merely as a starting point for private meditation.[30] The technique with which these images are displayed, and the response provoked in the reader/viewer, forms a marked contrast to classical ecphrastic technique. Paulinus guiding Nicetas past the pictorial programme in his portico recalls, quite probably by design,[31] the progress of Aeneas past the paintings of the Trojan War in Dido's temple to Juno;[32] but the differences between the two are instructive. In both cases, the viewer within the poem moves past a sequence of paintings which depict narratives already familiar to him—in the case of Aeneas, from (purported) personal experience; in the case of Nicetas, from his knowledge of the Bible. These narratives are also

distributive ('two verses over each door'). Walsh, *Letters* 2. 146, also prefers the distributive sense.

[28] *TLL.* 8. 670 s.v. *memoria* offers 'de actione reminiscendi' and suggests equivalence to 'recordatio': this is the sense which I have preferred here, *contra* Walsh, *Letters* 2. 146, who translates 'funeral monuments'. Although *TLL* 8. 682 attests this sense in two other passages of Paulinus (*Letters* 17. 2 and 32. 13), it seems to me quite clear from the context that the use here is in the contemplative rather than the material sense. This seems to be borne out by Lehmann's reconstruction of the Basilica Nova: 'Sviluppo', 82, fig. 7.

[29] A further telling example from the description of the building: though we are told almost nothing about the design of the martyrium, Paulinus writes a few lines on each of the martyrs whose relics are enclosed within it. *Poem* 27. 406–39.

[30] Note too the expressly exemplary purpose of the pictorial programme in the basilica: 'sanctasque legenti/historias castorum operum subrepit honestas/exemplis inducta piis . . .' *Poem* 27. 589–91.

[31] Note especially the phrase 'animum pictura pascit inani', at *Aeneid* 1. 464: Paulinus picks up this very particular use of 'pascit', this time with 'mentem' as object, at *Poem* 27. 515; he refers at the beginning of the section to the images as 'picturas', line 511 (again at line 516); the 'pictura . . . inani' of Virgil may well have suggested Paulinus' 'vacuis . . . figuris', commented on in note 21 above.

[32] Paulinus, *Poem* 27. 511–41; Virgil, *Aeneid* 1. 456–93.

presumed by the writers of the poems to be familiar to their readers: in the case of Virgil's readers, from the Homeric and post-Homeric epics; for Paulinus', from, once again, the Bible. The distinction, therefore, between reader and fictive viewer is already blurred in Paulinus' text, where the two are both drawing on the same extra-textual source of reference, while it remains sharply drawn in Virgil's. The contrast between the two *ecphraseis* is accentuated by their different purposes in their respective contexts. The pictures in Virgil, alluding to selected episodes in the Trojan War, are introduced primarily to show us their effect on Aeneas and to provide a dramatic preparation for and juxtaposition with the first entrance of Dido.[33] Aeneas' response to the pictures is made firmly within the context of the poem: he takes them, not as a call to action, but as a stimulus to grief, and reflects on them with the famous lament, 'sunt lacrimae rerum et mentem mortalia tangunt' ('[here are] tears in the nature of things, hearts touched by human transience').[34] The reflection which Paulinus expects his pictures to prompt is, however, of a very different nature. Not only is their aim avowedly, as we have seen, the instruction of the uneducated and the edification of the formerly ignorant; the pictures also invite the fictive viewer, and by implication the actual reader, to form moral judgements on their content and hence to instigate a certain, virtuous, course of action. Paulinus breaks off from his comparison of Ruth and Orpah to exclaim:

> nonne, precor, toto manet haec discordia mundo
> parte sequente deum vel parte ruente per orbem?
> atque utinam pars aequa foret necis atque salutis![35]

I ask you—doesn't this strife remain in the whole world, with one faction following God and the other rushing through the world to destruction? And would that the parties of death and of salvation were equal!

Virgil's *ecphrasis*, and the response of his fictive viewer to the depictions, is confined entirely within the economy of the poem and its textual referents.

---

[33] See the exposition of R. D. Williams, 'The Pictures on Dido's Temple (*Aeneid* 1. 450–93)', *CQ* NS 10 (1960), 145–51; reprinted in S. J. Harrison (ed.) *Oxford Readings in Vergil's 'Aeneid'* (Oxford, 1990), 37–45. Williams, however, fails to remark on the way in which the 'decrescendo' of the sequence to a portrait of the heroine Penthesilea, the 'bellatrix' and 'virgo' who 'audet... viris concurrere', prepares the scene with aptness and irony for the entrance of Dido.

[34] *Aeneid* 1. 462; I have used here the translation of C. Day Lewis (London, 1952).

[35] *Poem* 27. 537–9.

Paulinus' account, by contrast, is not textually circumscribed, but by stimulating reflection not only in the fictive viewer but also in the readers, expects to extend its effect beyond the textual into an active response in the world outside the text.

Of course, the link between the *tituli* for the edification of peasants and pilgrims and the *Natalicia* is particularly close, as the *Natalicia* are performance pieces, and themselves serve as textual intermediaries between events or objects and (actual) percipients. Like the *tituli*, but at greater length, they too label and interpret, directing the affective and moral response of the reader or hearer. Paulinus, as 'impresario'[36] of the cult of St Felix, works constantly to control interpretation of every facet of Felix's life and afterlife, as well as of his commemorative buildings; but this works in conjunction with his assumption that the audiences' response will not be a passive submission to direction, but an active embrace of that direction for themselves.

This expectation of active response to texts should not surprise, for at ← this period much of Christian practice was beginning to revolve around this type of response. Cassian, writing in the 420s, expressly provides instruction in techniques of meditation: 'hunc [versiculum] in opere quolibet seu ministerio vel itinere constitutus decantare non desinas. hunc et dormiens et reficiens et in ultimis naturae necessitatibus meditare' ('you should constantly chant this verse at any task, in ministry or travel. Ponder this verse both sleeping and waking and in the most extreme straits of nature').[37] The impetus behind the burgeoning genre of hagiography forms a very practical example of active reading: the writing of the Lives of saints takes for granted that literature may inspire and mould life.[38] We should remember that in the prototypical saint's Life, the *Life of Antony*, the starting point for his ascetic existence is his response to a biblical text:

... intravit in ecclesiam, et accidit ut tunc Evangelium legeretur, in quo Dominus dicit ad divitem: si vis perfectus[39] esse, vade, et vende omnia tua quaecunque habes, et da pauperibus, et veni, sequere me, et habebis thesaurum in coelis. Quo audito, quasi divinitus huiusmodi ante memoriam concepisset, et veluti propter se

---

[36] 'Impresario': see Trout, *Paulinus*, 197.

[37] See Cassian, *Conference* 10. 10. He later observes (10. 14) that the hearers found it far more difficult to meditate continuously on a single *versiculus* than 'per omne scripturarum corpus absque ullius perseverantiae vinculo varia passim meditatione discurrere'.

[38] See Peter Brown, 'The Saint as Exemplar', *Representations* 1 (1983), 1–25.

[39] My emendation from 'perfeleus', printed by Migne.

haec esset scriptura recitata, ad se Dominicum traxit imperium: statimque egres-
sus, possessiones quas habebat vendidit.[40]

... he went into the church; and it happened that at that moment the Gospel was
being read, in which the Lord says to the rich man: 'If you wish to be perfect, go,
sell all you possess, and give it to the poor, and come, follow me, and you will have
treasure in heaven' [Matt. 19: 21]. When Antony had heard this, as if he had
divinely received a previous memory of this type, and as if the passage had been
read out on his account, he took the Lord's command to himself: he went straight
out of the church, and sold the property which he possessed.[41]

We may also note the rising importance of preaching in the period, from
which great collections of sermons survive:[42] again, to craft and to respond
to a sermon involves drawing close connections—consciously or not—
between cognitive activity and action, mediated by the individual reception of the text. Finally, the developing practice of biblical commentary
shows again the importance of text and of active response to it, in this case
in literary form.[43]

To return to Paulinus' own circle, Augustine, in particular, espouses
the importance of an active response to scriptural texts: he ends an
unusually lengthy letter, addressing a number of scriptural questions
posed by his old friend Honoratus, with an exhortation to get into the
habit of reading holy scripture and, through meditation and prayer, to be
taught its meaning not by any man but by God:

sed ama etiam ecclesiasticas legere litteras et non multa invenies, quae requiras ex
me; sed legendo et ruminando, si etiam pure deum largitorem bonorum omnium

---

[40] *Life of Antony*, 2, quoted in the translation of Evagrius which would probably have been
the version known to Paulinus: PG 26. 835–976.

[41] This scriptural passage was also, of course, important for Paulinus: *Letter* 24. 5 ff. (to
Sulpicius) provides an extended discussion of ideas around it. The primary goal of a recent
doctoral study by Joanna Summers is to establish the details of Paulinus' response to this text
on both a practical and a theoretical level. She concludes that Paulinus' renunciation of wealth
did little to affect his position: 'The loss of property did not pose a problem for a man who
continued to rely on past sources of authority, education, friendships and his new-found
status within the church': Joanna Ceinwen Summers, *Paulinus of Nola and the Renunciation of
Wealth* (PhD thesis: King's College London, 1992), 405.

[42] Augustine's sermons, for example, fill two volumes of Migne (PL 38–9)—and this does
not include such works as the *Enarrationes in Psalmos*; more sermons were discovered in 1990
by François Dolbeau, and have recently been surveyed by Henry Chadwick in 'New Sermons
of St. Augustine', *JThS* 47 (1996), 69–91. Unfortunately only one sermon of Paulinus himself
survives: entitled 'De Gazophylacio', it is printed by Hartel as *Letter* 34.

[43] See Vessey, *Ideas of Writing*; he points out that a more apt phrase might be 'ideas of
reading-and-writing' (intro., xv): the active response to the Bible is critical.

depreceris, omnia, quae cognitione digna sunt, aut certe plurima ipso magis inspirante quam hominum aliquo commonente perdisces.[44]

But enjoy reading Christian writings, and you will find few things to ask of me; but by reading and pondering, if you also pray candidly to the God who bestows all good things, you will learn through and through everything which is worth knowing—or certainly more things—with the inspiration of God himself rather than with reminders from any man.

He is prepared to implement this approach to scripture in the most unlikely situations: he gives the same advice in a letter to the young girl Florentina, who is so young and unsure of herself that her mother has written to Augustine on her behalf to ask for scriptural instruction.[45] In both cases, this advice involves abrogation of the human authority to which the appeals for interpretation are made in favour of divine illumination through direct appeal to God. This is the express conclusion of *De Magistro*,[46] and lies also behind the philosophical discussion at the end of the *Confessions*:

Ita cum alius dixerit: 'hoc sensit, quod ego', et alius: 'immo illud, quod ego', religiosius me arbitror dicere: 'cur non utrumque potius, si utrumque verum est? et si quid tertium et si quid quartum et si quid omnino aliud verum quispiam in his verbis videt, cur non illa omnia vidisse credatur, per quem deus unus sacras litteras vera et diversa visuris multorum sensibus temperavit?'[47]

And so, when one person says: 'He [Moses] meant the same as I do', and another says, 'No, the same as I do', I think it more Christian to say: 'Why not both, if each is true? Indeed, if anyone sees a third meaning and a fourth and some completely different truth in these words, why should we not believe that Moses saw all these things when the one God, through him, organized holy Scripture to appear in true and diverse aspects to many people's senses?'

The paradoxical corollary to this emphasis on the textual—both the text of the Bible and the responses to it in spoken or written form—is, therefore, a reiteration of the primacy of the spiritual over the temporal realm. The

---

[44] Augustine, *Letter* 140. 85. For Honoratus as an old friend of Augustine's, see *De Utilitate Credendi* 1. 13. On Augustine's approach to reading, see Brian Stock, *Augustine the Reader: Meditation, Self-Knowledge, and the Ethics of Interpretation* (Cambridge, MA/London, 1996).

[45] Augustine, *Letter* 266. 4: 'Proinde tanto me certius, tanto solidius, tanto sanius gaudere scias de fide et spe et dilectione tua, quanto minus indigueris non tantum a me quicquam discere sed ab ullo prorsus hominum.'

[46] *De Magistro* 11 (38): 'de universis autem, quae intelligimus, non loquentem, qui personat foris, sed intus ipsi menti praesidentem consulimus veritatem . . .', which is Christ.

[47] Augustine, *Confessions* 12. 31. 42.

meditative or prayerful response of the individual is given authority over the interpretation of human mentors precisely because it entails a looking inwards to God.[48]

Given this paradox of a distaste for the literal coupled with close attention to 'the letter',[49] it is not surprising that Paulinus baulks at the idea of providing Sulpicius with a literal representation—in this case, a portrait of himself. He complains that Sulpicius is clearly doting on him 'tamquam avus circa serum nepotem' ('like a grandfather on a late-born grandson'),[50] and continues:

quid enim tibi de illa petitione respondeam, qua imagines nostras pingi tibi mittique iussisti? obsecro itaque te per viscera caritatis, quae amoris veri solatia de inanibus formis petis? qualem cupis ut mittamus imaginem tibi? *terreni hominis an caelestis?* scio quia tu illam incorruptibilem speciem concupiscis, quam in te rex caelestis adamavit.... sed pauper ego et dolens, quia adhuc terrenae imaginis squalore concretus sum ... utrimque me concludit pudor: erubesco pingere quod sum, non audeo pingere quod non sum; odi quod sum et non sum quod amo.[51]

What response should I make you for the petition in which you ordered me to have my portrait painted and sent to you? And I beseech you by the depths of my love, what compensation for true love are you seeking from hollow appearances? What sort of image do you want me to send to you? *The image of the earthly man, or the heavenly one?*[52] I know that you eagerly desire that incorruptible form, which the heavenly king loved so deeply in you. ... But I am poor and wretched, for I am still congealed in the filth of my earthly image ... Shame hems me in on either side: I blush to paint what I am, I don't dare to paint what I am not; I hate what I am, and I am not what I love.

Several things about this passage are remarkable. First, there is the clearly expressed dualism of the spiritual and temporal images, and the hierarchy in which they are placed. Worse, to send a portrait would be to send an image of an image, the 'imago terrena', a shameful and pointless exercise. Second, the passage forms one of the few clear indications in Paulinus' letters that he was aware in more than the vaguest way of neo-Platonic

[48] Not a conclusion which appealed to Jerome, who insisted (*Letter* 58) on the need for exemplars.

[49] Compare again the cross described in the eleventh *Natalicium*, which provides 'prompta fides' for those gazing at it 'comminus'. *Poem* 19. 662 and 661.

[50] Perhaps the metaphor derives from Paulinus' rejection of Ausonius' claims: Ausonius, *Letters* 24. 111 appeals to Paulinus with 'mea maxima cura', used by Venus at *Aeneid* 1. 678 of Ascanius—her grandson.

[51] *Letter* 30. 2; the 'late-born grandson', *Letter* 30. 1.

[52] Compare 1 Cor. 15: 49.

thought, for it recalls the passage with which Porphyry elects to begin the *Life of Plotinus*, in which Plotinus refuses to authorize the painting of a portrait of himself, asking: ' "Is it not enough to carry about the simulacrum that nature has put around me, that you ask me also to consent to leave behind me a more enduring simulacrum of a simulacrum, as though it were some work for public show?" '[53] (Significantly, the attempts of both men to remain unportrayed are confounded: Carterius steals a sketch of Plotinus by memorizing his face while attending his lectures; Paulinus is depicted by Sulpicius in his baptistry at Primuliacum.[54] Does this merely emphasize the hollowness of portraiture: how far removed from reality will be an *eidolou eidolon* not even ratified by the presence of its object as a sitter? Or does it show the irrelevance of earthly reality to a spiritually inspired representation?) Third, there is the explicit connection between the practice of loving and the formation of a more spiritual self, in which Paulinus depicts himself as woefully incomplete.[55] The literal representation is irrelevant, compared with the spiritual self towards which Paulinus is striving.[56]

The letter proceeds to a consideration of the paradoxical possibility of being simultaneously blind and sighted, starting from the passage of Genesis after Adam and Eve have eaten of the tree of knowledge: 'aperti sunt oculi eorum [Gen. 3: 7]', 'and their eyes were opened'. Paulinus continues: 'ora ergo, mi frater, ut utrumque in me operetur dominus, caecet videntem meum, ne videam vanitatem, et inluminet non videntem, ut videam aequitates' ('So pray, my brother, that the Lord may effect both things in me: that he blind my seeing eye, to prevent me from seeing

[53] Porphyry, *Life of Plotinus* 1. I quote from the translation of M. J. Edwards (deleting a 'that' after 'enough', which is presumably a misprint), in 'A Portrait of Plotinus', *CQ* 43 (1993), 480–90. This article forms an extremely interesting point of departure for seeing the similarities and differences between Plotinus' position and that of Paulinus. 'The portrait', writes Edwards, ' . . . is a symbol of the illusory world of sense above which Platonism strives to raise the soul' (481)—very much the context of Paulinus' argument here.

[54] *Life of Plotinus* 1; Paulinus, *Letter* 32. 2.

[55] This connection is in fact brought out even more clearly in the passage omitted after 'adamavit'. Later, Augustine quotes the 'erubesco' passage back to Paulinus to show a similar awareness of himself as profoundly sinful—an example both of the memorability of Paulinus' epigrammatic words and of the extensive dissemination of his letters. Augustine, *Letter* 186. 40.

[56] This again recalls a remark of Edwards': 'For anyone who adhered to [Platonism] in late antiquity, matter was the formless half-reality at the vanishing-point of truth and understanding,' 'Portrait', 487. For more on the ethical relationship between *similitudo* and *imago*, see the discussion of Paulinus, *Letter* 24. 9, in Chapter 6.

vanity, and that he enlighten the eye that does not see, so that I may see justice').[57] Once again, the idea of representation is, quite naturally, associated with sight; but it is only the spiritual version of seeing that Paulinus finds important. He ends the letter with the statement that God has painted his image 'non in tabulis putribilibus neque ceris liquentibus, sed "in tabulis carnalibus cordis" [2 Cor. 3: 3] tui' ('not on tablets that perish or on wax that melts, but on the fleshly tablets of your heart'). This ultimate preference for the spiritual over the literal image has also introduced the epistolary description of Paulinus' basilica with which we started: Paulinus undertakes it 'ut in hoc quoque nostra coniunctio *figuraretur*, quae iungitur animis et distat locis' ('so that in this too may be *configured* our connectedness, which joins us in mind while we are physically separated').[58] The purpose of the description of the basilica is not to create an image of the church itself, but a *figura*—almost a visual testimonial—of Paulinus' and Sulpicius' love. In fact, when there is an extended passage in the letters of Paulinus describing things or events, it is always inserted expressly to serve an abstract, spiritual purpose: so, for example, the consolatory description of Pammachius' almsgiving at St Peter's— which, it will be remembered, was not even witnessed by Paulinus.[59]

Paulinus also seems to have no doubt that memory operates by means of mental images. His denial of a portrait to Sulpicius continues:

hic etiam, si tantus amor est visibilia quoque captare solatia, poteris per magistras animi tui lineas vel inperitis aut ignorantibus nos dictare pictoribus, *memoriam* illis *tuam, in qua nos habes pictos*, velut imitanda de conspicuis adsidentium vultibus ora proponens.[60]

Here too, if you so love to grasp at visible sources of comfort, you will be able to describe me, even to painters who are inexperienced or who don't know me, through the guiding outlines in your mind, laying before them *your memory, in which you hold a depiction of me*, just like a face to be copied from the visible countenance of a sitter.

Memory contains a visual image so clear that it can apparently be imparted verbally to a third party; yet Paulinus feels that a portrait of his external self would be irrelevant. More generally, there obtains in the letters of

---

[57] *Letter* 30. 5. 'aperti sunt oculi eorum' from the same letter, 4.

[58] *Letter* 32. 10.

[59] *Letter* 13. 11–15. The passage begins: 'videre enim mihi videor tota illa religiosa miserandae plebis examina . . . ' The description of the arrival at Nola of Melania the Elder, which will be discussed later in the chapter, is another palmary example.

[60] *Letter* 30. 6.

Paulinus an anomalous situation whereby material images are eschewed, while the language in which spiritual ideas are expressed remains unabashedly imagistic and symbolic. How is this to be accounted for?

To seek an answer at the most general level, a recent remark by J. J. O'Donnell on Augustine's *De Doctrina Christiana* is illuminating:

> Most readers have accepted Augustine's assertion that the literal sense is prior to the allegorical, but the most unsettling thing about the book is the way it really suggests the exact opposite: that figurative use of language is natural, and the desire to take figurative language literally is a disordered interpretation conditioned by seeing texts on a page, where irony and metaphor can leak away.[61]

In *De Doctrina Christiana*, Augustine is more engaged with developing a systematics of representation, while Paulinus responds very directly to figurative language. My contention is precisely that for Paulinus the 'figurative use of language is natural',[62] and that through it, despite the limitations of the written word, which can appear to fix meaning and demolish nuance, irony and metaphor do not leak away, but can be constantly and vividly present. It remains to explore what, for Paulinus, is meant by 'figurative use of language', and how it seems to affect his connections of thought. This is of necessity a somewhat question-begging exercise, as, while it is immediately apparent that Paulinus fills much of his letters with material which does not immediately seem valid or justified by context, and whose function is decidedly unfamiliar, it also assumes that we can at least begin to analyze and explicate such use of language in conventional, communicable terms.[63]

Two things above all are accomplished by the figurative use of language and the imagistic connections of thought which we see throughout the letters of Paulinus. First, the paradoxes through which Christianity

---

[61] Review of R. P. H. Green (ed. and trans.), *Augustine: On Christian Doctrine* (Oxford, 1995): *Bryn Mawr Review* 96.3.15. Compare a comment of Jaş Elsner, discussing the same issue from an art historian's angle: naturalism has 'no natural [*sic*!] psychological or physiological priority'. Elsner, *Art and the Roman Viewer: the Transformation of Art from the Pagan World to Christianity* (Cambridge, 1995), 13.

[62] This also resonates with an observation of Averil Cameron: 'If it is the nature of ultimate truth to be hidden, it will be revealed only through signs, linguistic or otherwise; in other words, Christian language and Christian rhetoric will be of their very essence figural.' In *Christianity and the Rhetoric of Empire: The Development of Christian Discourse* (Berkeley/Los Angeles/London, 1991), 159.

[63] However, the validity of written criticism of music, for example, is not vitiated by the fact that there will always remain something which music alone can express and words cannot.

expresses itself are best captured and most fruitfully juxtaposed by the use of images. Second, with any specific image or idea there comes a matrix of associated images, and hence an extraordinarily wide and fluid potential for the assigning of meaning. It has not generally been appreciated that Paulinus' *catenae*, his 'chains', of biblical allusion and imagery have any purpose beyond the cosmetic. Even a sympathetic commentator writes: 'Unfortunately Paulinus does not always discipline his literary talent, and at times what starts as a fruitful biblical meditation degenerates into a riot of dissonant metaphors and extravagant conceits'.[64] But by refusing to restrict patterns of thought to linear processes, Paulinus finds it possible to achieve a far greater level of associative simultaneity.

Let us first study in more detail the delight in paradox that is so characteristic of Christian writings of this period, and not least of the letters of Paulinus[65]—a delight that should hardly surprise (Christ himself having chosen to teach in parables which were often paradoxical in force), but whose development reaches a remarkable level of sophistication in the fourth century. Paulinus uses paradox in a number of ways. An obvious application arises when it is used to capture especially significant moments and persons. So, for example, the potential conversion of Licentius is characterized in paradoxical terms: 'vincetur vel invitus . . . ne mala victoria vincat, si maluerit in perniciem suam vincere quam pro salute superari' ('he will be won over, even though he doesn't wish it, lest he should win by an evil victory, if he prefers winning for his damnation to being overpowered for his salvation').[66] Similarly, paradox encapsulates a Christian emperor: Paulinus has gladly undertaken the work of his panegyric on Theodosius, 'ut in Theodosio non tam imperatorem quam Christi servum, non dominandi superbia sed humilitate famulandi potentem, nec regno sed fide principem praedicarem' ('so that in Theodosius I might preach not the emperor so much as the servant of Christ, endowed with power not through the arrogance of domination but through the humility

---

[64] Walsh, *Letters* 1. 18.

[65] Averil Cameron has done much to highlight the importance of paradox within fourth-century Christian discourse in *Christianity and the Rhetoric of Empire*, especially ch. 5, 'The Rhetoric of Paradox': 'A great deal of Christian discourse . . . necessarily attempts to express the paradoxical, to describe in language what is by definition indescribable. . . . Not simply the status of propositions about God, but *the very nature of language* were at issue' (156–7, my emphasis). Cameron's specific examples are primarily drawn from the discourse surrounding the Virgin Mary, and virginity more generally, and hence have little overlap with the material adduced here.

[66] *Letter* 7. 3.

of service, a prince by virtue of his faith, not his realm').[67] Paulinus'
delight at the personification of paradox overflows in his description of
the arrival of Melania the Elder at Nola. She is dressed in dark rags and
riding a pony; she is surrounded by richly clad senators on caparisoned
horses: 'vidimus dignam deo huius mundi confusionem, purpuream ser-
icam auratamque supellectilem pannis veteribus et nigris servientem' ('we
have seen this world rightfully confounded for God: purple silk and gilded
trappings doing obeisance to old black rags').[68] The abstract moral is dwelt
upon in the letter: temporal poverty bespeaks—and yields—spiritual
riches.

We may note the way in which this mode of expression complements,
yet surpasses, the classical love of antithesis.[69] But for Christians of this
period there is a far more pronounced scope of relevance: the way in which
paradoxical expression echoes the paradoxes enacted in the life of Christ
and in his message. Northrop Frye remarks on 'the linguistic fact that
many of the central doctrines of... Christianity can be grammatically
expressed only in the form of metaphor. Thus: Christ *is* God and man;
in the Trinity three persons *are* one ...' and so on; he goes on to instantiate
the 'use of concrete paradox that enlightens the mind by paralyzing the
discursive reason'.[70] In the letters of Paulinus we are looking at the results
of absorbing this way of thought utterly into one's patterns of expression.

A striking example of such absorption occurs at the conclusion of one of
Paulinus' letters:

ergo illum amemus, quem amare debitum est. illum osculemur, quem osculari
castitas est. illi copulemur, cui nupsisse virginitas est. illi subiciamur, sub quo
iacere supra mundum stare est. propter illum deiciamur, cui cadere resurrectio est.
illi conmoriamur, in quo vita est.[71]

Therefore, let us love him: to love him is a duty. Let us kiss him: to kiss him is
chastity. Let us be joined to him: to have married him is virginity. Let us be
subject to him: to lie beneath him is to stand above the world. Let us be thrown

[67] *Letter* 28. 6.

[68] *Letter* 29. 12.

[69] Antithesis was, of course, particularly beloved of the rhetorical tradition: see A.D.
Leeman, *Orationis Ratio: The Stylistic Theories and Practice of the Roman Orators Historians
and Philosophers* (Amsterdam 1963) *ad loc.*

[70] Northrop Frye, *The Great Code* (reissued: Harmondsworth, 1990), 55. Frye's emphasis.

[71] *Letter* 23. 42. The expression of ideas in extravagant paradoxes has persisted throughout
the Christian tradition, especially in its more metaphysical thinkers: this passage calls to mind
one from John Donne: 'Take mee to you, imprison mee, for I/Except you' enthrall mee,
never shall be free,/Nor ever chaste, except you ravish mee.' Donne, *Holy Sonnets* 14.

down because of him: to fall for him is resurrection. Let us die with him[72]: in him is life.

It is by the paradoxical use of mundane images that the spiritual is evoked. The antitheses designedly suggest the limitations of language in its descriptive and referential functions, and by implication the limitations of conventional forms of rational analysis: the reader is thrown up against the possibility of something beyond language. This phenomenon of mundane paradox, widespread in the letters of Paulinus, reflects and extends the ideas of Christian friendship explored earlier, in which paradoxically inverted expectations become guarantors of the friendship's spirituality.

We may observe parenthetically that there are immense possibilities for witty juxtaposition and self-parodying expression in the pursuit of paradox and metaphor, and that these possibilities are not lost on Paulinus. One might have thought that Sulpicius' request that Paulinus should write inscriptions for his basilica would demand a certain lapidary seriousness; but the verses suggested for the baptistry end: 'Hinc senior sociae congaudet turba catervae;/Alleluia novis balat ovile choris' ('At this point, let the older crowd of the initiated throng rejoice too; "Alleluia!" bleats the fold with its new choirs').[73] And Paulinus affects a tone of horror at the potential juxtaposition of his own portrait in the baptistry with that of Saint Martin:

Sed in eo metuo, ne operibus tuis, quibus iniqua viarum saecularium dirigis et clivosa conplanas, ex illo, de quo semper conqueror affectu in nos tuo, salebram offensionis inmisceas, quod splendidos devotionis in Christo tuae titulos nostris nominibus infuscas et iustis laboribus hanc iniquitatem inseris, ut locum sanctum etiam vultibus iniquorum polluas.[74]

But I am afraid that because of your affection for me, of which I always complain, you may combine a horrible stumbling-block with the work in which you straighten the uneven parts of earthly ways and smooth the hilly ones, by darkening the radiant *tituli* that bespeak your devotion to Christ with my name, and introducing into your worthy labours the sinfulness of polluting the sacred place with ill-matched faces.

Note too the joking application of the scriptural reference in 'iniqua... dirigis et clivosa conplanas': the allusion to the 'vox clamantis in deserto' (the 'voice of the one crying out in the wilderness'), implies that Sulpicius

[72] *TLL* 3. 1936 s.v. *commorior* cites this passage under 'mori simul cum aliquo (*tam proprie quam in imagine*)'—my emphasis.
[73] *Letter* 32. 5.
[74] *Letter* 32. 2.

is preparing his baptistry as a 'way' to Christ—and that the figural presence of Paulinus will ruin the progress.[75] However, after more in this vein—'nonne tu lactis et fellis poculum miscuisti?' ('Surely you have mixed a cup of milk and bile?')—Paulinus comforts himself: obviously Martin's face is there as an example, and his own as a terrible warning!

The *Natalicia* prove themselves, once again, truly performance pieces with their use of humour to beguile or gently mock their audience. Because the single life-span of St Felix was not enough to cleanse Nola of its sins, God made him carry on his work after death 'potiore via' ('by a more potent route').[76] Meanwhile, Felix and his Lord enjoy a joke even in heaven: when a Nolan peasant, deprived of his oxen, comprehends Felix in a liberal attribution of blame, and threatens to die on the threshold of his shrine, 'sua cum domino ludens convitia risit' ('[Felix], joking with God, laughed at the accusations made against him').[77]

This leads us to elaborate on the conclusion of the first two chapters, that the nature of the letters themselves—with the metatextual 'performance' around them which I have dubbed their 'nexus of communication'—is of performance pieces, though performances aimed at an audience with a more subtle grasp of Latin and textual reference. The letters should be seen, not as inert, but as living texts for the enactment of Christianity.

I conclude this compressed selection of examples with a further delightful instance of Paulinus' wit in *Letter* 23, to Sulpicius. This is the longest of Paulinus' surviving letters, and takes the form of an extraordinarily extended imagistic meditation on biblical aspects of the theme of hair—a conceit prompted by the fact that the letter-carrier Victor, in the course of serving Paulinus, has apparently shaved Paulinus' head.[78] At one stage, Paulinus exclaims, 'sed ut totam de capillis texamus epistolam . . .' ('but, to weave the whole letter from hair . . .').[79] And he does.

---

[75] Compare Isa. 40: 3–4.

[76] *Poem* 19. 289.

[77] *Poem* 18. 316. Paulinus' account of the episode as a whole is an exercise in the delightfully absurd: for example, the oxen when restored ruin their master's clothes by greeting him 'spumosa per oscula', 'with slobbery kisses' (*Poem* 18. 419). Margit Kamptner discusses Paulinus *Poem* 18 in terms which in many ways resonate with my observations here: 'Paulinus *Poem* 18: Sources, Models and Structure', unpublished paper delivered at International Medieval Congress, Kalamazoo (May 1999).

[78] Victor, and his personification of Martin in his services to Paulinus, is discussed in Chapter 1. Victor himself is the focus of much of the wit in this letter—for example, when he shows Paulinus' brethren that one may mortify the spirit just as well by eating as by fasting—'voluit . . . ut non solum ieiunio sed et cibo humiliare animam disceremus' (*Letter* 23. 7)!

[79] *Letter* 23. 14.

This chapter has discussed the meditative and creative practices of reading and viewing which grew up around patterns of thought relying on imagistic juxtaposition; we have seen the way in which they went far beyond the functional to produce a world-view in which symbolic and spiritual connections were considered more real than literal ones, and in which the literal was only accorded significance in proportion to its evocation of such spiritual connections. But what was the impact of these patterns of thought? What, more precisely, were the mechanisms by which they operated; and what was their theological significance?

5

Imagines intextae: images interwoven in the text

The image of weaving with which we closed the previous chapter is not an idle metaphor: it encapsulates Paulinus' actual practice. His use of—principally scriptural—images is precisely a multidimensional weaving. It seems that Paulinus was renowned in his circle for the thematic meditations that result—it is possible to infer that Delphinus, for example, regularly requested letters in this form[1]—and we now move on to discover why.

Instead of giving piecemeal examples of Paulinus' complex use of images in these thematic meditations, I shall explore two longer extracts in some depth; for it is precisely in their extended form that these imagistic *catenae* are so remarkable. Both these extracts are taken from that letter to Sulpicius which was woven entirely from hair: it is the longest, and probably the most dense, of Paulinus' figural *jeux d'esprit*. An extraordinary intensity of imagistic association is maintained for nearly fifty paragraphs of Hartel's text. It seems that this was lengthy even for medieval readers—in four of the six manuscripts of Paulinus' letters, a division is made in *Letter* 23 between chapters 9 and 10—and I know of no extended modern attempt to engage with what Paulinus might have been attempting to do in this work.

The first extract is chosen simply to illustrate and explicate Paulinus' extraordinarily convoluted, yet vivid, use of images; the second, from a little later in the same letter, explores the considerable theological implications of this practice. In both we see, once again, the delight in paradox and the fluidity of meaning on which I remarked in Chapter 4.

---

[1] Certainly, as noted in Chapter 1, Paulinus begins one letter to him: 'Accepimus litteras sanctae affectionis tuae, quibus iubes nos in epistulis, quas ad te facimus, aliquem praeter officii de scripturis adicere sermonem, qui tibi thesaurum nostri cordis revelet.' There follows an association of images round the idea of the *thesaurus* and of laying up treasure (drawing on Matt. 6: 19–20): *Letter* 10. 1.

Summa igitur ope enitamur ita nos conparare, ut divini capitis, quod nobis per gratiam dei Christus est, crines et aurum esse mereamur. ex ipso enim capite pullulat illa caesaries, de qua scriptum est: 'capillatura eius ut greges caprarum' [S. of S. 4: 1]. et bene illorum potissimum animalium nomine designantur greges Christi, quorum maxime usus in lacte est, quia omnis qui credit deum Christum totam trinitatis plenitudinem in eo, quem pater 'unxit spiritu sancto' [Acts 10: 38], fide pietatis amplectitur. et ideo ipsa 'mater omnium viventium' [Gen. 3: 20], Christi corpus ecclesia, suco pietatis exuberat, et 'bona ubera eius super vinum' [S. of S. 1: 1]. in quo opinor significari, quod dulcior sit libertas gratiae in lacte misericordiae quam in vino iustitiae legis austeritas. 'littera enim', inquit, 'occidit', vides censurae merum; 'spiritus autem vivificat' [2 Cor. 3: 6], vides uberum munus et lactis effectum. sed hoc, ut tu mavis intellegi, semen detur,[2] quo prima nascentium multra coalescit. bona igitur ubera, quae 'pastor bonus, qui pro ovibus animam suam posuit' [John 10: 11], illis inmulsit infantibus, de quorum ore perfecit laudem sibi, ut destrueret inimicum boni et defensorem mali.

  Ex harum caprarum gregibus erat ille vir gregis, qui parvulos Christi nondum aptos solidiori cibo teneris lactabat alimentis, quibus dicebat: 'lacte vos potavi, non esca; nondum enim poteratis, sed nec adhuc potestis' [1 Cor. 3: 2]. cum autem huius lactis alimonia creverimus, firmatis primum fidei conceptione vestigiis adolescemus in robur iuventae, et confirmata per fidem caritatemque patientia levabimus manus nostras in actionem robustiorem operibusque virtutum velut cibo fortiore vivemus, ut efficiamur et illi crines, de quibus scriptum est: 'crines eius abietes nigrae sicut corax' [S. of S. 5: 11] id est corvus, sed bonus iste corvus nec ille ad arcam revertendi inmemor, sed ille pascendi prophetae memor, cui bene conparantur illarum abietum aemuli crines, de quibus dicit: 'abietes bonae et nigrae, adducentes naves Tharsis';[3] unde nunc corax iste non noctis sed luminis corvus est, cuius colore speciosi crines sunt ideo 'sancti, genus regale et sacerdotale' [1 Pet. 2: 9], quibus divinum caput ut ostro gloriae suae purpurat, quia et iuvenalis gratia in huius praecipue coloris capillo florentem vestit aetatem.[4]

So let us strive with the greatest effort so to prepare ourselves, that we may deserve to be the hair and the gold of the divine head, which is, by the grace of God, our Christ. For from that very head sprouts the hair, of which it is written: 'his hair is like flocks of goats'. And the flocks of Christ are particularly aptly denoted by the name of those animals whose greatest use is for milking, because everyone who

---

  [2] This is an extremely vexed line. Hartel reads 'hoc, ut tu mavis intellegi, semini detur', which is attested in none of the manuscripts. Walsh emends, again without manuscript support, to 'sed hoc ... serum indicetur'. I have used here the reading of O; the rest (bar M, in which the sentence is missing—though Hartel, mysteriously, gives an alternative spelling in M for 'multra') read '... ut tu magis intellegis emendetur'.
  [3] Hartel gives III Reg. 5: 8 and II Paral. 9: 21 as origins for this composite quotation; but neither is very close, and neither, interestingly, mentions the colour black: this seems to be Paulinus' own addition.
  [4] *Letter* 23. 27–8.

believes that God, and Christ, and the whole fullness of the Trinity, are in him whom the Father has anointed with the Holy Spirit, is embraced by the faith of piety. Likewise, the actual 'mother of all living things', the Church which is the body of Christ, abounds in the milk of piety, and 'her breasts are good beyond wine'. This, I think, means that the freedom of grace in the milk of mercy is sweeter than the harshness of the Law in the wine of justice. 'For the letter', he says, 'kills'—the wine of condemnation, you see; 'but the spirit gives life'—the gift of the breasts and the effect of milk. But this, as you prefer it to be understood, may be given as the seed, with which the first milk of the newborn is formed.[5] So the breasts are good on which the good shepherd, who laid down his life for his flock, suckled those children from whose mouths he perfected praise for himself, that he might destroy the enemy of good and defender of evil.

That herdsman was from flocks of these goats, that man who suckled on soft foods the little ones of Christ who were not yet fit for more solid nourishment; he would say to them: 'I have given you milk to drink, not food; you used not to be capable of eating it, and you still are not'. But when we have grown, through the nourishment of this milk, we shall progress to youthful strength with our footsteps first strengthened by the conception of faith, and, our endurance affirmed through faith and love, we shall raise our hands to more powerful action, and we shall live on the stronger food, as it were, of virtuous deeds, so that we too may become the hair, of which it is written: 'his hair is fir-trees black as the *corax*'—that is, the raven, but the good raven: not the one who forgot to return to the ark, but the one who remembered to feed the prophet, to whom is aptly compared the hair like fir-trees, of which scripture says: 'good black fir-trees, bringing the ships to Tarshish'; so now that *corax* is not the raven of night but of light, and hair made beautiful by its colour is therefore 'sacred, of royal and priestly descent'—hair which empurples the divine head as with the dye of its own glory, because a young man's grace clothes the flower of youth in hair of this colour above all.

There are three main scriptural strands whose interpretative resonance is interwoven through the first of these paragraphs. The first derives from the Song of Songs, the song of the anonymous bridegroom to his beloved, then commonly interpreted as the song of Christ to *ecclesia*, the Church.[6] The second is the image of Christ as head of the Church, intermingled with images of the head of the bridegroom/Christ, and of his hair. The third is the image of the milk of the goats—introduced through the

---

[5] Gillian Clark has suggested to me that Paulinus' image here is of the (male or female) seed, which triggers the transformation of maternal blood into milk: she cites Aulus Gellius 12. 1, and Favorinus' argument for the influence of paternal seed on maternal milk, in support. This is by far the best explanation of this passage which I have come across.

[6] For the history of interpretation of the *Song of Songs*, see E. Ann Matter, *The Voice of My Beloved: The Song of Songs in Western Medieval Christianity* (Philadelphia, 1990).

bridegroom/Christ's hair 'like flocks of goats'—which represents in turn
the milk of the Church, of Christ, and of the New Testament and its
spiritual interpretation of the Old Law. Each of these strands develops and
extends the available matrix of reference in a manner which is simultaneously elusive and startlingly vivid. They also resonate backwards and
forwards in the context of the letter, as well as outwards to their scriptural
origins. So, for example, when first the hair of the bridegroom is equated
with gold, this looks back to the previous paragraph, where the bridegroom's golden hair (S. of S. 5: 11) is said to be the gold from which the
coin of the saints is struck: hence the desire to become such hair. Paulinus
then introduces the hair 'like flocks of goats', and proceeds to develop that
image: the milk-yielding goat also represents the Church; the milk of
mercy produced by the Church is superior to the wine of the old Law—
encapsulating once again the pivotal letter/spirit antithesis.

   The implicit contrast between spirit and letter also embraces the
dichotomy of *ecclesia* and *synagoga*, the Church of the New Testament
as opposed to the Synagogue of the Old (though at the same time, of
course, *synagoga* is also the *typos* of *ecclesia*). The *typos* of Christ as the
head whose body is the Church (as at Eph. 1: 22–23), which also
runs through this paragraph, is the image which we saw to be so critical
to the notion of Christian friendship, a particularly happy resonance in
the context of a letter to Sulpicius. At the end of the passage the *typos* of
Christ the good shepherd is also introduced; if my interpretation of the
confused penultimate sentence is correct, we have an image of milk
combined with spirit/seed to create a life-giving force for the flock of
the good shepherd—'life-giving' both literally, physically, and as a
metaphor of salvation. This reading is endorsed by a startling passage in
the ninth *Natalicium*, in which Paulinus casts himself as a sheep whose
udders (*ubera*) become distended as he gazes upon the salvific
'fountain' that is Nicetas. Again, the spirit gives 'the gift of life'—which
is milk.[7]

   The second paragraph continues the image of shepherd and goats; but
now the shepherd is not Christ, but Paul, linked with Christ as being from
among the flocks of Christ who received the salvific milk as well as himself
articulating an ongoing tradition of nourishing the faithful with spiritual
milk ('I have given you milk to drink . . . '). Paul is identified as chosen by
God from the 'goats'—the Jews, who are to be separated at Judgement

---

[7] *Poem* 27. 266–8: 'sic ego Niceta viso quasi fonte reperto/sicut ovis sitiens ad viva fluenta
cucurri/aridus et sensi mea protinus ubera tendi . . . '

Day from the Christian sheep; but the goats as the bridegroom/Christ's hair are still a present image, reinforcing the integrated interpretation of Old and New Testaments. The milk represents the nourishment of the spiritually immature (the 'milk' of the New Covenant still echoes behind the image); more solid food represents the good deeds on which they will grow strong, while the phrase 'the *conception* of faith' recalls the earlier image of the seed generating the new-born children and the milk on which they are suckled. Those who thus become strong through virtuous deeds become the hair like 'fir-trees black as the *corax*'—once again, the hair of the bridegroom in the Song of Songs. This time it is evoked in its blackness, the blackness of the virtuous raven who fed Elijah in the wilderness, not of the vicious raven who failed to return to Noah after the Flood; and the potential virtue of blackness is supported with an allusion to the goodness of the black firs used for ship-building. Paulinus brings this passage to a close with a flourish: blackness is light (which also resonates with S. of S. 1: 4, 'nigra sum, sed formosa'); and it may be elided with the sacred colour purple, and the sheen of a young man's hair—returning again to the youth and beauty of the bridegroom/Christ.

This is an excellent example of the sheer bravura of Paulinus' imagistic display. Similar complex connections of thought, drawn through symbolically significant images, continue throughout this and many of his letters. The extremely dense style of the passage also immediately draws attention to the way in which the idea of active reading must be further developed: for such writing is incomprehensible without considerable knowledge, not just of the Bible, but of the tradition of its typological interpretation.[8] But this does not wholly capture the difference from the way in which readers such as Paulinus would have responded to the classical texts through which they had been educated: many classical texts, after all, require likewise an appreciation of complex intertextual relationships for their satisfactory interpretation. The difference seems rather to lie in the expected psychology of reading: the sense of the text, not as an end

---

[8] On typological interpretation, see Leonhard Goppelt, *Typos: The Typological Interpretation of the Old Testament in the New*, trans. Donald H. Madvig (Grand Rapids, MI, 1982; first published 1939). The fullest study of this overall tradition remains, to my knowledge, that of Henri de Lubac, *Exégèse Médiévale: les quatre sens de l'écriture* (4 vols.: Paris 1959–64). Beryl Smalley provides a convenient summary at the beginning of *The Study of the Bible in the Middle Ages* (Oxford, 1952). See also the recent study, heavily influenced by the reading of Northrop Frye, by Tibor Fabiny, *The Lion and the Lamb: Figuralism and Fulfilment in the Bible, Art and Literature* (Basingstoke/London, 1992).

in itself, but as a conduit, however imperfect,[9] of a truth that lies beyond the
textual.[10] These works demand a reader who is highly educated within an
appropriate matrix of reference, but as a means to an end: to equip him or
herself to look beyond the letter to the spirit, beyond the literal to the
spiritual. This runs exactly counter to the explicit message of Paulinus'
letters: the fiction actively sustained is of an unintellectual programme of
ascetic behaviour, whereas his prose style presupposes a great deal of
Christian erudition; but here again, we see Christian paradox in practice.[11]

The expectation of active reading is well exemplified by the independent way in which Paulinus deals with typological signification. In the
above passage, the phrase 'in quo *opinor* significari' ('in which, *I think*, is
signified...') is not idly used. As observed earlier, the logic of active
reading serves to endorse the validity of individual interpretation, and now
and then Paulinus will self-consciously depart from a traditional reading
in order to substitute his own. An excellent example of this occurs in
another letter to Sulpicius: he adverts to the image of Jacob wrestling with
the angel, and continues,

in quo tametsi principaliter sacramenti salutaris praefiguratio esse videatur ... atta-
men in huius nostri nunc ratione sermonis eatenus usurpanda videtur historia,
quatenus imaginem evangelicae praeceptionis operata est, ut illo videlicet exemplo
intellegamus non posse nos esse idoneos ad congrediendum deo, cui utique con-
gredimur, cum verbum eius inplere nitimur et in virtutes divinas imitatione ipsius
praevalere conamur.[12]

In this, even though generally it may be seen as a prefiguration of the sacrament of
salvation, in the current rationale of my argument it seems that the story should be
used insofar as it creates an image of the evangelistic precept, that plainly by that
example we may understand that we, as ourselves, cannot be fit to meet with God,
but that we certainly do meet with him when we strive to fulfil his word and try by
imitating him to excel in divine virtues.

---

[9] This surely is one of the reasons why so much commentary on the material aspects of
texts survives from the fourth century: because of reflection on the limitations of texts as
'conduit'. (See, for example, Evaristo Arns, *La technique du livre d'après saint Jérôme* (Paris,
1953).) Augustine's reflections on signs, and on the limitations of language, in such works as
De Doctrina Christiana and *De Magistro* would have been prompted by the same concern.

[10] Giselle de Nie is at present developing ideas on the psychology of reading in a far more
sophisticated fashion than I am currently equipped to do: see especially her 'Word, image and
experience in the early medieval miracle story', in A. Remael et al. (eds.) *Language and Beyond*
(Amsterdam, 1997).

[11] Cameron, *Christianity and the Rhetoric of Empire*, 155, remarks on this type of practical
paradox in fourth-century Christianity.

[12] *Letter* 24. 8.

Like Augustine, Paulinus consistently shows an awareness of the multi-
plicity of meanings in the images he employs: witness his distinction
between the good and bad ravens. More extravagantly than Augustine,
however, he is also inclined to assign meaning in symbolic terms which
draw upon typological figures: so, in the letter under scrutiny, he is at
pains to explain how a soul may be both black and good:

Sed et nunc eruditae ad apostolicam fidem animae abietes sunt nigrae et bonae;
nigrae vero iam non de peccato, ut puto, magis quam adhuc vel de inhabitatione
corporea vel de exercitationis internae quasi bellico pulvere vel pulverulento
sudore nigrantes; bonae tamen propter spiritalem etiam in noctibus corporum
conversationem.[13]

But now too souls formed to the apostolic faith are good black fir-trees; they are
really black not, I think, from sin, but from still being blackened by their bodily
habitation, or by the martial dust, so to speak, of internal struggle, or by dusty
sweat; and they are good because of the spiritual way of life of their bodies even at
night.

'Etiam in noctibus' is presumably inserted to emphasize that night's
association with blackness does not mar the soul[14]—or is it a reference
to the night of spiritual struggle? The explanation of black as good also
once again calls on S. of S. 1: 4, 'nigra sum, sed formosa', and the context
of the Song of Songs invoked earlier in the letter.

In recent years, more attention has been paid to the way in which the
visual arts of late antiquity expect to elicit such a complex and educated
response than to similar uses of figuralism in literature. John Onians
initiated the exploration of the rise at the time of non-literal tendencies
in viewing: he goes so far as to state that 'The vitality of Christianity
depended partly on its insistence that people should disregard the evidence of their eyes'.[15] Michael Roberts has espoused a contrary position:
'In late antiquity what seems to have happened is that the referential
function of language/art lost some of its preeminence; signifier asserts
itself at the expense of signified.'[16] However, it seems clear that exactly the

---

[13] *Letter* 23. 30. Notice another formula denoting departure from traditional interpretation in 'ut puto'.

[14] Compare 'non noctis sed luminis corvus', *Letter* 23. 28 above.

[15] Onians, 'Abstraction and Imagination in Late Antiquity', *Art History* 3 (1980), 1–24;
quote from 20. A notable development of the subject for the Eastern tradition: Herbert
Kessler, ' "Pictures Fertile with Truth": How Christians Managed to Make Images of God
Without Violating the Second Commandment', *Journal of the Walters Art Gallery* 49/50
(1991/92).

[16] Roberts, *The Jeweled Style: Poetry and Poetics in Late Antiquity* (Cornell, 1989), 72.

opposite trend is in play: the signified is, if anything, far more important than before (being of the spiritual realm), but its relationship with the signifier is negotiated differently, in a non-literal manner. To attempt a detailed comparison of the traditions of expression in the visual arts and the literature of late antiquity lies beyond the scope of this study, but a few general comments may validly be made.

The representational art of the period shows a marked preference for abbreviated scenes—for a compressed, summary account of a biblical theme in a single *mise-en-scène* as opposed to an extended sequential narrative account.[17] We see this particularly on the sarcophagi of the fourth century and the ivory tablets of the first half of the fifth;[18] on the fourth-century ivory casket known as the Brescia lipsanotheca; and on the renowned carved doors from the church of Santa Sabina in Rome (*c.* 430).[19] This type of scheme bears a startling similarity to Paulinus' allusive use of typological motifs: likewise, a single mode or moment or aspect of a narrative is fixed upon, thereby not only hinting at its own narrative context but, through typological resonance, recalling others. Moreover, although it does not always seem to be the case, such abbreviated scenes are often juxtaposed in such a manner as to suggest parallels between them. There is an excellent example of this in a set of panels from an ivory casket of *c.* 420–30, now in the British Museum, London.[20] Two of them are particularly dense in imagery. On the first, Christ carries his cross against a twofold background, a depiction of Pilate washing his hands and of Peter with the cock who crowed three times: the two images are unified by their grim symbolism of the denial of Christ. On the second, the death by hanging of the sinner Judas is juxtaposed directly with the death by crucifixion of the redemptive Christ. The other two panels form a neatly contrasted pair: the Marys at the tomb suggests despair at the death

---

[17] See the description of Erich Dinkler in Kurt Weitzmann (ed.) *Age of Spirituality: Late Antique and Early Christian Art, Third to Seventh Century* (New York, 1979), 396–448.

[18] For a comprehensive survey of Roman sarcophagi, see Giuseppe Bovini and Hugo Brandenburg, *Repertorium der christlich-antiken Sarkophage*, Vol. I: Rom und Ostia, ed. Friedrich Wilhelm Deichmann (Wiesbaden, 1967). The sarcophagus of Junius Bassus has been studied with particular thoroughness: see Elizabeth Struthers Malbon, *The Iconography of the Sarcophagus of Junius Bassus* (Princeton, 1990). For the ivory tablets, see Wolfgang Fritz Volbach, *Elfenbeinarbeiten der Spätantike und des frühen Mittelalters* (Mainz, 1976).

[19] Brescia lipsanotheca: see André Grabar, *Christian Iconography: A Study of Its Origins* (Princeton 1968), plates 333–7; detail in Volbach, *Elfenbeinarbeiten*, Tafel 57 Nr. 107. Doors of S. Sabina: Grabar, *Christian Iconography*, plates 195 and 338–9.

[20] Volbach, *Elfenbeinarbeiten*, Tafel 61 Nr. 116. One of these appears on the cover of this book.

of Christ; the portrayal of doubting Thomas, the absolute affirmation of his resurrection. These are my own interpretations; but André Grabar has elucidated a similar programme of interactive juxtaposition for the doors of S. Sabina: though their original placement is doubtful, 'there are obviously pairs of panels . . . [whose] form and content make them like the two leaves of a diptych'. He takes as an example two panels directly comparing the miracles of Moses with those of Christ: for example, the provision of quails and manna for the children of Israel in the desert parallels the multiplication of the loaves and fishes.[21]

We see in the example of the ivory panels and of the doors of S. Sabina how crucial a role the Bible performs as the textual intermediary providing the link between the images; a further example shows how the resonances of the mediating text may be even more complicatedly realized. This example is drawn from a bowl of the period.[22] It bears only two images: the three Hebrews leaving the fiery furnace and Joseph escaping from Potiphar's wife. The connection between them remains obscure unless one resorts to an account of the tempting of Joseph in *The Testament of the Twelve Patriarchs*, an apocryphal development of biblical themes and a text known to Origen and Jerome, in which Potiphar's wife—or the lust which she inspires—is described as a 'burning flame'.[23] Cox Miller has recently remarked on the same phenomenon with reference to frieze sarcophagi: '. . . groups of figures are not tied together organically; rather *they are unified by the theological message to which all of them point*: in Kitzinger's striking formulation, such a frieze is "like a line of writing which required the viewer's active participation" to discern the unifying narrative which the discrete sculptural groups exemplify again and again.'[24]

---

[21] Grabar, *Christian Iconography*; quote from 142.

[22] Fourth-century, Tunisia, earthenware (now in Mainz). See Weitzmann, *Age of Spirituality* Item 415, 464–5; the commentator remarks on the 'visual parallelism between Joseph's flight and that of the Hebrew youths', as well as the 'thematic parallelism' between the two images.

[23] From the 'Testament of Joseph on Self-Control', 2. 2: '. . . and I struggled with a shameless woman who was urging me to transgress with her; but the God of Israel my father protected me from the burning flame'. *The Testaments of the Twelve Patriarchs*, ed. M. de Jonge (Leiden, 1978), 145. For Jerome and Origen's knowledge of the text, see intro., xxx–xxxi.

[24] Patricia Cox Miller, ' "Differential Networks": Relics and Other Fragments in Late Antiquity', *JECS* 6 (1998), 113–38 (my emphasis). This excellent article parallels many of the observations which I am making here; its emphasis on *ecphraseis* for written evidence is, however, to my mind slightly misleading—largely because *ecphraseis* at this period were written by conscious classicizers or archaizers (hence her reliance on Ausonius), while the 'dissonant echoing' she highlights is a characteristically Christian aesthetic.

It is particularly relevant to the writings of Paulinus that a textual intermediary between percipient and image should be required for the full interpretation of visual symbolism: we have already seen how his strongly textual emphasis in comprehension of the visual arts may be contrasted with his vividly imagistic style of writing.[25] Jaş Elsner has recently argued that 'In exegetic terms images do what texts cannot.... The instantaneous, non-diachronic nature of the image (what should perhaps be called its *iconicity*) collapses the totality of these narratives and narratives about narratives into a single space and time'.[26] But I wish to argue that this is precisely what texts *were* able to do, because of the mental equipment and intellectual customs of their writers and readers. (Indeed, Elsner tacitly admits that this is so by using the biblical exegesis of Gregory of Nyssa to 'read' the programmes of the mosaics of the Monastery of St Catherine at Mount Sinai.) The matrix of imagistic association around particular images or ideas—as we saw in the long passage from Paulinus quoted above—allows for non-linear and, indeed, synchronic patterns of thought.[27] Such techniques of suggestive juxtaposition force us to rethink assumptions about narrative continuity.

For that matter, we have to ponder the validity of a sharp distinction between the textual and the imagistic. Certainly, we tend to think of images as somehow prior to texts, more pristine; for Paulinus, it seems to have been the other way around: the 'pristine' source of the Bible prompted a flow of images which could be textually or visually expressed—or both, as we saw in the iconographic programme of his basilica. The virtue of images lies precisely in their lack of subordination

---

[25] Henry Maguire emphasizes the importance of textual directives to the viewer of Byzantine mosaics, *contra* the emphasis of Onians on the active initiative of the viewer (talk: Pontifical Institute of Mediaeval Studies, Toronto, March 1996); it seems to me that these alternatives are far from mutually exclusive—indeed, that they are complexly interrelated.

[26] Elsner, *Art and the Roman Viewer*, 119–120 (Elsner's emphasis). Despite my disagreement with this specific extract, the two cardinal points of Elsner's study seem to me to be extremely valuable: his emphasis on the participation of the viewer in interpretation; and his consistent appreciation that, for Christian art, the artistic endeavour served as a starting point for spiritual reflection, not as an end in itself.

[27] Margaret Miles has remarked on the same phenomenon in discussing the fourth-century symbolism surrounding baptism—as rebirth, as enlightenment, as cleansing: 'These interpretations visually work together as adding to and glossing one another, although they may, if analyzed verbally, seem contradictory.... [They] were visually presented simultaneously, enriching one another as aspects of a fundamentally ineffable experience...' From *Image as Insight*, 57.

to any literal sense; at the same time, they evoke a nimbus of textual association.

Transmuting the relationship between the textual and the imagistic is part of realizing the inherence of the spiritual in the temporal, because of the imaginative power of visualization that has to be called upon to make that transition.[28] Imagistic thought was in some degree essential to the paradoxical doctrines of Christianity, for such thought had the capacity to make logically incompatible ideas cohere.

This is well illustrated by my second extract from the expansive *Letter* 23, which has at its climax a textual crux of immense theological significance:

quod [regnum mortis], vivente semper, ut vivit, Christo et ante carnalem adventum suum in maiestate naturae suae apud dominum patrem deo verbo, tamen dispositis in ordinem suum saeculis ab Adam usque ad Moysen, mortis potestas licentia bacchante regnaverat et de lege intellecto nec evitato peccato creverat, hoc regnum rex regum et dispensator temporum dei filius passione sua divisit ac diruit, deus 'factus sub lege', ut subiugatos legi solveret, 'factus per mulierem' [Gal. 4: 4], sed mulierem sexu, virginem partu, ut sanctificaret utrumque sexum creator utriusque, suscipiendo verbum, nascendo per feminam.[29]

Though Christ is always living, as he does live—even before his fleshly advent—in the majesty of his nature as God the Word in the house of the Lord his father, yet in the generations arrayed in order from Adam right down to Moses, the power of death had ruled over this [mortal kingdom], and had increased from the apprehension of the Law and the failure to avoid sin: this kingdom the king of kings and disposer of ages, the son of God, divided and destroyed through his own passion: he was made God under the law, so that he should free those subjected to the law, 'made through a married woman', but a woman [only] in gender, a virgin in childbirth, so that the creator of both genders might sanctify both, by taking on the word and being born through a woman.

The crux concerns the object of 'suscipiendo' ('by taking on'). Here, Hartel prints 'verbum' ('word'); Walsh and Santaniello correct to 'virum' ('man'). The solution at first sight seems obvious. Hartel has been misled by his consistent preference for the testimony of the earliest surviving manuscript (O) into favouring its mistaken reading 'verbum' over the 'virum' contained in all other manuscripts and branches of the tradition; Walsh and Santaniello sensibly restore the correct reading,

---

[28] See again Giselle de Nie on the subject of creative visualization in Gregory of Tours and Venantius Fortunatus: 'Iconic Alchemy: imaging miracles in late sixth-century Gaul', *SP* 30: *Ascetica* (1997), 158–66.

[29] *Letter* 23. 14.

'virum'. It is clear that the context is insisting upon the gender inclusive-
ness of Christ; so we would expect to find a man as the object of our first
gerund to balance the woman governed by our second.

However, we must consider what Paulinus meant by 'verbum' in the
context of Christ's incarnation; and the second paragraph of this very
letter addresses this question.

> ... benedicimus dominum, *dei verbum* deum, qui sicut in ipso illo homine, quem
> gessit, ita in nostris mentibus gradus quosdam corporeae aetatis exequitur: *nascitur*
> *crescit roboratur senescit.* sed orandus, ne in nobis diu aut iugiter parvulus et
> infirmus et pauper sit.[30]
>
> ... we adore the lord God *word of God*, who just as in that actual human body,
> which he wore, so in our minds pursues certain stages of corporeal existence: *he is*
> *born, grows, becomes strong, and grows old.* But we should pray that he may not be
> small and weak and impoverished in us for a long time, or continually.

In other words, from almost the beginning of this letter, word and body
are already closely linked. The physical embodiment of Christ as *verbum* is
taken very seriously; and at the same time the transition from body to
mind—from the physical to the metaphysical—is made here without a
hint of dislocation. One can attribute properties to the Word which are
normally attributed to human bodies: the Word grows strong, or old, or is
little and poor. Indeed, the choice of verbs—especially of 'roboratur' and
'senescit'—is of those particularly linked to embodied experience.

It will come, by now, as no surprise that the paradoxical link between
the incorporeal Word and embodied Christ is made by love. This letter
itself sets out to be an active proof of the love between Paulinus and its
addressee, Sulpicius. It begins with the challenge, already cited in Chapter
3: 'quid extorques, ut te plus amemus? crescere summa non recipit' ('why
do you extort that I should love you more? Plenitude does not admit of
increase'), and continues some lines later, 'quid enim fieri diligentius in
deo et proximo potest, quam quod in nobis exhibes Christo?' ('for what
can happen more lovingly[31] in God and neighbour, than what you display
to Christ in us?'). God, Paulinus goes on to say, *is* both God and neighbour, God 'by the majesty of his nature', neighbour 'by his assumption of
ours'.[32] Thus both the first and second commandments of the new
covenant, the familiar commandments to love God and neighbour
(Matt. 22: 37–40), are embraced in Paulinus' and Sulpicius' love for

---

[30] *Letter* 23. 2.   [31] Construing 'diligentius' as the participial adverb from *diligo*.
[32] All quotes from *Letter* 23. 1.

each other in Christ, *and* in the incarnation which makes Christ 'both God and neighbour', and therefore the fullest possible object of love.

But in the earthly realm Paulinus does have something to add to his love for Sulpicius. Now, he says, Sulpicius has surpassed himself and come to Paulinus 'supergressa humanitate' ('with surpassing humanity'). The ambiguity of 'humanity'—'kindness' or 'human nature'?[33]—is clearly intentional; meanwhile, 'supergressus' is also used in *Letter* 21 (to Amandus), where it seems to mean 'went beyond': John 'went beyond' archangels and all created things to focus eagerly upon the creator himself.[34] Maybe, in some ways, plenitude does admit of increase. The form which the 'surpassing humanity' takes is that of the letter-carrier Victor: it will be remembered from Chapter 1 that 'when he came to us in the name of God and *in your persona*, we received him with close affection and great rejoicing'.[35]

The extraordinary audacity of this metaphor bears investigation: for surely the 'surpassing humanity' evokes the incarnation of Christ himself. And Victor evokes the figure of Christ in other ways as well. He brings both 'contubernium spiritale' ('spiritual companionship'), and 'corporeus famulatus' ('ministrations to the body').[36] In fact, through his services to Paulinus, his physical ministrations *become* spiritual companionship—and when Victor washes Paulinus' feet 'et ego dominum Iesum *in fratre Victore* veneratus' ('I actually revered Christ *in brother Victor*').[37]

This begins to anticipate the subject of my final chapter; but it is the nature of that immanence—*in* brother Victor—that is crucial to Paulinus' association of *verbum* with *vir*, and to the theological significance of his figuralism: and we shall here make a preliminary foray into the process of its valorization.

It is no coincidence that *Letter* 23 is one of Paulinus' wittiest literary productions. Its insouciant use of metaphor is inseparable from Paulinus' sheer joy in the potentialities of his own word-play. The audacity of the association of Victor with Christ is typical of the audacity of Paulinian

---

[33] *TLL* 6. 3. 3075–83 interprets *humanitas* first as 'natura humana', then *speciatim* as 'substantia humana Christi'—but also notes it as a term of general approval, of the positive in human nature. All these meanings are bound up in the use of *humanitas* here.

[34] *Letter* 21. 3: '... archangelos quoque et omnes desuper creaturas virtutes principatus dominationes thronos supergressus in ipsum se creatorem ardua mente direxit...'

[35] *Letter* 23. 3: 'fratrem Victorem in nomine dei tuaque persona ad nos venientem intima affectione et magna gratulatione suscepimus'. Cited Chapter 1, text to n. 98.

[36] Mentioned in that order, *Letter* 23. 3.

[37] *Letter* 23. 5. This is the passage which begins 'servivit ergo mihi, servivit, inquam...'.

metaphor. These metaphors are established and developed with a confidence that belies their originality, and masks the fact that he is doing
nothing less than proposing an alternative spiritual reality. And if that
juxtaposition of 'spiritus' and 'res', soul and matter, seems paradoxical,
that is entirely appropriate.

To return to the complexity of Paulinus' use of metaphor and imagery—as well as to the theme of hair—we may look at the sustained
use of the image of Samson which surrounds the extract containing the
'verbum'/'virum' crux. The treatment of Samson goes well beyond any
simple schematic of type and antitype, into a rich and variegated use of
metaphor drawn from every episode of his story. The *catena* of associations is introduced with a delightfully absurd image prompted by Victor's
shaving of Paulinus' head. This must refer to complete shaving, and not
just a part-tonsure, because of the image developed from it: Paulinus asks
Victor and Sulpicius to make a point, in their prayers, of shaving him of
the sins which are more numerous than the hairs of his head and make his
soul uncombed.[38] But then, Paulinus goes on, there is also the hair of
gratia spiritalis ('spiritual grace'), and we should beware of that 'inimica
novacula', that 'hostile razor' the devil, who might take it away—as
Delilah did Samson's.

quod patiantur necesse est qui *suam feminam id est carnem viro suo hoc est spiritui* in
dei leges non subiugant et tamquam malesuadae coniugi molles mariti fluentibus
animis adquiescunt, degeneres ab illo magistro, qui mox ut agnovit Christum, inter
ipsa militiae rudimenta magni certaminis victor 'non adquievit carni et sanguini'
[Gal. 1: 16].[39]

They must necessarily suffer this who do not subjugate *their wife—that is the
flesh—to her husband—that is the spirit*—according to the divine laws, and acquiesce
like weak-willed husbands with undiscliplined minds to a seductive wife, falling
short of that teacher [Paul] who, as soon as he acknowledged Christ, victorious in
the great struggle at the very beginnings of his service 'did not give way to flesh and
blood'.

We sinners, Paulinus goes on to insist, should pay attention to Samson's
corruption by a faithless wife, because we carry the same burdens *spiritaliter* as he *carnaliter*. (The passage presents rather a harsh juxtaposition
with the apparent opportunities earlier that the redemptive 'creator of
both genders might sanctify both'.) The cutting of the hair of grace

---

[38] 'anima inpexa', *Letter* 23. 10—the notion of sins as dreadlocks of the soul I find
eminently memorable.
[39] *Letter* 23. 11.

reduces humankind to the life of beasts—blinkered, like an animal at the mill-wheel—so that they shan't realize their circular path. This, of course, recalls the episode in Samson's life when he is captured by the Philistines and his eyes put out, and he is made to grind corn (Judg. 16: 21). But, just as hair grows back again, so will the spirit become whole again 'gratia reflorente' ('with the renewed flourishing of grace').[40]

So, 'to weave this whole letter out of hair', let us follow that strong man of God right to his end—for in his blindness and death we marvel at the sacraments of divine mystery *praelineata*, delineated in advance. He struck down more enemies as he died than in the whole of his previous life— hence prefiguring Christ's passion.

This introduces the passage of the 'verbum'/'virum' crux; but Paulinus has not yet finished with the Samson story. For Christ is also 'that lion in whose mouth, after his death, we find honey'—'quid enim dulcius dei verbo?' ('for what is sweeter than the word of God?')[41] Samson, of course, killed that lion on his way to court Delilah; on his way back, he turned out of his road to see the lion's corpse, and 'ecce examen apum in ore leonis erat ac favus mellis' ('and behold, there was a swarm of bees in the lion's mouth, and a honeycomb') (Judg. 14: 8). Samson as the prefiguration of Christ must, then, be assimilated to the lion—but, as he killed the Christ-lion, he must also be a prefiguration of the Jews. As Samson went to seek his marriage with Delilah, he needed to kill the lion: so the marriage between Christ and the Church could not be performed without killing the lion from the tribe of Judah. Later, we have yet another interpretation of Samson: 'morte Samso commori disco hostibus meis, hoc est mortific-ando carnem meam simul interficere peccatum' ('by the death of Samson I learn to die with my enemies, that is, by mortifying my flesh simulta-neously to kill sin'); moreover, by the blindness of Samson I am illumin-ated 'ad intellectum bonum' ('to good understanding'), for when Samson called God to his aid in the temple of the Philistines he showed that the eyes of his mind, the 'oculos mentis', were unharmed.[42]

Once again, the paradoxical tensions between and within the different interpretations are positively exploited rather than being smoothed over; once again, we see Paulinus refusing to claim any of the interpretations as the primary one. It is as if—to develop the art-historical parallel—we have

---

[40] *Letter* 23. 13.
[41] *Letter* 23. 16. It is another interesting slippage of signification here that Christ produces the Word instead of *being* the Word.
[42] All from *Letter* 23. 18.

a sequence of abbreviated scenes: each contains a common figure, in this case that of Samson, but in each case that figure is differently, often contrarily, contextualized. (It will, in fact, be noticed that the material model—in which a variety of figures resonate against a common context of spiritual meaning—has been neatly inverted.) The very refusal to adjudicate between the scenes, the acceptance of the fluidity of meaning between one and the next, is one of the great strengths of Paulinus' biblical interpretation—and, indeed, one of the things that makes his exegesis exceedingly difficult to pin down and write about. Paulinus does not treat biblical paradox as a problem to be solved; he does not merely accept it; he embraces and internalizes it—and the result is a sort of revelation by metaphor.

Revelation by metaphor is once again a contradiction in terms that bears immense significance at the centre of its contradiction. The implication is that Paulinus, like the beast—or Samson—has been forced to plod round in a circle grinding the corn of temporal affairs: now, he attempts to throw off the blinkers of spiritual blindness and yield himself to the centrifugal forces pushing him away from the circle. To put it another way: Paulinus is precisely trying to break out of the 'circular path' of conventional, temporal 'reality', and to move off on the spiritual tangents which construct an alternative reality. He is creating, as it were, a spiritual ontology.

These tangents must, of course, be infinite in number—for Paulinus' rendering of the Bible is endlessly multivalent: and as he refuses adjudication between versions, so he refuses closure. But the tangents (contravening their true mathematical properties) touch each other at various points, not just at their starting point, and they may become self-contradictory—as we have seen with the sudden transformation of the *figura* of Samson from Christ to Jew. But that, it seems, is part of the point, that multiple meanings carry their own contradictions within them. The effect, in the end—to shift my own metaphor—is more of a web, an astonishing, multilayered interconnection of meaning. It involves a profound rejection of linearity, of conventional linear modes of exposition and argumentation—and it is this, it seems, that modern readers (and that may well comprehend most readers of Paulinus since his death) have found so rebarbative.

It is the use of metaphor that makes this rejection of linearity possible—for, again paradoxically, only in the visual, supposedly 'surface' properties of metaphor can the multivalence of meaning be so economically captured. This quality of metaphor, and particularly of Paulinus' use of it—what

Matthias Skeb calls 'Anschaulichkeit', visualizability[43]—is crucial to the creation of Paulinus' spiritual ontology. We are inured by time and habit to the full realization of what extraordinary statements 'the word made flesh' and 'God made man' are:[44] Paulinus, however, makes the paradox inherent in those statements central to his entire notion of reality. He manages simultaneously to preserve, and to dwell upon, their freshness, while making these extraordinary equations seem entirely natural. 'Verbum', it seems, is actually interchangeable with 'virum'—and a whole web of meaning is opened up by that interchangeability.

The interchangeability of 'verbum' and 'virum' is well illustrated by the continuation of our original passage.

itaque mortem ipsam moriendo destruxit, 'solvens', ut scriptum est, 'inimicitias in carne sua et faciens utrumque unum' [Eph. 2: 14 and 16] id est hominem et deum, *quem* in se ipso conexuit deus et homo Christus Iesus, in quo utriusque substantia naturae discordiam posuit et unificantis gratiae aeternum foedus agnovit. . . . hic [Christus/Samarites] *hominem suum* praetermissum a praeviis nec curatum miseratus accessit et *iumento suo hoc est verbi incarnatione suscepit* et oleo gratiae et vino passionis suae commendatum stabulario, perfecto illi magistro gentium, in duobus testamentis denarii mercede sanavit, redditurus illi et beatae virginitatis de innumeris huius boni fructibus uberes gratias et innumerabiles coronas, quia hoc consilium praecepto adiciens de suo supererogauit.[45]

And so he destroyed death itself by dying, as it is written, 'abolishing the enmity in his own flesh and making the two one', that is, man and God, *whom* Christ Jesus as God and man bound together in himself, in whom the essence of each nature laid aside its disharmony and acknowledged the eternal bond of unifying grace. . . . He [Christ/the Samaritan] took pity on *his own man* who had been passed by and not cared for by the earlier men, and approached him, and supported him *on his packhorse—that is, on the incarnation of the word*—and, when he had been handed over with the oil of grace and the wine of suffering to the inn-keeper, that perfect teacher of the gentiles [Paul again], Christ cured him in two Testaments with the payment of a *denarius*, giving him thereafter (from the innumerable fruits of this benefit) the rich grace and innumerable crowns of virginity, because he paid out this teaching in addition, from his own example.

In Christ, the substance of each nature—man and God—laid down its essential unlikeness and acknowledged the eternal bond of unifying grace.

---

[43] See Skeb, *Christo vivere*, 201 and 283: in both places he speaks of Paulinus' need for the visualizable, his 'Bedürfnis nach Anschaulichkeit'. Pp. 198–208 cover similar ground to my discussion here, with an emphasis on Paulinus' movement 'per visibilia ad invisibilia'.

[44] Following from Frye's observation, Chapter 4, n. 70.

[45] *Letter* 23. 14 (continued).

Note the reflexivity of the passage, revolving round that central relative pronoun 'quem': its antecedents, logically, are both man and God, but made one—hence the singular pronoun, symbolizing their unification; but the subject of the verb in the relative clause is also both 'man' and 'God' as Christ, who linked the two natures: so in the remarkable identity of subject and object—God and man joined together man and God—that joining is verbally enacted.

This difficult reflexivity continues as Christ is likened to the Good Samaritan: he approached 'hominem suum' ('his own man'), and supported him with his pack-horse 'hoc est verbi incarnatione' ('that is, *with the incarnation of the word*'). In what sense can the man taken on by Christ the Samaritan be 'suum', his own? His own, because made by him—which applies well to Christ, but hardly to the Samaritan—or his own, because of the recognition (proleptic, in the case of Christ) of their common humanity?[46] And how can the pack-horse, the 'iumentum', be the incarnation of the Word? One answer is that humankind is supported and ratified by Christ's choice to take on human form; but there is, I think, further significance to the 'iumentum': it is like Samson, or the beast at the millstone—'quia dignus est opere iumentario' ('because he [Samson] deserved a pack-animal's labour')[47]—blinded or blinkered and confined to the endless circularity of temporal meaning; this, it seems (in the continuation of the passage), contrasts with Christ's gift to humankind of the 'rich grace and innumerable crowns of blessed virginity', that is, of living for spiritual meaning. His own example of virginity represents the divine part of him: and by that example, he leaves the spiritual riches of virginity as an option for all. So, Christ unites within himself both the literal, temporal and temporally bounded word, and the eternal Word which contains every meaning and refuses closure. Eternal meaning—Christ as *verbum*—embraces within itself its own temporality. The word embraces embodied properties—'nascitur crescit roboratur senescit'—but is still the Word.

The embodied Word is evoked with another passage of extreme paradoxical reflexivity:

... hic leo de tribu Iuda pro nobis victor, ex ore nos adversi leonis eripiens, ideo venatur ut servet, capit ut absolvat, frangit ut solidet, mandit ut integret, hoc in nobis edens quo corrumpimur. quamobrem optemus huius leonis praeda fieri, ne simus praeda leonis inimici.... cibus autem Christi esse non possumus, nisi

---

[46] Sacchinus, in the 1622 Antwerp edition of Paulinus, clearly saw this problem and sidestepped it by conjecturing 'saucium' in place of 'suum'.
[47] *Letter* 23. 12.

faciamus voluntatem eius, ut vicissim et ipse nobis cibus fiat, in quo semper vivimus, si ad eius praecepta vivamus. sic ergo de potente exit dulce ...[48]
this lion from the tribe of Judah is victorious for us: let him snatch us from the mouth of the opposing lion and hunt so that he may save us, capture to release us, break to strengthen us, devour to make us whole, eating in us that by which we are corrupted. So we should desire to be the prey of this lion, so as not to be prey to the enemy's ... But we cannot be the food of Christ, unless we do his will, so that in turn he himself may become food for us, in whom we live for ever, if we live according to his precepts. This is how sweetness comes from the mighty ...

Spiritual meaning, then, is connected with these deeply reciprocal forms of embodiment and eating. Man consumes the word: the word encompasses man, and is yet encompassed by him. None of this is so richly expressed as by Paulinus' own *catena* of paradoxical images, which make possible the absorption, the internalization, of the sweet but strange Word of God.

So, for Paulinus, 'verbum' *is* 'virum': though the 'virum' of the manuscripts should probably stand, Hartel's 'verbum' is not so extraordinary a choice after all. His reading happens to reflect the central focus of Paulinus' thought. The word is immanent in man, as man in the word:[49] spiritual meaning encompasses temporal meaning, and temporality is immanent in the spiritual. These complex moves are realized above all by the creative juxtaposition of images. And once the old temporal reality with no spiritual perspective has been displaced,[50] realities are not hierarchical, but are complementary and interdependent, linked by an endless web of meaning. The close links between this and Paulinus' non-hierarchical structure of deeply interdependent friendships, which we have already explored, will be immediately apparent.

In his second letter to Paulinus, Jerome invites him, rather patronizingly, to learn to understand the inner meaning of scripture:

Totum quod legimus in divinis libris nitet quidem et fulget etiam in cortice, sed dulcius in *medulla* est. Qui esse vult nuculeum frangit nucem.... Si haberes hoc *fundamentum*...nihil pulchrius, nihil doctius, nihilque latinius tuis haberemus voluminibus.[51]

[48] *Letter* 23. 16.
[49] I am reminded of an epigrammatic observation made by Colette to Proust, in a letter of 1895: 'The word is not a representation, *but a living thing*'. Quoted in Edmund White, *Proust* (London, 1999), 6; my emphasis.
[50] We may note that this is where Paulinus quietly elides the epistemological stage of the argument: there is no attempt to *prove* that the 'old temporal reality' has been displaced beyond the repeated affirmation of New Testament revelation.
[51] Jerome, *Letter* 58. 9.

Everything which we read in the holy books shines, certainly, and gleams even on the surface, but is even sweeter at the *core*. If you want to eat the kernel, crack the nut. . . . If you had this *foundation*, . . . we would have nothing more beautiful, more learned, more Latinate than your books.

It is sweeter at the core: 'quid enim dulcius dei uerbo?' ('for what is sweeter than the word of God?'). Was the style of expression which Paulinus developed, and which is shown *par excellence* in *Letter* 23, his answer to Jerome's behest? If so, he outmastered the self-styled master of interpretation. Note that Jerome makes a sophistic shift here from 'medulla', core, to 'fundamentum', foundation. For a moment, it seems, he recommends the type of non-linear thinking and appreciation of immanence which Paulinus so joyfully espouses—but Jerome cannot even begin to sustain it: he supports the injunction with a tired old proverb from Plautus[52]—what a contrast with Paulinus' infinite play of metaphor!—and slips immediately back into the comfortably hierarchical conventions of linear thought and its reliance on vertical construction from a solid foundation. Paulinus, however, spent the rest of his epistolary life playing amid the sweetness of that scriptural kernel. Truly, spiritual meaning was to be found at the paradoxical centre of metaphor.

So Paulinus' use of images is not, as has traditionally been thought, mere redundant embellishment, but is fundamental to the expression and practice of his faith. This is how he translates the literal and mundane into the spiritual; how he moves towards the transcendent. His imagistic *catenae* represent his ongoing effort to realize the mysteries at the heart of Christianity. His resistance to adjudication between versions, and to closure of meaning, is an attempt to sketch the multifarious richness of the divine. We have already seen how such a world-view could transform a simple exchange of letters or declaration of friendship into a symbolically significant statement about participation in the Christian community. In the final chapter, we will explore the implications of this world-view for its participants' notions of self.

---

[52] Plautus, *Curculio* 1. 1. 55: 'qui e nuce nuculeum esse volt, frangit nucem.'

6

Homo interior: the inner self

All the principal themes explored in the preceding chapters impinge on the idea of the self—of how a person configures and situates him or herself in the world. If spiritual bonds are superior to and in some sense more real than physical ones, what implications does that have for the relationship of mind to body as constitutive parts of a person? If connections of thought revolve around imagery and visualization, how does a person relate to the unvisualizable, or in other words, the divine? If a friend is conceived of as another self, then what is that self? And if letters are circulated within a far-flung community configured as 'members of one body' by people who are in the strongest possible sense representing their dispatchers, what are the implications for personal identity?

It may be objected that to speak of 'the self' and of 'personal identity' for this period is to import to it anachronistic psychologies—particularly in the absence of a specific vocabulary for the concepts. A general defence against this type of objection was offered many years ago by Marrou: 'A word, an idea, are analytical tools; they may be of recent invention, but the reality which they allow to be singled out may have existed for a long time.'[1] This 'réalité' has often, in connection with ideas of the self, proved more elusive than might be supposed, given the pervasive and often-repeated assumption that only in the early modern period did the 'self' or the 'individual' emerge as concepts which could be isolated and interrogated. David Aers has recently supplied a delightfully polemical attack on this idea.[2] He vigorously counters the notion that 'All [medieval]

[1] 'Un mot, une idée, sont des instruments d'analyse; ils peuvent être d'invention récente, mais la réalité qu'ils permettent d'isoler peut avoir existé depuis bien longtemps.' *Saint Augustin et la fin de la culture antique* (4th edn. Paris, 1958), 549. Marrou is defending the importation of 'l'idée de culture' to a study of late antiquity.

[2] 'A Whisper in the Ear of Early Modernists; or, Reflections on Literary Critics Writing the "History of the Subject"', in David Aers (ed.), *Culture and History 1350–1600. Essays on English Communities, Identities and Writing* (Detroit, 1992), 177–202. I am grateful to Andrew Taylor for drawing my attention to this article.

writing was a version of the simplest homiletic *exemplum* in its representations of human beings', exposing this idea as the product of a search for
'master narratives', which demands the creation of an antithetical state
out of which the narratives may be said to have their beginning. Although
his aim is to prove that it is meaningful to speak of subjectivities in the
late medieval period, his argument (which ties 'the subject' especially
to Christian penitential practice) is also valid for late antiquity, and
indeed insists that 'The place to which anyone seeking to write a
history of interiority and the subject must return is St Augustine's *Confessions*'.[3]

Moreover, as the *Confessions* show, what has come to constitute our
vocabulary of personhood is in fact nascent at this period. The concept of a
friend as another self was expressed, with a remarkable lack of ambiguity,
through the use of personal pronouns. So in the renowned account of
Augustine's early, prematurely-terminated friendship: 'Mirabar enim
ceteros mortales vivere, quia ille, quem quasi non moriturum dilexeram,
mortuus erat, et me magis, *quia ille alter eram,* vivere illo mortuo
mirabar' ('I was amazed that other mortals were living, because he,
whom I had loved as if he were not going to die, was dead; and I was
still more amazed that I was alive while he was dead, *because I was another
he*').[4] Similarly, Ambrose (again in the context of death, this time that
of his brother) speaks of having lost 'melior mei portio' ('the better part of
myself ').[5]

But a more specialized vocabulary was also emerging. Early Christian
thinkers, for example Tertullian and Hippolytus, use the terms *persona* or
prosopon in their original grammatical or dramatic sense—as a participant
in, or subject of, conversational exchange—as Pierre Hadot says, 'sans

---

[3] Quotes from Aers, 'Whisper', 181 and 182 respectively. The phrase 'homo interior' was
already in circulation through the New Testament letters of Paul: so Rom. 7: 22: 'conde-
lector...legi Dei secundum interiorem hominem (*kata ton eso anthropon*)'. Paul's usage
revolves round the relation of the 'interior' to the spiritual and the 'exterior' to the carnal,
discussed below.

[4] Augustine, *Confessions* 4. 6. 11. Augustine goes on to echo Horace (*Carm.* 1. 3. 8) with the
words that his friend was 'half his soul', and to suggest, 'et ideo forte mori metuebam, ne totus
ille moreretur, quem multum amaveram'—a thoroughgoing example of the interpermeability
of selves, which will be discussed below.

[5] Ambrose, *De Excessu Fratris* 1. 6. Both Augustine and Ambrose are richly aware of the
classical precedents for this type of expression—which in its turn suggests that it is equally
valid to speak of a 'sense of self' in the classical period, even if that sense is rather different
from that evinced in Christian writers. See now Christopher Gill, *Personality in Greek Epic,
Tragedy, and Philosophy* (Oxford, 1996).

véritable contenu conceptuel'.[6] Moreover, at least since the second-century *Institutiones* of Gaius, which draw a distinction between 'persona', 'res', and 'actio', the word *persona* had been enshrined in Roman legal tradition: here *persona* seems to mean something like 'human agent' (as legal subject), without entailing any comment on interior processes.[7] However, by the fourth century the terms *persona* and *prosopon* were taking their place in trinitarian theology, and being used to refer to Christ as an incarnate manifestation of an essential, but incorporeal, unity.[8] In a world profoundly concerned with the negotiation of its relationship with the divine, it was a small and logical, but nonetheless significant step from this usage to using *persona* to express the mixture of spiritual and corporeal in everyone. John Rist points to the precise moment in Augustine's writing at which this transition is made: in *Letter* 137, of 411, for the first time he uses *persona* to express the body/soul relationship:

Sic autem quidam reddi sibi rationem flagitant, quo modo deus homini permixtus sit, ut una fieret persona Christi, cum hoc semel fieri oportuerit, quasi rationem ipsi reddant de re, quae cotidie fit, *quo modo misceatur anima corpori, ut una persona fiat hominis.*[9]

So some people demand that we give them an account of how God could be mixed with man so that the single *persona* of Christ should result, when this only needed to happen once, as if they could give an account of the thing which happens daily: *how a soul may be mixed*[10] *with a body, so that one human person should result.*

Besides the specific details of the constitution of *persona*, a generalized sense of interiority indisputably obtains. The first exchange of letters between Augustine and Paulinus reveals a non-specific sense of the body–soul relationship which is thrown into relief by the process of

---

[6] See Pierre Hadot, 'De Tertullien à Boèce: le développement de la notion de personne dans les controverses théologiques', in Ignace Meyerson (ed.), *Problèmes de la Personne*, Colloque du centre de recherches de psychologie comparative XIII (Paris 1973), 123–34; quote from 128. This section of my argument is indebted to his account.

[7] For Gaius' *Institutiones*, see W. M. Gordon and O. F. Robinson (trans.), *The Institutes of Gaius*, Texts in Roman Law (Ithaca NY, 1988).

[8] Hadot, 'De Tertullien à Boèce', 129; the origins of *persona/prosopon* 'fûrent oubliées au profit d'un sens ontologique'.

[9] Augustine, *Letter* 137. 11. Rist draws attention to this passage in *Augustine: Ancient Thought Baptized* (Cambridge, 1994), 100. Contrast 1 Cor. 15: 44: 'Si est corpus animale, est et spiritale'; but the passage goes on to make clear that, for Paul, the earthly and spiritual properties are still entirely separate: 'Igitur, sicut portavimus imaginem (*eikona*) terreni, portemus et imaginem caelestis' (1 Cor. 15: 49).

[10] It is not the coexistence, but the *mixture* of the elements of soul and body which is so remarkable here.

negotiation of distance. There is in these letters a strong sense of the potential for spiritual communication, but at the same time a sense that such communication is incomplete without a more conventional familiarity with the 'homo exterior'. Paulinus approaches Augustine with an appeal to the power of spiritual communication: 'denique nunc etsi sermone, non tamen tamquam et affectu rudes scribimus teque vicissim in spiritu per interiorem hominem quasi recognoscimus' ('in short, I am now writing, perhaps in unburnished language, but not accordingly with unburnished affection, and, as it were, recognizing you spiritually through the inner man');[11] and Augustine memorably replies:

O bone vir et bone frater, latebas animam meam. Et ei dico, ut toleret, quod adhuc lates oculos meos; et vix mihi obtemperat, immo non obtemperat.... Quo modo ergo non doleam, quod nondum faciem tuam novi, hoc est domum animae tuae, quam sicut meam novi?[12]

Oh noble man and noble brother, you used to be hidden from my soul. And I ask it how it could bear that you are still hidden from my eyes; and it scarcely submits— no, it does not submit to me.... So how could I not grieve that I don't yet know your face—that is, the house of your soul, which I know like my own?

Augustine refuses to relinquish his sense that extra familiarity is granted by knowledge of his correspondent's physical appearance; in fact, he was to continue throughout his life to treat the body as necessarily part of the self, and to wrestle with the theological consequences.[13] The later correspondence with Paulinus provides two palmary examples of this attitude. In a letter of 404, he expresses a wish to talk ('conloqui') with Paulinus, 'tamquam si praesens praesenti inter dulces loquelas obderem' ('as if with each of us present I were enveloped in delightful conversation'); and later still, answering (c. 414–16) a barrage of theological queries from Paulinus, he exclaims, '...atque utinam praesens de me ista quaesisses!...cum

---

[11] Paulinus, *Letter* 6. 2.

[12] Augustine, *Letter* 27. 1. For a joking application of this outer/inner dichotomy, see Paulinus' tribute to the dreadful cooking of the letter-carrier Victor: 'verum spiritalis coquus interiorem hominem cibare doctior, quo destrueret escam gulae, non siligine nobis pultes sed farina confecit aut milio', *Letter* 23. 6.

[13] See Rist, *Augustine*, 94: 'From the time of his conversion, Augustine wished to maintain *both* that it is man's soul which is created in the image of God, *and* that man himself is some kind of composite of two substances, a soul and a body' (Rist's emphasis). Later, Augustine came to emphasize Eph. 5: 29: 'Nemo enim unquam carnem suam odio habuit': to reject the body would be 'a desertion of the love for the body which God has intended' (ibid., 110). This emphatic embrace of the body, made in the context of his debate with the Manicheans, surely also formed for him a significant stage in his own move away from Manicheism.

enim interrogando disputas, et quaeris acriter et doces humiliter' ('. . . and I wish you had been present to ask me these things! . . . for when you debate through questions, you ask shrewdly and you teach humbly').[14] Paulinus shows a similar anxiety actually to see his prior acquaintances in his early correspondence. His pressing invitations to Sulpicius—'et invitare non desinam. veni ad nos . . .' ('I shan't stop inviting you. Come to me . . .')[15]—have already been discussed in Chapter 3, where it was argued that subsequently the longing for the physical presence of his friend was resolved by reinventing the friendship as existing on a purely spiritual plane. An intermediate stage of this process is seen in a letter to Delphinus of early 401, in which Paulinus attempts to console himself (a 'tenue solatium') for the absence of his former mentor with an exercise in spiritual visualization. Delphinus' appearance is conjured through meditation while writing: 'ut dum ad affectionem tuam litteras facimus, toto in faciem tuam corde defixi subito te obliviscamur absentem . . .' ('so that while I am writing to your dear self, as I concentrate entirely in my heart on your image I suddenly forget that you are absent . . .')[16] But Paulinus moves on to reiterate the superiority of spirit to body:

itaque hac eadem lege, qua verior circumcisio quae in corde quam quae in carne concisio et praesentia firmior quae spiritu quam quae corpore iungitur et cohaeret sibi, semper tecum sumus tuque nobiscum.[17]

And so by this same law, in which a circumcision in the heart is more true than a cut[18] in the flesh, and a spiritual presence is stronger than that which is physically joined and fused, we are always with you and you with us.

For Paulinus, the spirit is always and unequivocally superior to the flesh in the configuration of the self, and as time goes on the corporeal

---

[14] Augustine, *Letters* 80. 2 and 149. 23 and 34 respectively.

[15] Quote from *Letter* 11. 14.

[16] Paulinus, *Letter* 20. 1. He says a little earlier that even if his burning thirst for Delphinus is not slaked, 'tamen proposita interioribus oculis conspectus atque conloquii tui imagine mitigamus'. This is paralleled in the propemptikon for Nicetas, written in the previous year: 'nunc abi felix, tamen et recedens/semper huc ad nos *animo recurre*' (*Poem* 17. 317–18).

[17] Paulinus, *Letter* 20. 1 again.

[18] TLL 4. 63 notes that *concisio* is characteristically associated with *circumcisio*, and cites, alongside the above passage, Paulinus, *Letter* 50. 3, to Augustine (erroneously cited as *from* Augustine rather than *to* him): '. . . non glorianti in concisione carnis, sed in circumcisione cordis'. This is Goldbacher's text, where Hartel's merely repeats 'circumcisione': in support of Goldbacher's reading, we may note that once again *circumcisio* is paradoxically appropriated to the spiritual context. The scriptural text that lies behind this is, of course, the *locus classicus* of Rom. 2: 29, and Paul's 'circumcisio cordis in spiritu, non littera'.

becomes increasingly insignificant in comparison with the spiritual and symbolic. In later instances of negotiating physical absence the shift to spiritual interpretation has actually been realized. Of Victricius' failure to make the journey from Rome to Nola to see him, Paulinus writes:

fateor enim me huius boni damno non solum contristatum sed et confusum fuisse; numquam enim magis mihi ipsi, ne dicam aliis, manifestata fuerant peccata mea, quam quod mihi de tam proximo 'vultus tui lumen' [Ps. 4: 7] inviderant.[19]

For I confess that I wasn't just thoroughly saddened by the loss of this blessing, but actually brought up short; for never have my sins been made more apparent to me—not to mention other people—than by begrudging me the 'light of your countenance' from so near by.

It is typical that a physical circumstance should be interpreted as spiritual direction. (Clearly, there are issues of public reputation at stake too—but they, if anything, fortify the spiritual message, by intensifying Paulinus' humiliation at his unworthiness.) The presence or absence of Victricius is seen in entirely symbolic terms: his journey to Nola would have been significant, not as an opportunity for a meeting in the flesh, but as a benediction and an affirmation for Paulinus. Paulinus, however, concludes that 'etiam si ad nos usque venisses, aeque tamen a sanctitate tua longe fuissemus' ('even if you had come right up to me, I would still have been a long way away from your holiness'):[20] the symbolism of spatial displacement is more important than the fact.

While soul was always considered superior to body, the relationship of the one to the other was not necessarily one purely of hierarchical domination. Augustine wrote to Paulinus on the subject of the efficacy of prayer for the dead in *De Cura Pro Mortuis Gerenda*: although he argued that the outer show of prayer was less important than the 'invisibilis voluntas et cordis intentio' ('the invisible will and inclination of the heart'), he went on to add:

---

[19] Paulinus, *Letter* 37. 1. Note the persistent sense of place within a community that prompts the aside 'ne dicam aliis'.

[20] Paulinus, *Letter* 37. 1 again. Walsh, *Letters* 2. 178, renders 'even if you had come at all . . .', which destroys the antithesis. The ambiguity of 'a sanctitate tua' (title or quality?) seems to me to be entirely intentional. This utterly spiritual interpretation of the significance of a journey contrasts sharply with Paulinus' first request to Sulpicius for a visit, in which the journey is to be speeded by personal love: ' . . . quid de spatio agam? si nos desideras, via brevis est; longa, si neglegis.' *Letter* 1. 11.

...et nescio quomodo, cum hi motus corporis fieri nisi motu animi praecedente non possint, eisdem rursus exterius visibiliter factis ille interior invisibilis qui eos fecit augetur, ac per hoc cordis affectus, qui, ut fierent ista, praecessit, quia facta sunt crescit.[21]

...and in some way, although these physical movements could not be made without being preceded by some movement of the soul, that invisible interior which made them is intensified in its turn by those actions made externally visible, and through this the eager disposition of the heart, which preceded these things so that they should happen, increases because they have been done.

Here, therefore, a powerful reciprocity between inner and outer was envisaged: the actions of the body, though inferior to the volitions of the soul, may yet improve the soul's virtuous disposition. This was at the time almost certainly a concession to Paulinus' less intellectualized and more body-orientated point of view; but Augustine subsequently incorporated it into his own thinking.

In fact, the bodily part of the self is taken very seriously: we have already seen that this is so in the metaphorical sense by which Christians are members of Christ's body; but it is also true in terms of the personal and individual appreciation of the body. Daniélou has a sophisticated and utterly convincing reading of this valorization of the corporeal: he traces it to the central Christological problem of how the infinite (*aperigraptos*: the uncircumscribed) is to become personal—or the divine human. Only in the fourth century, he argues, does trinitarian theology begin to develop to address this, 'in which the concept of the person—that is, of the concrete, independent individual—is divorced from the idea of limitation'. By this paradoxical process Christ may be realized as simultaneously both divine (and therefore infinite) and personal; and reciprocally, 'the "personal" gets a purchase in the absolute being'.[22] It is against the background of this newly realized fluidity of the human self that we should read the texts of late antiquity.

[21] Augustine, *De Cura pro Mortuis Gerenda*, 5. 7. For a discussion of this exchange between Augustine and Paulinus, see Trout, *Paulinus*, 244–50.

[22] '...où on dissociera le concept de personne, c'est à dire de l'individu concret sub-sistant, de celui de limitation...'; '...le "personnel" prend pied...dans l'être absolu'. J. Daniélou, 'La notion de personne chez les Pères grecs', in Meyerson, *Problèmes*, 113–21; both quotes from 117. Though his emphasis is different from that of Hadot in the same volume, nevertheless the shape of his analysis is the same: the fourth-century wrestling with the problem of the incarnation brought with it a new appreciation of the nature of, and potential for, the physical, human self. (This, once again, is the issue reflected in the second passage discussed in Chapter 5.)

Another important area of theological debate, that concerning the resurrection of the body, was significant for ideas of how the body related to the soul. It was generally agreed that the self which was to be resurrected was not equivalent to the soul alone: Christ's resurrection had been corporeal, and therefore the body of Christians must in some way be involved when they too come to be resurrected. The practical details of this bodily resurrection were found to be inordinately complex, and were hotly debated; but it was indisputable that positive value must be assigned to the body if that was the form in which Christ had chosen to rise. Caroline Bynum has recently chronicled, in the context of a grand study of medieval ideas surrounding bodily resurrection, the near-obsession with physical continuity of the fourth-century Fathers; Augustine inherited this mantle, and 'His repeated emphasis on the yearning of the separated soul for body... becomes an important component of the medieval notion of flesh as essential to personhood.'[23] It was in fact Paulinus who wrote to Augustine—again in their earliest exchange—that only the fruit of the 'oculi temporalium expectatores' was denied them in correspondence; he adds: 'quamvis ne corporalis quidem gratia temporalis in spiritalibus dici debeat, quibus etiam corporum aeternitatem resurrectio largietur...' ('although not even corporeal grace should be called transitory in spiritual contexts, in which resurrection will bestow everlasting life on bodies too...').[24] Augustine's position on this issue became if anything more inclusive of the body in the course of his life: as we have seen, this was probably at least partially under Paulinus' influence.[25] In his *Reconsiderations*, he made it clear that he had revised the early opinions on resurrection expressed in his second treatise, *De Beata Vita*:

displicet autem illic... quod tempore vitae huius in solo animo sapientis dixi habitare beatam vitam, quomodolibet se habeat corpus eius... Quae sola beata vita dicenda est, ubi et corpus incorruptibile atque inmortale spiritui suo sine ulla molestia vel reluctatione subdetur.[26]

But in that work, it bothers me that I said that the blessed life resided in the wise man's mind alone during this life, in whatever state the body might be... This

---

[23] Caroline Walker Bynum, *Resurrection of the Body in Western Christianity, 200–1336* (New York, 1995): section on Augustine and resurrection, 94–104; quote from 100–101. Bynum gives a full account of the debates and preoccupations which I have merely alluded to above.
[24] Paulinus, *Letter* 6. 3.
[25] So Rist's discussion in *Augustine*, cited in n. 13 above.
[26] Augustine, *Reconsiderations* 1. 2.

alone should be called the blessed life, when the incorruptible and immortal body is subject to its own spirit without any revulsion or resistance.

Augustine's views on physical resurrection are, of course, set out most fully in the final book of the *City of God*;[27] the details of these need not concern us here, but there is one aspect extremely relevant to an epistolary focus. While time is to be obliterated in the heavenly state, it is clear from his discussion that spatial displacement is not:[28] distance is spiritually transcended.[29] This seems to bear out our conclusions about the spiritual significance of the negotiation of distance in letters, for it implies that in a spiritual context distance is not sufficiently important to merit dissolution.

Meanwhile, although we may infer that Paulinus took an orthodox position on the question of physical resurrection, he preferred to avoid discussion of the issue. When Augustine asks his opinion, he responds, 'at ego de praesenti vitae meae statu ut magistrum et medicum spiritalem consulo...' ('but I am seeking your advice as a teacher and spiritual doctor about the present state of my life...'), as he aims to die the (symbolic) death of the gospel voluntarily before reaching the 'carnalem resolutionem' ('dissolution of the flesh').[30]

But for Paulinus the inner/outer dichotomy is not always resolved into the relationship of body to soul, in which both are, at least potentially, benign partners in the creation of the self. He is if anything more likely to evoke another set of associations, the value-laden contrast of things of the flesh with things of the spirit that was to become in Western thought the characteristic configuration of the body/soul relationship. He calls on this idea when he rejects Sulpicius' request to him to have his portrait taken:

utinam conpleatur in me verbum illud evangelici Symeonis, ut fiat mihi Christus 'in ruinam et resurrectionem' [Luke 2: 34], ruina exteriori meo et interiori resurrectio, ut cadat in me peccatum, quod anima cadente consistit, et exurgat ille inmortalis, qui cecidit exurgente peccato. exterioris enim status interioris casus est, et ideo quando 'infirmatur exterior, qui intus est renovatur de die in diem' [2 Cor. 4: 16].[31]

---

[27] Augustine, *City of God* 22, especially ch. 29.

[28] '...vi et per corpora in omni corpore quocumque fuerint spiritualis corporis oculi acie perveniente directi.' *City of God* 22. 29.

[29] Though, naturally, neither category is relevant for God himself: 'Non enim quia dicimus Deum et in coelo esse, et in terra...aliam partem dicturi sumus eum in coelo habere, et in terra aliam: sed totus in coelo est, totus in terra; non alternis temporibus, sed utrumque simul, quod nulla natura corporalis potest.' *City of God* 22. 29.

[30] Paulinus, *Letter* 45. 4.

[31] *Letter* 30. 5.

May that word of Simeon in the gospel be fulfilled in me, that Christ should become a 'destruction and resurrection' to me, a destruction to my outer self and a resurrection to my inner, that sin, which endures while the soul perishes, might perish in me, and that immortal self may rise up, which has perished with the rising of my sin. For the outer self upright is the downfall of the inner, and therefore when 'the outer self is weakened, what is within is renewed from day to day'.

Where I have offered the translation 'self', the Latin seems probably to be omitting a personal pronoun: the rendering 'self' seems best to capture the sense, for the 'exterior' here referred to is not the body as such, but the base elements in the self as represented by engagement with affairs of the world; so the 'interior' represents virtuous withdrawal from the world to a realm of spiritual introspection.[32] This type of inwardness is that so memorably and fully expressed by Augustine in his *Confessions*, and it necessitates the antithetical creation of a symbolic exteriority, which though associated with is not identical to the body. This ascent to God through profoundly introspective means has been aptly dubbed by Charles Taylor 'radical reflexivity': it relies on the assumption that through introspection one may gain access not to something more perfectly personal but, ultimately, to something essentially shared.[33] Augustine succinctly exhorts his reader to participate in such 'radical reflexivity' in order to attain truth in *De Vera Religione*: 'Noli foras ire, in te ipsum redi. In interiore homine habitat veritas' ('Don't go outwards, return into yourself. Truth lives in the inner man').[34] The emphasis of such a quest falls, notably, on the *process* of introspection rather than on any *fait accompli*. Paulinus clearly espouses these means of ascent to God through introspection, though nowhere in his writings are the ideas explored with the thoroughness and intensity that Augustine brings to them. One of his clearest statements, however, may be found in the important letter to Sulpicius of 400 in which he explores at length what he sees as the foundations for a Christian life:

---

[32] Walsh renders 'the outer *man*', etc. (*Letters* 2. 123); but 'self' seems to me to make the sense clearer.

[33] For 'radical reflexivity', see Charles Taylor, *Sources of the Self. The Making of the Modern Identity* (Cambridge, MA, 1989), 130. Contrasting Augustine's formulation of the self with that of Plato, Taylor writes, 'this same opposition of spirit/matter, higher/lower, eternal/temporal, immutable/changing *is* described by Augustine, not just occasionally and peripherally, but *centrally and essentially* in terms of inner/outer'. (128–9; 'is' emphasized by Taylor; other emphasis mine).

[34] Augustine, *De Vera Religione*, 39 (72).

quare totus labor et plenum opus nobis in observantia et expoliatione cordis nostri est, cuius tenebras vel abstrusas in eo inimici latebras videre non possumus, nisi *defaecato ab externarum rerum curis animo et intus ad semet ipsum converso*...[35]

So the entirety and fulness of our work lies in the scrutiny and refinement[36] of our heart, in which we cannot see the hidden shadows and darkness of the enemy, unless *our mind is purified from concern with outer things and turned inwards to itself*...

So, two broad meanings of the inner/outer dichotomy emerge: the intuitively available body/soul division, which is drawn upon in a wide variety of contexts; and the value-laden and symbolic dichotomy, pitting things of the flesh against things of the spirit.

But in the epistolary context a third element comes into play. The situation is not completed by the interplay of correspondents' desire to see each other in the flesh, however completely their souls may be revealed to each other—any more than their attitude to their bodies is summed up by the negative connotations implied by 'things of the flesh'. It is, of course, through the letter-carriers that the negotiation of distance is effected; and it is in the context of the writers' interrelationship with their carriers that a developing idea of the self may be seen, working out the psychological implications of Christians as members of one body. When considering the exchange of letters, the framework in which the self is configured has at least three relational points, the two correspondents and the person who carries the letter between them—who, as we saw in Chapter 1, comes on occasion to play a significant role in the lives of both parties.

This claim is repeatedly confirmed by the language in which carriers are described in the letters. Paulinus uses extremely striking formulations: Victor, in a letter to Sulpicius, is 'in te meus et in me tuus' ('mine in you and yours in me'); Romanus and Agilis are commended to Augustine 'ut nos alios' ('like second selves'),[37] and Augustine responds in kind:

---

[35] Paulinus, *Letter* 24. 9. Paulinus expresses very similar concerns in section 11: '[rerum] cura vel amor quoniam mentis ipsius praestringit aciem et animam ab interioribus suis abductam ad exteriora sollicitat, dicit etiam nobis per prophetam: vacate et videte...[Ps. 45: 11].'

[36] Opinions vary on text and sense for this word. Walsh, for unspecified reasons, reads 'exploratione' (*Letters* 2, 59). TLL 5. 2. 1905 s.v. *exspoliatio* cites this passage, and gives its sense as equivalent to *circumcisio*. TLL does, however, recognize that *expolitio* (from *expolire*) may have the alternative form *expoliatio*; and it is this sense which I have adopted here.

[37] Or 'like other mes'! Quotes from *Letters* 28. 1 and 6. 3 respectively.

Sanctos fratres Romanum et Agilem, aliam epistulam vestram audientem voces
atque reddentem et suavissimam partem vestrae praesentiae...cum magna in
domino iucunditate suscepimus.[38]

With great rejoicing in the Lord, we have received the holy brothers Romanus and
Agilis, your second letter, one which hears voices and gives back the sweetest part
of your presence.

The corollary to this language of complete interpenetration is expressed
even in cases where the carrier is previously unknown (evincing once again
the power of the spiritually pre-existing bonds of *amicitia*): Paschasius has
been empressed to Nola to carry a letter to Victricius,

non adrogantia pervicaci sed 'corde puro et fide non ficta' [1 Tim. 1: 5] nostrum
credentes esse quod tuum est teque ita vicissim reputaturum non ambigentes, *ut
illum non afuisse tibi duceres eo tempore, quo nobiscum fuisse cognosceres.*[39]

...believing, not in stubborn arrogance but 'in pure heart and unfeigned faith',
that what is yours is ours, and hence not doubting that you will think the same
thing in turn, *so that you should not consider him to have been away from you during the
time in which you know him to have been with me.*

Paulinus is astonished when Sulpicius complains that he has 'usurped' the
carriers: 'non enim a me alieni forent tecum manentes, qui totus es meus in
Christo domino, per quem sum invicem tuus...' ('for they would not be
remote from me while they remained with you, who are entirely mine in
Christ the Lord, through whom I am in turn yours...').[40]

The carriers are completely enveloped in the community of Christ as
'membra Christi': the most specific example of this is found in an early
letter to Sulpicius. The passage which remarks that Paulinus has in some
way seen Sulpicius, since 'the members of your body came to us in your
servants', has already been noted; but the precise implications of membership in the body of Christ are adumbrated later in the letter:

nam Vigilantius quoque noster in Campania et antequam ad nos perveniret et
posteaquam pervenit, vi febrium laboravit et aegritudini nostrae, *quia et ipse sociale
membrum erat*, socio labore conpassus est. denique ille catechumenus, *qui necdum
nostri corporis erat membrum*, vulnera nostra non sensit...[41]

---

[38] Augustine, *Letter* 31. 2. See further text to note 50 below.

[39] *Letter* 18. 1.

[40] *Letter* 27. 2.

[41] *Letter* 5. 11. This very physical working out of the implications of the 'membra unius
corporis' theme is far from unique to Paulinus. For example, Augustine, in his *Letter* 28. 1,
expresses an urgent desire to see Jerome; but consoles himself with the reflection that at least
Jerome has been seen by Alypius, and so in some sense by Augustine too.

For while our Vigilantius was in Campania, both before he reached us and after he arrived, he was afflicted with a violent fever and suffered my illness with me in a common affliction, *because he was actually a common limb*. As proof, the catechumen, *who was not yet a member of our body*, did not feel our pains . . .

Michel-Yves Perrin has recently reviewed much of the evidence for Paulinus' relationship with his carriers. He comments on the way in which Paulinus combines the notion of 'communion in Christ' with the classical *topos* of slaves as *membra* in the *domus* of their master (though this is to ignore the biblical antecedents for the idea of 'membra unius corporis', explored in Chapter 3 above),[42] and aptly observes, 'As true replacements (*lieu-tenants*) of their ascetic father, they could, in the strongest sense of the term, represent their mandate to the letter's addressee.'[43] Perrin concludes that the evidence invites one 'to suggest the hypothesis that Paulinus of Nola was peculiarly sensitive to personal interactions between people, as between people and God.'[44] But he takes his argument no further than this insistence on Paulinus' particular sensitivity to interpersonal relations; indeed, at one stage he seems to assert that there is no significance beyond the rhetorical to the language used of the carriers.[45]

While Perrin's gathering of the evidence is extremely useful, his conclusion stops short of acknowledging its full implications. Paulinus' comments on the letter-carriers reveal much about how he—and his correspondents—conceive of themselves. The possessive pronouns used of the carriers, the claim that such possession is held *in* Christ or another correspondent; the idea that while with a correspondent to whom the writer is spiritually bound they cannot be truly or entirely absent; the idea that they may somehow be their despatcher's eyes, his second letter, his other self—indeed, 'véritables lieu-tenants': all these, if taken

---

[42] Perrin, 'Courriers'; quote from 1032–3.

[43] 'En *véritables lieu-tenants* de leur père en ascèse, ils peuvent représenter, au sens le plus fort du terme, leur mandat auprès du destinataire de la lettre.' Perrin, 'Courriers', 1034; my emphasis.

[44] '. . . à proposer l'hypothèse d'une sensibilité singulière de Paulin de Nole aux médiations personnelles entre les hommes, comme entre les hommes et Dieu.' Perrin, 'Courriers', 1044.

[45] The 'rhetoric' assertion is made at Perrin, 'Courriers', 1042: the special place of the monastic letter-carriers and their characteristic epithet 'unanimus' bears predominantly on 'leur capacité essentielle de se conformer aux canons d'une rhétorique qui exige d'envelopper tout leur être . . .' It seems to me that this is logically inconsistent with Perrin's overall argument: if we can make claims, based on the letters, about the importance to Paulinus of his carriers and of human interaction in general, then we must be considering that language of the letters can point to a reality beyond the rhetorical.

seriously, lead us to remarkable conclusions. They bespeak a notion of the self which, while located in individuals, is essentially unboundaried, for it is profoundly relational. The earthly aspects of the self create the individual boundaries; but it is far more important that selves may be truly interpermeable in their spiritual communion. This is how such extravagant language may be used of the carriers: they perform their role less as individuals than as extensions of the correspondents' selves.

We may observe that a profoundly relational idea of the self seems to be paralleled in Augustine's far more philosophical development of the theme. Brian Stock, discussing Augustine's *De Trinitate* and its formulation of his ideas of the self, points to the term *appellatio relativa*, used of temporal facets of the divine, which 'underpins his [Augustine's] subsequent reflections on the relational nature of self-knowledge'. Stock later emphasizes the possibility that relationality and autonomy may be co-existent: 'Clearly . . . what one sees within oneself one sees individually, and the fact that we understand ourselves relationally does not rule out the possibility of an autonomous self.'[46] A passage may be selected from *De Trinitate* to underline this point. It discusses the relationship of love and knowledge in the mind:

Mens . . . amore quo se amat potest amare et aliud praeter se. Item non se solam cognoscit mens sed et alia multa. Quamobrem non amor et cognitio tamquam in subiecto insunt menti, sed substantialiter etiam ista sunt sicut ipsa mens *quia et si relative dicuntur ad invicem, in sua tamen sunt singula quaeque substantia.*[47]

The mind can also love something else beyond itself with the love with which it loves itself. Likewise, the mind does not know itself alone, but many other things too. Wherefore, love and knowledge do not exist, as it were, in subjection to the mind; but they also exist as substances, just as the mind itself does: *for even if they are mutually predicated relatively, yet they each exist individually in their own substance.*

In this formulation too, ideas of the self come down to the negotiation of the human and the divine: human as against divine knowledge of the self; human limitation combined with divine limitlessness.

This profoundly relational notion of the self is not uniquely linked with the circumstances of epistolary exchange—but it may well have originated from them; and the parallel with Augustine may be no coincidence. We can draw a more general connection with the pursuit of a consistently and

---

[46] Stock, *Augustine the Reader*, 248 and 256.   [47] *De Trinitate* 9. 4 (5).

ideally communitarian form of existence in the monastic way of life.[48] Luc
Verheijen has made this connection explicit in his study of the monastic
Rule of St Augustine.[49] Indeed, he actually shows that Augustine's
changing interpretation of the word *monos* at the root of *monachus*,
monk—from *monos* as 'cor simplex' to a collective notion of the 'anima
una et cor unum'—can be traced precisely to the inspiration of Paulinus,
and the terms of his commendation of the letter-carriers Romanus and
Agilis.[50] Paulinus' interpretation of Acts 4: 32a,[51] Verheijen goes on to
show, becomes the foundation of Augustine's idea, not just of monastic
community, but of the Christian community in general.[52]

If Paulinus did indeed inspire Augustine with his vision of the unanimity of Christians in Christ—and there is no reason to suppose that he did
not—then his influence, through Augustine, on spiritual life and thought
at the end of the fourth century (and for some time beyond) is immense. It
makes Jerome's scornful aside to Paulinus in his second letter doubly
ironic: 'sin autem cupis esse quod diceris, monachus, id est solus, quid
facis in urbibus quae utique non sunt solorum habitacula sed multorum?'
('now if you wish to be what you are called, a monk, that is a solitary, what
are you doing in the cities which are certainly not habitations of solitaries
but of multitudes?')[53] But Jerome, it seems, was striving for his own
reasons to create an etymology—and to demarcate boundaries—for *monachus* which the word had in fact never possessed.[54]

---

[48] This, notably, is precisely a connection which Perrin wishes to deny: he insists that the
prevalence of the adjective 'unanimus' with reference to monks has little to do with 'la
solidarité naissante d'un *ordo* monastique en voie de constitution'. 'Courriers', 1042.

[49] Luc Verheijen, *Nouvelle Approche de la Règle de Saint Augustin* Collection de Spiritualité Orientale et Vie Monastique 8 (Abbaye de Bellefontaine, 1980); see especially chs. 4 and
6. I am indebted to Conrad Leyser for drawing my attention to this work.

[50] i.e. Paulinus *Letter* 6. 3: 'sunt enim, velim credas, unum cor et una in domino anima
nobiscum'. (Note that Verheijen's page references for this passage are incorrect: it is 41–2 in
Hartel's CSEL volume.)

[51] Acts 4: 32a: 'Multitudinis autem credentium erat cor unum, et anima una'.

[52] '... grâce à une Lettre de Paulin de Nole, Augustin a appris à donner à *anima una et cor
unum* une signification plus collective et à comprendre le terme dans le sens de l' "unanimité"
et de la "concorde" entre plusieurs personnes'. Verheijen, *Nouvelle Approche*, 104; for
detailed argument, see 81–4. This interpretation was for Augustine 'un grand pas en avant
dans sa vie théologique et spirituelle' (84). See also Lawless, *Monastic Rule*, 158.

[53] Jerome *Letter* 58. 5.

[54] See E. A. Judge, 'The Earliest Use of Monachos for "Monk" (P. Coll. Youtie, 77) and
the Origins of Monasticism', *JbAC* 20 (1977), 72–89. He suggests that the name *monachus* was
originally given to ascetics living within civil communities, and only later came to be applied
to those who withdrew from them (85)—ascetics in cities were, of course, the focus of

We have already seen that Paulinus' whole influential notion of Christian unanimity was intimately bound up with his development of the new ideas of *amicitia*.[55] We may now move a step further: a constant awareness of participation, not only in a literal earthly community, but in a spiritual community, imbued with symbolic significance, of people mutually striving towards a better knowledge of God, could—indeed, in spiritual terms, should—lead to a sense of self in which personal boundaries are only of secondary importance.

It should not, then, be surprising to have found that notions of public and private for Christians in late antiquity have different content from those of today. If it is automatically assumed that the primary characteristic of the self is its relationality, then naturally a sense of privacy will be quite differently demarcated—and, indeed, will be assigned negative value. So Verheijen observes, 'with respect to the soul, one should repudiate every "private" and temporal feeling'.[56] It is the public—indeed, the publishable—that will be associated with the spiritual;[57] for as nothing can be held in privacy from God, so nothing should be withheld from one's community in God.[58]

To say that for Paulinus the self is fundamentally relational is not just to echo Charles Taylor's famous dictum, 'one cannot be a self on one's own'. This, of course, remains true; but I am trying to capture something a stage more thoroughgoing than his envisaged formation of the self within

particular vitriol from Jerome (see *Letter* 22. 34). Again, I am indebted to Conrad Leyser for the reference to this article.

[55] It is extremely interesting that, immediately after the passage from *De Trinitate* quoted above, Augustine uses an example drawn from *amicitia* as illustration; '...relative ita dicuntur ad invicem...sicut duo amici etiam duo sunt homines, quae sunt substantiae; cum homines non relative dicuntur, amici autem relative'. He does, however, go on to say that the relationship between friends is not exactly parallel to that between *amor* and *amans*: one may cease being a friend while the friend still loves, but if *amor* ceases loving, it ceases to be *amor*. (Of course, an *amicus* who no longer loves is no longer an *amicus*: the distinction seems to be that *amicus*, unlike *homo*, does not count as a *substantia*.)

[56] '[On] devrait détester, à l'égard de son âme, tout sentiment "privé" et temporel.' Verheijen, *Nouvelle Approche*, 121.

[57] Note Trout's comments on the close relationship, for Paulinus, between 'outward signs' and 'inner commitment', *Paulinus*, 129–30.

[58] Robert Markus remarks on Augustine's realization, in the process of writing *De Genesi ad Litteram*, that 'Sin was a retreat into privacy. ...By it [sin] all community is fatally ruptured': hence, the monastic community 'living in concord and singlemindedness' becomes 'a microcosm of the City of God'. Markus, *End of Ancient Christianity*; quotes from 51 and 78 respectively.

ongoing 'webs of interlocution'.[59] It is crucial that the *ideal* notion of the self becomes, in Paulinus, one which is essentially in communion with other selves; for the Platonists and Neo-Platonists, the ideal self was the one which communed completely, *in solitude*, with the divine, and the goal of meditation and of all 'exercices spirituels'[60] was to attain that perfection of solitude.[61] For Paulinus and those he influenced, on the contrary, the self is essentially permeable to other selves, because it has been permeated by Christ; and what one is therefore depends fundamentally upon with whom one associates. Spiritual association is, of course, superior to temporal, and association with Christ superior to all; but both spiritual and temporal associations seem to work on the same model.

The implications of this are seen most radically in the context of conversion: conversion, that is, not merely to a nominal Christianity, but to the thoroughgoing commitment to a living interpretation of the Christian message which Paulinus embraced. In his letter exchange in verse with Ausonius—written between 389 and 394, just before Paulinus removed from Spain to Nola—we are fortunate to have one of the first extant literary accounts of personal conversion. (As Charles Witke writes, in his detailed study of literary aspects of the exchange, 'Ausonius himself was a conventional Christian; Paulinus was learning how to be a cultural Christian'.[62]) Here, too, are passages which contain Paulinus' most explicit account of his self-configuration subsequent to conversion.

The issue of Paulinus' apparent need to give an account of his conversion is an important one: it seems to be related both to his adoption of

---

[59] Taylor, *Sources of the Self*, 36. This dictum immediately precedes a protest against the fact that 'Modern culture has developed conceptions of individualism which picture the human person as, at least potentially, finding his or her own bearings within, declaring independence from the webs of interlocution which have originally formed him/her, or at least neutralizing them.' I have been much influenced by Taylor's discussion, and it has been instrumental in leading me to consider the possibility of less boundaried, more contextual notions of the self.

[60] The phrase is Hadot's: *Exercices spirituels et philosophie antique* (Paris 1981).

[61] Daniélou, in his discussion of 'la notion de personne', makes the related observation that, at least for the Greek fathers, waiting for 'libération eschatologique' replaced the desire of Greek philosophy for 'libération intérieure'—essentially a solitary undertaking. 'Notion de personne', 120.

[62] Charles Witke, *Numen Litterarum: The Old and the New in Latin Poetry from Constantine to Gregory the Great*, Mittellateinische Studien und Texte vol. 5 (Leiden/Cologne, 1971), 3–65; quote from 6. On Ausonius' 'conventional' Christianity, see also R. P. H. Green, 'The Christianity of Ausonius', *SP* 28 (1993): Latin Authors, 39–48.

letters as a central mode of Christian expression and to his own self-conception. In the correspondence with Ausonius, we can read a process whereby Paulinus' decision to live a more fully Christian life becomes intimately, even necessarily, connected with his desire to communicate the decision.[63] Certainly, Ausonius demands that Paulinus account for his silence—'quis tamen iste tibi tam longa silentia suasit?' ('But who is it that has urged so long a silence upon you?')[64]—but the fullness of Paulinus' response must have been unexpected. In answer to an epistolary poem of 74 lines,[65] Paulinus returns over 330 lines of poignant and detailed explanation and appeal (*Poem* 10). He does not comment explicitly on his desire to explain himself at such length; but passages in his early prose letters may hint at a motive. He asks Alypius most particularly to tell him 'omnem tuae sanctitatis historiam' ('the entire history of your holiness'),[66] including his family background and, above all, how he separated himself from his earthly mother and 'crossed over' to 'matrem filiorum dei prole laetantem' ('the mother of the sons of God who delights in her offspring'), Mother Church.[67] (The concern explicitly to change the sphere of reference of a word—in this case *mater*—is, as we shall see, paralleled in the correspondence with Ausonius.) Sulpicius, in *Letter* 1, is labouring to give an account 'pro meo ac tuo facto' ('on behalf of my deed and yours'): what, Paulinus asks, is the point, 'si non persuaseris hominibus non ad aedificationem suam, sed ad destructionem tuam tecum de opere dei disputantibus?' ('if you don't persuade the men who argue with you about the work of God not for their own edification but for your destruction?'). He goes on to say: 'multum interest, quinam isti sint quibus ratio reddenda sit' ('it makes a great difference who they may be to whom the account should be given')—whether they are receptive and eager to learn, or disdainful and

---

[63] Compare the emphasis of Ambrose, in *De Officiis Ministrorum*, on the importance of self-disclosure between friends: references and discussion in Konstan, *Friendship*, 150–1.

[64] Ausonius *Letter* 21. 62. Trout, *Paulinus*, 72–6 discusses the possibility that this demand was made the more urgent by Ausonius' suspicion that Paulinus might have become ensnared in Priscillianism.

[65] That is, assuming the traditional order of the poems (in which 'Proxima quae' precedes 'Quarta tibi') which Green, in his edition, has reversed. Trout summarizes the debate over this at *Paulinus*, 68, n. 84. I have used, throughout this reading, Green's edition of Paulinus *Poems* 10 and 11 in preference to that of Hartel; I give Hartel's variants in the notes.

[66] This request for a 'historia' is briefly discussed in Chapter 1.

[67] *Letter* 3. 4: the sentence begins, 'Specialiter autem hoc a te peto', 'I ask this particularly from you . . .'. Hartel records 'lactantem' as a variant for 'laetantem': this would make for a peculiarly Paulinian image, but would require the (far from impossible) emendation of 'prole' to 'prolem'.

faithless.[68] And in a letter which has not been securely dated, but which may well be early (not least because the same scriptural passages as in the proven early letters are frequently picked out for comment[69]), Paulinus writes to Aper:

Laetatus sum in his quae scripsisti mihi et secundum fidem tuam, quam corde conceptam ore testatus es. si me gratia domini participem tanti spiritus faciat, spero quia in domo domini ibimus, et quae communi spe fideque percepimus pariter intuentes in facie veritatis consona exultatione cantabimus hymnum...[70]

I was delighted at the things which you wrote to me, including those[71] concerning your faith, which has been conceived in your heart, as you witnessed with your mouth. If the grace of the Lord makes me a participant in so great a spirit, I hope that we shall go into the house of the Lord, and, seeing together in the countenance of truth what we have perceived with shared hope and faith, we shall sing a hymn with harmonious joy...

It seems that giving an account of one's arrival at conversion or coming to the Christian faith is, for Paulinus, a significant part of that conversion. The Christian tradition is relayed and fortified by accounts of personal experience, because the crucial thing about such experience is that it should be shared. Adjectives evoking shared experience abound in the letter to Aper: 'participes', 'communis', 'consonus'; we may note too the emphatic adverb 'pariter'. So the sharing of a conversion narrative—thereby enacting a participatory notion of selfhood—becomes a component part of being a Christian. The development of the Christian self is discovered and charted. It seems that Paulinus first puts this notion into practice under the pressure of Ausonius' persistent questioning. He tries, indeed, to embrace Ausonius within this new, participatory world-view: rather than complaining of his changed way of life, Ausonius should congratulate him that 'sic mea verti/consilia, ut sim promeritus Christi fore, dum sum/ Ausonii' ('that I have changed my modes of thought in such a way as to deserve to become Christ's, while I still belong to Ausonius').[72]

Despite this conciliatory move, in his exchange with Ausonius Paulinus is already coming to see his 'cultural conversion' and withdrawal as necessitating a break with the past and a rethinking of assumptions,

<hr/>

[68] *Letter* 1. 4.
[69] For example, that comparing *stultitia* and *sapientia*, commented on below.
[70] *Letter* 38. 1.
[71] This seems the best way of rendering the awkward 'et'. Hartel notes no variant readings in the manuscripts, but the usage is surprising.
[72] *Poem* 10. 150–52.

though it is not initially a foregone conclusion that Ausonius will be rejected along with that past. (Later, perhaps in view of the failure to communicate his purpose to Ausonius, Paulinus is more uncompromising: we may remember that he writes to Sulpicius, 'abscidatur ut inutilis dextera a corpore tuo, qui tibi in Christi corpore non cohaeret' ('let the man who is not joined to you in the body of Christ be cut off like a useless right hand from your body').[73]) The very detail of the account given to Ausonius, indeed, seems to be an attempt to draw him in to the participatory notions of Christianity.

> . . . quid me accusas? si displicet actus
> quem gero agente deo, prius est, si fas, [74] reus auctor,
> cui placet aut formare meos aut vertere sensus.
> nam mea si reputes quae pristina, quae tibi nota,
> sponte fatebor eum modo me non esse sub illo
> tempore qui fuerim . . .[75]

Why are you laying accusations against me? If you don't like the action I take with God as agent, the originator is—if I may—primarily responsible, whom it pleases to shape or to change my disposition.[76] For if you consider as mine the former characteristics, the ones known to you, I will freely acknowledge that I am not now the same person as I was at that time . . .

Given this sense of a change in values, it is no coincidence that in the early prose letters Paulinus frequently reverts to one of the cardinal passages that reflects the inversion of matters taken for granted in the world: 'Nonne stultam facit Deus sapientiam huius mundi? . . . quae stulta sunt mundi elegit Deus, ut confundat sapientes' ('Surely God has made foolish the wisdom of this world? . . . God has chosen the foolish things of the world, to confound the wise').[77]

---

[73] *Letter* 1. 5, in the context of Sulpicius choosing the audience to whom he should give his account of conversion. This echoes Matt. 18: 8, and is, it seems, the sinister reverse of the 'membra Christi' tenet.

[74] Witke comments unsatisfactorily on 'si fas', attributing its usage purely to a combination of tradition and metrical utility (*Numen Litterarum*, 51); but Paulinus must surely have been alert to the juxtaposition of pagan term and Christian God.

[75] Paulinus, *Poem* 10. 128–33.

[76] I have chosen to translate 'sensus' with the neutral 'disposition' to keep its interpretation as open as possible: in this context, the word suggests a multitude of meanings: sensibilities, thoughts (or ways of thinking), self-awareness. See especially *OLD* s.v. *sensus* 6, 9, and 5.

[77] 1 Cor. 1: 20 and 27; see, for example, *Letters* 1. 3; 5. 7; 38. 1. In a very similar context of the embattled assertion of Christian values, the passage is a critical one for St Patrick

To return to the exchange with Ausonius, this paradoxical break with the past to ensure interconnection of selves in the present is seen at the most fundamental level in a number of ways. First, Paulinus silently signals his change by enacting a deliberate rejection of epistolary expectations. Ausonius points out that he has sent four letters to Paulinus, 'officium sed nulla pium mihi pagina reddit' ('but no page returns its faithful duty to me').[78] The expectations of the *officium* of correspondence were outlined in Chapter 1; though Paulinus has not received Ausonius' letters, the fact is that this *officium* has gone unperformed for three years ('trieteride', as Paulinus himself terms it in his reply[79]), even though at least an annual exchange was generally expected. Paulinus could, after all, easily have written anyway (as he apparently wrote twice in one year to Augustine at the beginning of their correspondence). However, not only does Paulinus fail to perform the *officium* of correspondence, he does not apologize for his silence.

Second, we see Paulinus' reappraisal of his relationship with the world of his correspondent through his deliberate—and deliberately signalled— changes in the semantic range of certain emotive words. Ausonius' feeling that Christian culture can be simply grafted on to the classical is perhaps encapsulated by his sudden inclusion of 'celebri ... frequens ecclesia vico' ('a church packed with the festive village'), in an otherwise conventional *locus amoenus* description.[80] Similarly, towards the end of the same poem, God the Father and Christ the Son are invoked almost as an after-thought—and both, instead of being named directly, are alluded to by circumlocution: 'certa est fiducia nobis,/ si genitor natusque dei pia verba volentum/accipiat, nostro reddi te posse precatu...' ('my faith is firm, if the progenitor and the offspring of God receive the pious words of the desirous, that you can be returned through my prayer...').[81] Paulinus,

---

in his *Confession*: see Catherine Conybeare, 'Re-Reading St. Patrick', *JMLat* 4 (1994), 39–50.

[78] Ausonius, *Letter* 21. 3.

[79] *Poem* 10. 103.

[80] Ausonius, *Letter* 24. 86. This is well discussed by Witke, *Numen Litterarum*, 31.

[81] Ausonius, *Letter* 23. 32-4 and 24. 104-6. Green prints this poem, of which two substantially different versions have come down to us, as two separate letters: a short response to Paulinus, and a more extensive and elaborate version written for public circulation and self-defence. (See Green, *The Works of Ausonius*, 654–6 for an explanation.) This is contrary to Green's editorial practice elsewhere, and seems to create as many problems as it solves: to whom, for example, is Ausonius justifying himself, more than to Paulinus?

however, is at pains to demonstrate to Ausonius that his Christian commitment has changed the scope of language, and he articulates the
response of *Poem* 10 round several resonant words used, in their former
senses, by Ausonius. Ausonius accuses Paulinus of 'nostri ... oblivio caeli'
('forgetfulness of our region'), and of burying in Spain his 'patrios ...
honores', his 'paternal [but also, of course, senatorial] honours'.[82] But
Paulinus corrects him:

> nec mihi nunc patrii est, ut vis, oblivio caeli,
> qui summum suspecto patrem, quem qui colit unum
> hic vere memor est caeli.[83]

Nor am I now forgetful, as you put it, of my father's region, as I look up to the
highest Father, and the man who worships Him alone is truly mindful of
heaven.

With the interposed 'ut vis', Paulinus signals directly his revision of
Ausonius' words. The passage is almost impossible to translate aptly:
'patrii ... caeli' combines the terms of Ausonius' two accusations—'senatorial'/'paternal' and 'region'—to make a third term, effectively 'homeland'. Yet the next line revises completely the referents of 'patrii ... caeli':
it can now only refer to the heaven of God the Father—of which Paulinus
is truly 'memor'. These lines are immediately followed by another attempt
to embrace Ausonius within the semantic range, with a direct address to
him as 'pater'.[84] Paulinus seems to be indicating a more inclusive semantic
strategy—but one in which the Christian sense is always foremost. He
takes a similar approach earlier in *Poem* 10, again in direct response to
Ausonius, who has written, 'nec possum reticere, iugum quod libera
numquam/fert pietas ...' ('and I cannot keep silent, because free loyalty
does not wear a yoke').[85] Once again, owing to the multi-layered resonance
of the words used, the passage is almost untranslatable: 'pietas' refers to
his sense of affectionate duty towards Paulinus as friend and pupil;
'libera' to the unrestrained nature of that 'pietas', but also to its nature
as subsisting between 'liberi', gentlemen. But Paulinus rebuffs the claim

---

[82] Ausonius, *Letter* 21. 52 and 21. 61.

[83] *Poem* 10. 193–5. At line 193, Hartel gives 'nec mihi nunc patrii visa est oblivio caeli ...'
Witke, I think, misses the point of the Christian appropriation of 'caeli' (*Numen Litterarum*,
55).

[84] Note that Paulinus finally transfers both terms to Felix: 'tu *pater* et *patria* et domus et
substantia nobis ...' *Poem* 15. 15.

[85] Ausonius, *Letter* 21. 48–9.

by once again consciously extending the semantic range, this time of 'pietas':

> pietas abesse Christiano qui potest?
> namque argumentum mutuum est
> pietatis, esse Christianum, et impii,
> non esse Christo subditum.[86]

How can affectionate duty be lacking from a Christian? For to be a Christian is evidence of piety, and likewise it is a mark of the impious not to be subject to Christ.

'Pietas' becomes the characteristic, not of gentlemen, but of all Christians—who are, in fact, not 'liberi', but 'subditi' to Christ and to his easy yoke.[87] Here too Paulinus goes on immediately to call Ausonius 'pater'. This forms part of his response to a climactic set of claims by Ausonius, 'ego sum tuus altor et ille/praeceptor primus, primus largitor honorum' ('I am your foster-father and that first teacher, the first dispenser of honours'), to which Paulinus replies with a corresponding trio: 'patrone praeceptor pater' ('patron teacher father').[88] The implications, at this stage, are clear: Ausonius retains a connection with Paulinus; but the words used to describe him are susceptible first to another, Christian interpretation.

Paulinus attempts to integrate Ausonius into his new, Christian sense of relationalism. At the same time, it becomes incumbent on Paulinus, in his desire to communicate his own position, to state his (new) self-conception. This necessitates exploring—at any rate implicitly—issues of individuation of selves in the context of their connectedness or relationalism. In a particularly striking passage, he strives to express his sense of the interpermeability of selves with God:

> deusque nobis atque pro nobis homo
> nos induendus induit,
> aeterna iungens homines inter et deum
> in utrumque se commercia.[89]

---

[86] *Poem* 10. 85–8.

[87] As at Matt. 11: 30: 'Iugum enim meum suave est, et onus meum leve'. Ausonius' final farewell, 'Discutimus, Pauline, iugum' (*Letter* 23/24. 1), must, ironically, have brought the *iugum* of Christ to Paulinus' mind, especially as Ausonius offers the description 'leve... positu'. Compare Paulinus' epithalamium: 'Christe Deus... / ... moderare levi subdita colla iugo', *Poem* 25. 3–4.

[88] Ausonius, *Letter* 22. 33–4 and Paulinus, *Poem* 10. 96 respectively.

[89] *Poem* 10. 53–6. I am indebted to Sister Mechtild O'Mara for suggesting the subsequent translation of this extremely difficult passage. Hartel gives 'nos induendo se exuit' at line 54, and 'in utroque se commercia' at line 56.

We have to clothe ourselves in his divinity, and for our sake he had to be clothed in our humanity; God has clothed himself in us, covenanting an eternal exchange with each other between men and God.

The extraordinarily interwoven word-order, with 'deus' and 'homo' embracing 'nobis atque pro nobis' in the first line, and 'aeterna . . . commercia' embracing the entire second clause; the verbal insistence on interrelationships, with the repetition of 'nobis' in reciprocal applications ('by' and 'for' us) and the near-redundancy of 'in utrumque se'; the resolutely singular verbs, despite the fact that both 'deus' *and* 'homo' serve as subjects (and in the case of 'induendus', require subtly different construals): all these emphasize the complex and continuous interrelationship between God and humankind, and anticipate the more developed expression of these concepts which we have traced in *Letter* 23.

Given the permeability of man to the divine, and vice versa, Paulinus also tries to show how he is linked with Ausonius through their mutual interconnection with God. He first pays tribute to Ausonius' immense influence in his household, and then sets their friendship in the context of an approach to Christ through love, which enables a mutual attempt to join with Christ:

> hoc mea te domus exemplo coluitque colitque
> inque tuum tantus nobis consensus amorem est,
> quantus et in Christum conexa mente colendum.[90]

By this pattern, my household has revered and continues to revere you, and I have as great a feeling for your love as for Christ, who must be worshipped with linked minds.

This remarkable passage appears to place Paulinus, Ausonius, and Christ in an equal tripartite relationship, connected by love; and if there is a semantic shift to a more Christian sense of *colo* (which my translation implies), it is not explicitly signalled. Testimony to the levelling power of love is supplied later in the letter: 'si iungor amore, / hoc tantum tibi me iactare audebo iugalem' ('if I am yoked by love, of this alone shall I presume to boast: that I am your yoke-mate');[91] but the inclusion of Christ in this level relationship seems a radical step. Can the implication be that Christ's love—and the love for Christ—is found complete in all who love each other in Christ? That the same plenitude is found in the individual as

---

[90] *Poem* 11. 17–19. Hartel omits 'est' in line 18.

[91] *Poem* 11. 39–40; Hartel gives 'iungar' in line 39. Again, I am indebted to Sister Mechtild O'Mara for this translation.

in a community of individuals? Then the relationalism of selves—at least, of Christian selves—is a given, because all have the same plenitude in the light of their love of Christ, and yet by the same token individuation can be sustained, because each person individually loves Christ, as he them. We may compare, once again, the more explicit account of Augustine—which, once again, may well have developed from Paulinus' lead:

Huius enim templum simul omnes et singuli templa sumus, quia et omnium concordiam et singulos inhabitare dignatur; non in omnibus quam in singulis maior, quoniam nec mole distenditur nec partitione minuitur.[92]

For we are all his [God's] temple together, and we are his temples individually too, because he graciously inhabits the union of all as well as individual people. He is no greater in the whole than in individuals, since he is neither increased by mass or diminished by sub-division.

It seems to be some such resolution of individuation with an all-embracing relationalism that Paulinus is, albeit imprecisely, envisaging at the end of his final letter to Ausonius:

> ... videbo corde, mente complectar pia
>   ubique praesentem mihi.
> et cum solutus corporali carcere
>   terraque provolavero,
> quo me locarit axe communis pater
>   illic quoque animo te geram,
> neque finis idem, qui meo me corpore,
>   et amore laxabit tuo.[93]

[As long as I live,] I shall see you in my heart, and shall embrace you, everywhere present to me, in my pious mind. And when I am released from the bodily prison, and fly away from the earth, in whatever part of heaven our common Father places me, there too I shall bear you in my soul, and the end which will release me from my body shall not also release me from your love.

Witke suggests that Paulinus asserts here that *amicitia* will last forever, while promising no letters to nourish it.[94] But as we have seen, the appeal to seeing a correspondent in his heart, 'ubique praesentem mihi', is to become a far from empty claim for Paulinus; so too, the statement of the validity of an enduring love. This passage seems to represent the final attempt to incorporate Ausonius into his new view of the world.

---

[92] Augustine, *City of God* 10. 3.   [93] *Poem* 11. 55–62.
[94] Witke, *Numen Litterarum*, 42.

In the end, however, we see that Paulinus could not have sustained further communication with Ausonius. The two men's goals in life are now incommensurable: Paulinus cannot express the sense of self generated by his conversion in terms which Ausonius can accept. Ausonius replies, 'Discutimus, Pauline, iugum . . . / discutimus, sed tu tantum reus' ('Paulinus, we are shattering our yoke . . . We are shattering it, but you alone are responsible').[95] In the image of the yoke is summarized the critical difference between Ausonius' classical notion of friendship, and the Christian one which Paulinus is beginning to devise. While the yoke invokes a certain relationality of selves, it is a far less thoroughgoing one than obtains for Paulinus—who wishes to acknowledge the conjunction, not just of two selves, but of the entire Christian community. Ausonius' image also concedes—as the 'membra unius corporis' does not—that under certain circumstances this relationality of selves is no longer tenable. It is tempting to read a further line—'acceduntque alienae pondera librae'—as explicitly acknowledging that Paulinus' scale of values has changed: the sense would then be, not just that Paulinus has shattered the yoke, but that he is now piling the weights from another, alien scale upon Ausonius.[96]

The difference between the two men is again encapsulated later in the letter. Ausonius invokes classical *adynata* to argue that if the bow of Ulysses and the spear of Achilles were easy to handle, then 'mens altera' could destroy their bond; but Paulinus has shown that Odysseus and Achilles are now simply irrelevant to him—and hence 'mens altera' *can* destroy the bond.[97] The series of self-corrections (for it seems that each statement about Paulinus' state of mind revises the immediately preceding one), strengthened by repetition of 'mea', creates a tetracolon crescendo, building up to the mind created by and belonging to God, which is yet most truly Paulinus' own: 'mens nova mi, fateor, mens non mea, non mea quondam, / sed mea nunc auctore deo . . .' ('I have a new state of mind,

---

[95] Ausonius, *Letter* 23. 1 and 6. Even this, of course, shows their different sphere of reference in the use of the image of the yoke: Green draws our attention to Ausonius' reminiscence of Theocritus 12. 15, while Paulinus, as has been remarked at note 87 above, is more liable to recall Matt. 11: 30.

[96] Ausonius, *Letter* 23. 12/24. 26. Green says firmly of 'libra' ad loc., 'not "balance", but "weight"', arguing that 'the dominant image of the yoke continues'; but he has just glossed 'munus' in the preceding line as 'the tasks of correspondence', so does not himself offer an entirely consistent interpretation of this ambiguous passage.

[97] The fourth *Natalicium*, *Poem* 15, represents in many ways a further moving on from, and rejection of, Ausonius' terms: 'non ego Castalidas, vatum phantasmata, Musas / nec surdum Aonia Phoebum de rupe ciebo; / carminis incentor Christus mihi, munere Christi / audeo peccator sanctum et caelestia fari.' *Poem* 15. 30–33.

I confess, not my own mind—or rather, formerly not my own, but now mine with God as its originator').⁹⁸ Paulinus' ultimate rejection of Ausonius has tended to baffle and sadden commentators, as it did Ausonius himself; but, given that Paulinus had come to believe that his Christian self was constituted in and moulded by association with his spiritual confrères and with Christ, he could not have sustained further communication with Ausonius. Ausonius wrote more truly than, perhaps, he knew, 'Vertisti, Pauline, tuos, dulcissime, mores' ('you have changed your ways, my sweetest Paulinus').⁹⁹

Yet this correspondence sets a pattern for enacting Christian tenets in literary form as well as in life, and seems to be instrumental in creating Paulinus' view of epistolary endeavour as the heart of Christian communication. Certainly, the epistolary form provides an ongoing enacted metaphor for the self which is at once individuated and relational, in the interrelations of correspondents, carriers, and Christ. Perhaps the processual, open-ended nature of epistolary form appealed to Paulinus, rather than the firm statement expected of a treatise or commentary. Perhaps also Paulinus came to be suspicious of literary closure of meaning, and so worked hard to establish a stance which though literarily expressed is not completed by its literary expression—paralleling his general concern with moving beyond the material realm.

As we see even from these early examples of Paulinus' thought on the Christian self, the permeability of the self is indissolubly bound up with its moral properties: hence the link drawn by Paulinus between desert and possession or permeation by Christ. The fact that the self is accessible to Christ accounts for its potential for improvement: Christ has the power 'aut formare meos aut vertere sensus' ('either to shape or to change my disposition'). In the second letter of Christian instruction to Crispinianus, Paulinus observes that Christ has the power to make his followers 'et heredes et imaginis suae conformes et gloriae participes' ('his heirs, formed to his image and participating in his glory').¹⁰⁰

---

⁹⁸ *Poem* 10. 142–3. Note the central repetition of 'non mea', each time with a subtly different sense: Paulinus' mind is now not his own because it is God's—and was 'quondam' not his own because it was *not* God's! This anticipates the argument of Augustine *Letter* 258, quoted at the beginning of Chapter 3. Paulinus has directly rejected classical models at *Poem* 10. 19–22: 'quid abdicatas in meam curam, pater,/redire Musas praecipis?/negant Camenis nec patent Apollini/dicata Christo pectora'.

⁹⁹ Ausonius, *Letter* 21. 50.

¹⁰⁰ Paulinus, *Letter* 25*. 1.

But being formed in the image of Christ is only the starting point for the amelioration of the self. It is not the *imago*, but the *similitudo* of Christ that we must seek to achieve in our own lives. Unusually for Paulinus, he gives a clear exposition of the difference between the two:

nam et idcirco descendit ad nos, ut ad illum adscenderemus, ideo conformatus est corpori carnis nostrae, quae peccato serviebat, ut nos conformaret corpori carnis suae, quae peccatum non fecit, ut vere ad originalem gloriam reformemur, *si divinam similitudinem Christi imitatione capiamus.* nam in Adam solam nobis imaginem remansisse ipsa, quae opificium divinae manus narrat, Genesis ostendit, in qua similitudo cum imagine dei in ipso adhuc hominis faciendi molimine nominatur, sed capite subsequenti, quo iam factus homo tantum ad imaginem dei scribitur, similitudinem quasi peccaturo fuisse subtractam indicat profecto futuri praescientia, ut reservaretur hominibus in Christo, qui per oboedientiam pietatis suae reconciliavit patri mundum, quem inconciliaverat primi parentis inoboedientia.[101]

For it was for this reason that he descended to us, that we should ascend to him, and likewise he took on the bodily form[102] of our flesh, which was enslaved to sin, that he should make us like his fleshly body, which did not sin: thus might we be truly reformed to original splendour, *if we take on the divine likeness of Christ by imitation.* For Genesis itself, which tells the work of the divine hand, shows that only the image remained to us in Adam: in Genesis, the word 'likeness' is used with 'image of God' in the actual effort of making man [Gen. 1: 26], but, given that the point immediately follows by which man once made is only described as in the image of God, knowledge of the future declares without doubt that 'likeness' had been taken away from Adam, because he was going to sin, so that it might be stored up for men in Christ,[103] who through his pious obedience reconciled with the Father the world which the disobedience of the first father had alienated.[104]

Thus the Christian's desire for himself is to move beyond the image of Christ to his likeness. Despite the importance of the imagistic, in moral improvement the image is only the starting point: the aim must be to be

---

[101] Paulinus, *Letter* 24. 9 (to Sulpicius).

[102] *Conformare* is glossed at *TLL* 4. 249 as 'similem reddere, aptare', with three other citations in the same sense from Paulinus. I have despaired, however, of preserving the parallelism in the translation which is suggested by the Latin 'conformatus est ... conformaret'.

[103] Walsh translates 'men *living* in Christ'; but it seems to me that the phrase 'in Christo' is purposely ambiguous: the potential for 'likeness' may be afforded through Christ's incarnation, or through the permeability of men to Christ—or both.

[104] Blaise offers an apt translation of this particular passage: 'le monde que la désobéissance de notre premier père avait éloigné de Dieu'. See under *II inconcilio*, 425. (*TLL* 7. 1. 998 gives merely 'dolo seducere'.)

like Christ in every respect through imitation of him, not to be content with the superficial image. We may remember that the purpose of this letter is to alleviate Sulpicius' guilt at not having sold all he possessed (as in the passage from Matt. 19: 21). 'Sane considera ipsa ... verba domini', Paulinus advises, 'et videbis te principia pro fine posuisse' ('ponder carefully the actual words of the Lord, and you will see that you have taken the beginnings for the end').[105] For the point of the passage is not the injunction to sell one's property—which might be construed as imitation of Christ's image—but Christ's final command, 'et veni, sequere me' ('and come, follow me'). It is in the following of Christ that his *similitudo* is to be found.

We begin to see how this permeability of the self to Christ is bound up with the interrelations of human selves in the above-mentioned letter of instruction to Crispinianus:

quomodo autem probare possum aliter quia diligam te sicut et me, nisi idem tibi cupiam, quod mihi optimum iudicavi, id est ut renuntiantes huic saeculo et omnibus pompis et inlecebris vanitatis eius fugiamus ab ira ventura et confugiamus ad unicam generis humani salutem, Iesum Christum ...[106]

For how else can I prove that I love you as myself, if not by wishing the same thing for you that I have judged best for myself, namely that we should renounce this world and all its vain display and enticements and flee from the wrath to come, and take refuge in the only salvation of the human race, Jesus Christ ...

The relationship between two people is thus gauged by their common pursuit: to attempt to improve themselves by striving towards the *similitudo* of Christ. The injunction 'et veni, sequere me' is applicable in the temporal realm too, so long as the *imitatio* occurs in the pattern of Christ. Certainly, Paulinus' language in a letter to Augustine is utterly Christological:

utinam ergo sic dirigantur viae meae post vestigia tua, ut exemplo tuo solvens calciamentum vetus de pedibus meis disrumpam vincula mea et liber exultem ad currendam viam, quo possim adsequi mortem istam, qua tu mortuus es huic saeculo, ut vivas deo Christo vivente in te, cuius et mors et vita in corpore tuo et corde et ore cognoscitur ...[107]

Thus may my paths be directed in your footsteps, so that by your example I might slip off my old shoes from my feet and burst my chains and rejoice in freedom to run the course, to attain that death, by which you have died to this world so that you may live for God with Christ living in you: his death and life are discerned in your body and heart and mouth ...

---

[105] Paulinus, *Letter* 24. 5.   [106] *Letter* 25*. 1.   [107] Paulinus, *Letter* 45. 4.

This, then, is the practical function of the profound relationalism of selves: to give meaning to a life in Christ, which may be realized in part by imitation of other humans. The command 'diligas proximum tuum' makes other people an essential part of the Christian life: it ends by making them also an essential part of the Christian self, by the parallelism— fostered in Christ—of love and imitation. Relational configurations of onself become the proof of Christian perfectibility.

Yet, paradoxically, while the self is perfectible—for striving towards the *similitudo* of Christ would be meaningless were it not so—perfection does not lie in the power of the individual. It is only through divine grace that such perfection may be achieved. Grace is, by its very nature, necessarily communicable, and yet it is indivisible; as such, it forms an essential part of the model for connectedness of selves. Paulinus uses *gratia* to convey the idea of his connection with Victricius through the carrier Paschasius: he has brought him to Nola 'ut . . . diutius quasi quadam tuae gratiae portione frueremur', 'so that we may enjoy for a little longer some portion, as it were, of your grace.'[108] The awareness of such grace constantly impinges on the Christian's idea of self: Augustine gives a succinct expression of this sense in the final paragraph of *De Trinitate*:

Domine deus une, deus trinitas, quaecumque dixi in his libris de tuo agnoscant et tui; si qua de meo, et tu ignosce et tui. Amen.[109]

Only Lord God, God the Trinity, whatever I have said in these books from your self, may your people acknowledge it; if anything from my own self, both you and yours pardon it. Amen.

Paulinus echoes this sentiment in a letter to Sulpicius of 397: 'quid ille miser habeat, qui se non habet? *Non enim se habet qui plus de se quam de deo sperat . . .*' ('what would that poor man possess, who does not possess himself? *For he does not possess himself who expects more from himself than from God . . .*').[110] Only by the grace of God can the relational self, the paradoxical *cor unum* of the followers of Christ, be completed.

[108] *Letter* 18. 1.
[109] And see again Augustine's first letter to Paulinus, *Letter* 27. 4 (only the errors in his writing are his).
[110] *Letter* 11. 13.

Appendix: The contents of Hartel's manuscripts and the dating of Paulinus' letters

The oldest surviving manuscript of Paulinus' letters is dated by Hartel to the tenth century.[1] It contains, except for the consolatory letter to Pammachius, only letters addressed to correspondents in Gaul, and predominantly those in Aquitaine: hence Fabre's observation that 'Il est donc probable que c'est en Aquitaine qu'elle s'est formée'.[2] The letters are arranged according to correspondent: the ten letters to Sulpicius open the manuscript, followed by five to Delphinus, six to Amandus (the order of the two presumably accounted for by Delphinus' seniority), and eleven *singillatim* (in fact twelve in the modern numeration, but the beginning of 33 is joined with the end of 13).[3] The prose letters are completed with the letter to Jovius, followed by the poem also addressed to him.[4] Within these groupings, no apparent order is adhered to (by contrast with the early manuscripts of Augustine's letters, which, while also grouped according to addressee, are arranged chronologically within the subdivisions[5]). The emphasis on Gallic addressees might suggest a provenance in Gaul. However, the temptation to identify this manuscript as a direct descendant of Sanctus' 'adnotatio epistolarum'[6] should be resisted, not

---

[1] Hartel Praef. vi; the manuscript is Codex Parisinus 2122, 'O' in Hartel's apparatus. This is perhaps from an eighth-century archetype: Fabre, *Chronologie*, 4. My account of the manuscripts here is based predominantly on the information in Hartel, Praef.

[2] Fabre, *Chronologie*, 5.

[3] The order of the letters in O:
to Sulpicius, 5, 24, 23 (divided into two parts), 11, 1, 22, 30, 28, 29, 31
to Delphinus, 10, 20, 19, 14, 35
to Amandus, 36, 12, 9, 2, 21, 15
singillatim, 37, 18, 38, 39, 44, 42, 33, 13 (joined with preceding letter), 34, 43, 32, 16

[4] *Letter* 16; *Poem* 22.

[5] See D. de Bruyne, 'Les anciennes collections et la chronologie des lettres de saint Augustin', *RBén* 43 (1931), 294–5 (conclusions (5) and (6)); also Lietzmann, 'Entstehungsgeschichte', 303–4, concluding that Augustine personally collected and edited his early correspondence.

[6] Mentioned in the Introduction, text to note 68.

least because neither the letter to Sanctus nor the one jointly addressed to Amandus and to presumably the same Sanctus, which immediately precedes it in Hartel's edition, is included. They are, however, to be found in the other five manuscripts which, together with the tenth-century one, comprise our only *testimonia* for most of Paulinus' prose letters. The remaining manuscripts fall essentially into two groups. Hartel's PFU[7] are all dated to the fifteenth century. P contains the same letters as O, in the same order, but adds letters 40, 41 (the letter to Sanctus), 4, 6, 3, 7, and 8. F repeats this sequence, adding five letters from Augustine to Paulinus and *Letter* 50 from Paulinus to Augustine. U retains the sequence, organizing it formally into five *libri*, except that the exchange with Augustine and the preliminary letter from Paulinus to Alypius are extracted to form the first *liber*.[8] (The second book, the letters to Sulpicius, intriguingly adds Ausonius' poem to Paulinus 'Quarta tibi haec...',[9] and attributes it to Sulpicius.) The other two manuscripts, L and M,[10] share an ordering for the letters which is quite different from PFU— though interestingly they preserve the order of PFU for the letters 'ad diversos', with some additions at the end.

These manuscripts typically contain only one of the *carmina*, Poem 22, which goes with the letter to Jovius in PFU but is divorced from it in LM. Interestingly, the earliest manuscript also contains the metrical exchange between Ausonius and Paulinus[11] and a few of the other *carmina*,[12] which are generally missing from the remaining manuscripts of the letters.[13] This leads Hartel to posit an archetype which contains 'epistulas plurimas'[14]—presumably the prose letters of O, with the few extra common to

---

[7] P: codex Parisin. lat. papyr. 9548.
F: Laurentianus plut. 23. cod. 20 memb. 259.
U: codex Urbin. lat. 45 membr. f. 203.
[8] The first book comprises *Letters* 4, 6, 50, 3 followed by Augustine's letters; *Libri* 2–5 are, therefore, the letters to Sulpicius; to Delphinus; to Amandus; and 'ad diversos' (with the letters to Augustine removed).
[9] Ausonius, *Letter* 21.
[10] L: codex Lugdunensis 535 membr. 4° f. 131.
M: codex Monacensis membr. 26303.
[11] Paulinus, *Poems* 10 and 11 in Hartel's edition, along with Ausonius, *Letters* 17–23/24 (the two last being the two different versions, supplied by Green, of the last poem in the correspondence).
[12] *Poems* 24, 31, 17, 9, 7 and 8 in Hartel's edition.
[13] Although F, P and U contain Ausonius' 'quarta tibi haec...' (*Letter* 21 in Green's edition).
[14] Hartel, Praef. xiv.

the other manuscripts (for example, the letters to Sanctus)—but none of the poems except 22; he argues that the *carmina* in O derive from a separate source.[15] His *stemma* is thus constructed with three separate lines of descent from the archetype: that of O; that of PFU, through a mediating source; that of LM, again through a mediating source. This is not entirely satisfactory. It seems problematic, indeed, question-begging, to posit a single archetype from which O descends directly but from which the scribe of O elected not to copy some of the material. Moreover, the source of the *carmina* in O remains unexplained. It seems far more likely— particularly in the light of my observations in the Introduction about the lack of a definitive 'collection' of the letters in Paulinus' own time— that O represents one tradition, LM another. PFU appear to derive their ordering from O's tradition, though probably not directly from O itself, but clearly have another source for material as well. A more exact relation than this, given the absence of surviving intermediaries, is hard to determine. However, even this conclusion may lead us to suppose that Hartel's reliance on O, his 'codex optimus',[16] is ill-founded. Even if there was originally a single archetype, which seems unlikely, there is no reason to suggest that a reading from O is more authoritative, or closer to the archetype in any way except chronologically. In several cases, Hartel's support for O has led him to print rather eccentric readings; where these have a bearing on my argument, I have addressed them *ad loc*.

The remainder of the letters printed by Hartel has been preserved for us in other collections. The preservation of the exchange with Augustine has already been mentioned (though it is also, as we have seen, present in PFU); manuscripts of Jerome give *Letters* 25 and 25* to Crispinianus (originally attributed to Jerome) and Letter 26 to Sebastianus, as well, of course, as Jerome's side of the correspondence with Paulinus.[17] The letters to Marcella and Celancia, also from the Hieronymian tradition, first crept into the Paulinian corpus in the printed edition of Rosweyd and Sacchinus in 1622; they are presented by Hartel in an Appendix, but were only briefly thought to be by Paulinus. There are also *Letters* 46 and 47, introduced from codices of Rufinus. Reinelt argues vigorously that these are inauthentic;[18] Fabre reviews the evidence to conclude that, even if the attribution is not certain, it is 'vraisemblable' that these letters are from Paulinus, and Walsh says briskly that Reinelt's suggestion 'has little validity'.[19] I prefer to follow Fabre and Walsh, and read these letters as authentic.

---

[15] Hartel, Praef. xiv.   [16] Hartel, Praef. xv.   [17] That is, Jerome, *Letters* 53, 58, and 85.
[18] Reinelt, *Studien*, 45–52.   [19] Fabre, *Chronologie* 88–97; Walsh, *Letters* 2. 355.

Not only is the 'corpus' of Paulinus' letters a posthumous construct, but the system of numeration which has become canonical has equally dubious foundations. It bears no relation to either of the predominant orders in which the letters are presented in the manuscript tradition, but instead represents an early attempt to establish a chronological order for the letters. By the time of Hartel's edition in 1894, this chronology had already been substantially reconsidered; yet despite his open disdain for the edition of Lebrun which, in 1685, had first suggested the order, he effectively enshrined it in tradition by replicating the numeration, justifying this eccentric decision on the grounds that Migne had already followed Lebrun, and that it would be more convenient for the men (*sic*) who were working on the letters if he did the same.[20] Fabre was scathing about this evasion of responsibility: '... it is staggering to see that Hartel doesn't even pose the question of chronology, in either his articles or his edition.'[21] He does, however, acknowledge that the very proliferation of chronological studies of Paulinus' letters 'is sufficient proof that the question hasn't entirely been resolved'.[22]

I have not attempted to add to these chronological studies, or to engage in the debates raging round the precise dating of early events in Paulinus' life. The current situation is that Trout has defended Fabre's scheme in the face of the revisions of Desmulliez; Perrin considers Trout's arguments inconclusive, and prefers to let Desmulliez' chronology stand.[23] Trout has now produced an early chronology which I take as definitive in two appendices to his *magnum opus*.[24] Otherwise, where I cite dates, I use the traditional scheme of Fabre.[25] For this type of study, establishing a precise absolute date for any given letter is less important than acknowledging a relative chronology to facilitate the charting of changes in modes of thought or expression. In Fabre's table, the most significant deviations in relative chronology from the order of the letters printed by Hartel are

[20] Hartel, Praef. xxvi. Even in 1948, Fabre comments (*Chronologie*, 2, n. 4), 'Le mot *virorum* est divertissant!'

[21] '... on est stupéfait de voir que Hartel ne pose pas même la question [de chronologie], pas plus dans ses articles que dans son édition.' Fabre, *Chronologie*, 3.

[22] '... prouve suffisament que la question n'a pas été entièrement résolue'. Fabre, *Chronologie*, 4.

[23] See Fabre, *Chronologie*; Trout, 'Dates of the ordination of Paulinus'; J. Desmulliez, 'Paulin de Nole. Études chronologiques (393–7)', *RecAug* 20 (1985), 35–64; Perrin, 'Courriers'.

[24] See Trout, *Paulinus*, 273–92: Appendix B, 'Early Chronology and *Cursus Honorum*' and Appendix C, 'Select Chronology'.

[25] See Fabre, *Chronologie*, esp. 137.

that two of the despatches to Amandus and Delphinus are considered to predate the rest of the surviving letters (*Letters* 35 and 36 being dated to 390–92 and *Letters* 9 and 10 to 393); and that *Letter* 29, the account to Sulpicius of the visit of Melania the Elder, is placed in the same year (400) as the *tours de force* of *Letters* 23 and 24, and prior to *Letter* 27.

At the end of all this, we can say with reasonable confidence that we have fifty authentic letters of Paulinus around which to base this study of his thought: from Hartel's total of 51 we should subtract *Letter* 34, which is in fact the sermon 'de gazophylacio', and *Letter* 48, which is so small a fragment as to be useless for my purposes; at the same time, we should remember to add the second letter to Crispinianus, 25*.

SELECT BIBLIOGRAPHY

PRIMARY SOURCES

Ambrose, *Letters: Epistulae*, ed. Faller, CSEL 9, 1–3 (Vienna, 1968–1982).
———— *De Officiis Ministrorum*, PL 16, cols. 25–194.
Augustine, *Confessions: Confessionum libri XIII*, ed. Verheijen, CCSL 27 (Turnhout, 1981).
———— *De Beata Vita*, ed. Green, CCSL 29 (Turnhout, 1970).
———— *De Civitate Dei* (from the Teubner edition of Dombart and Kalb), CCSL 47 and 48 (Turnhout, 1955).
———— *De Cura Pro Mortuis Gerenda*, ed. Zycha, CSEL 41 (Vienna, 1900).
———— *De Doctrina Christiana*, ed. Martin, CCSL 32 (Turnhout, 1962).
———— *De Magistro*, ed. Daur, CCSL 29 (Turnhout, 1970).
———— *De Ordine*, ed. Green, CCSL 29 (Turnhout, 1970).
———— *De Trinitate*, ed. Mountain, CCSL 50 (Turnhout, 1968).
———— *Letters: Epistulae*, ed. Goldbacher, CSEL 34, 44, 57–58 (Vienna, 1895–1923), and Divjak, CSEL 88 (Vienna, 1981).
———— *Reconsiderations: Retractationes*, ed. Mutzenbacher, CCSL 57 (Turnhout, 1984).
Ausonius, *Works*, ed. with introduction and commentary, Green (Oxford, 1991).
Cassian, *Conferences: Conlationes*, ed. Petschenig, CSEL 13 (Vienna, 1886).
Cicero, *Laelius de Amicitia*, ed. Combès (Paris, 1975); also edited with introduction, translation, and commentary by Powell (Warminster, 1990).
———— *Letters: Epistulae ad Familiares*, ed. Purser, OCT (Oxford, 1982); *ad Atticum*, vol. I ed. Watt, vol. II ed. Shackleton Bailey, OCT (Oxford, 1965 and 1961).
Councils: *The Canons of the First Four General Councils of Nicaea, Constantinople, Ephesus and Chalcedon*, ann. Bright (Oxford, 1892).
Epigrammata Damasiana, ed. Antonio Ferrua (Rome, 1945).
Eucherius of Lyons, *Epistola paraenetica ad Valerianum cognatum de Contemptu Mundi et Saecularis Philosophiae*, PL 50. 711 ff.
Eutropius, *Epistula de Contemnenda Haereditate*, PL 30. 45–50.
Evagrius tr., [Athanasius] *Vita S. Antonii*, PG 26. 835–978.
Gaius, *The Institutes of Gaius*, trans. Gordon and Robinson: Texts in Roman Law (Ithaca NY, 1988).
Gregory the Great, *Dialogues*, ed. de Vogüé, SC 251, 260, and 265 (3 vols.: Paris, 1978–80).

Gregory of Tours, *Liber in Gloria Confessorum* and *Liber in Gloria Martyrum*, ed. Krusch, MGH Scriptores Rerum Merovingicarum 1. 2 (1885), 484–561 and 744–820; both translated by Van Dam (Liverpool, 1988).

Jerome, *Contra Vigilantium*, PL 23. 353–68.

————— *Letters: Epistulae*, ed. Hilberg, CSEL 54–56 (Vienna, 1910–1918).

Paulinus, *Letters: Epistulae*, ed. Hartel, CSEL 29, 1 (Vienna, 1894).

————— *Le Lettere*, ed. Giovanni Santaniello (2 vols.: Naples, 1992).

————— *Poems: Carmina*, ed. Hartel, CSEL 30 (Vienna, 1894).

Pliny, *Letters: Epistularum Libri Decem*, ed. Mynors (Oxford, 1963).

Prudentius, *Psychomachia*, ed. Cunningham, CCSL 126 (Turnhout, 1961).

Sedulius, *Epistola ad Macedonium*, ed. Huemer, CSEL 10 (Vienna, 1885).

Sulpicius Severus, *Vita et Epistulae Martini*, ed. and tr. Fontaine, SC 133–5 (Paris, 1967–1969).

Symmachus, *Letters: Epistulae*, ed. Seeck, MGH Auctores Antiquissimi 6, 1 (1883).

The Testaments of the Twelve Patriarchs, ed. de Jonge (Leiden, 1978).

Uranius, *De Obitu Paulini*, PL 53. 857–66.

Victricius, *De Laude Sanctorum*, ed. Mulders and Demeulenaere, CCSL 64 (1985).

SECONDARY SOURCES

Aers, David, 'A Whisper in the Ear of Early Modernists; or, Reflections on Literary Critics Writing the "History of the Subject" ', in David Aers (ed.), *Culture and History 1350–1600. Essays on English Communities, Identities and Writing* (Detroit, 1992), 177–202.

Annas, Julia, 'Aristotelian Political Theory in the Hellenistic Period' in André Laks and Malcolm Schofield (eds.), *Justice and Generosity: Studies in Hellenistic Social and Political Philosophy*, Proceedings of the Sixth Symposium Hellenisticum (Cambridge, 1995), 74–94.

Arns, Evaristo, *La technique du livre d'après saint Jérôme* (Paris, 1953).

Austen, Jane, *Jane Austen's Letters*, ed. Deirdre le Faye (Oxford/New York, 1995).

Basson, André, 'A Transformation of Genres in Late Latin Literature: Classical Literary Tradition and Ascetic Ideals in Paulinus of Nola' in Ralph W. Mathisen and Hagith S. Sivan (eds.), *Shifting Frontiers in Late Antiquity* (Aldershot/Brookfield VT, 1996), 267–76.

Bastiaensen, A. A. R., 'Le cérémonial épistolaire des chrétiens latins', *Graecitas et Latinitas Christianorum Primaeva* Suppl. II (Nijmegen, 1964), 7–45 (index 89–90).

Boissier, Gaston, *La Fin du Paganisme: étude sur les dernières luttes religieuses en occident au quatrième siècle* (2 vols.: Paris, 1894).

Bovini, Giuseppe, and Hugo Brandenburg, *Repertorium der christlich-antiken Sarkophage*, Vol. I: Rom und Ostia, ed. Friedrich Wilhelm Deichmann (Wiesbaden, 1967).

Brown, Peter, *Augustine of Hippo* (London, 1967).

———— *The Cult of the Saints: Its Rise and Function in Latin Christianity* (Chicago, 1981).

———— 'The Saint as Exemplar', *Representations* 1 (1983), 1–25.

Bruggisser, Philippe, *Symmaque ou le rituel épistolaire de l'amitié littéraire* (Fribourg, 1993).

Brunt, P. A., '*Amicitia* in the Late Roman Republic', *PCPS* 191 NS 11 (1965), 1–20.

Bruyne, D. de, 'Les anciennes collections et la chronologie des lettres de saint Augustin', *RBén* 43 (1931).

Bynum, Caroline Walker, *The Resurrection of the Body in Western Christianity, 200–1336* (New York, 1995).

Cameron, Alan, 'The Fate of Pliny's Letters in the Late Empire', *CQ* NS 15 (1965), 289–98.

Cameron, Averil, *Christianity and the Rhetoric of Empire: The Development of Christian Discourse* (Berkeley/Los Angeles/London, 1991).

Casati, Giuseppe, 'S. Agostino e S. Paolino di Nola', *Augustinianum* 8 (1968), 40–57.

Chadwick, Henry, 'New Sermons of St. Augustine', *JThS* 47 (1996), 69–91.

Clark, Elizabeth, 'Friendship between the Sexes: Classical Theory and Christian Practice', in *Jerome, Chrysostom and Friends: Essays and Translations*, Studies in Women and Religion 11 (New York/Toronto, 1979), 35–106.

———— *The Life of Melania the Younger* (New York/Toronto, 1984).

———— *The Origenist Controversy: The Cultural Construction of an Early Christian Debate* (Princeton, 1992).

Clark, Gillian, ' "The bright frontier of friendship": Augustine and the Christian Body as Frontier', in Ralph W. Mathisen and Hagith S. Sivan (eds.), *Shifting Frontiers in Late Antiquity* (Brookfield, VT, 1996), 217–29.

———— 'Victricius of Rouen: *Praising the Saints*', *JECS* 7 (1999), 365–99.

Cloke, Gillian, *This Female Man of God: Women and Spiritual Power in the Patristic Age, AD 350–450* (London/New York, 1995).

Constable, Giles, *Letters and Letter-Collections*, Typologie des Sources du Moyen Age Occidental 17 (Turnhout, 1976).

Conybeare, Catherine, 'Re-Reading St Patrick', *Journal of Medieval Latin* 4 (1994), 39–50.

———— 'Did Woman have a Beata Vita?', unpublished paper delivered at the International Medieval Congress, Leeds (July, 1997).

———— 'Spaces Between Letters', in Kathryn Kerby-Fulton and Linda Olson (eds.), *Reading Women: New Approaches to Female Literacy in Late Antiquity and the Middle Ages* (forthcoming).

Courcelle, Pierre, *Les lettres grecques en occident de Macrobe à Cassiodore* (Paris, 1943).

———— 'Les lacunes dans la correspondance entre s. Augustin et Paulin de Nole', RÉA 53 (1951), 253–300.

———— *Recherches sur les 'Confessions' de S. Augustin* (new edn.: Paris, 1968).

Cox Miller, Patricia, ' "Differential Networks": Relics and Other Fragments in Late Antiquity', *JECS* 6 (1998), 113–38.

Curtius, Ernst Robert, *European Literature and the Latin Middle Ages*, tr. Willard R. Trask (repr. Princeton, 1990).

Daniélou, Jean, 'La notion de personne chez les Pères grecs', in Ignace Meyerson (ed.), *Problèmes de la Personne*, Colloque du centre de recherches de psychologie comparative XIII (Paris, 1973), 113–21.

De Nie, Giselle, 'Iconic Alchemy: imaging miracles in late sixth-century Gaul', *SP* 30 (1997): Ascetica, 158–66.

———— 'Word, Image and Experience in the Early Medieval Miracle Story', in A. Remael et al. (eds.), *Language and Beyond* (Amsterdam, 1997).

Desmulliez, J., 'Paulin de Nole. Études chronologiques (393–397)', *RecAug* 20 (1985), 35–64.

Duval, Yves-Marie, 'Les premiers rapports de Paulin de Nole avec Jérôme: moine et philosophe? poète ou exégète?' *Studi tardoantichi* 7 (1989), 177–216.

Edwards, M. J., 'A Portrait of Plotinus', *CQ* 43 (1993), 480–90.

Elsner, Jaş, *Art and the Roman Viewer: the Transformation of Art from the Pagan World to Christianity* (Cambridge, 1995).

'Epistolographie', *RE* Suppl. V, 185–220.

Erdt, Werner, *Christentum und heidnisch-antike Bildung bei Paulin von Nola mit Kommentar und Übersetzung des 16. Briefes*, Beiträge zur Klassischen Philologie 82 (Meisenheim, 1976).

Fabiny, Tibor, *The Lion and the Lamb: Figuralism and Fulfilment in the Bible, Art and Literature* (Basingstoke/London, 1992).

Fabre, Pierre, *Essai sur la chronologie de l'oeuvre de saint Paulin de Nole* (Paris, 1948).

———— *Saint Paulin de Nole et l'amitié chrétienne* (Paris, 1948).

Fontaine, Jacques, 'Valeurs antiques et valeurs chrétiennes dans la spiritualité des grands propriétaires terriens à la fin du IVe siècle occidental', in *Epektasis: mélanges patristiques offerts au Cardinal Jean Daniélou* (Paris, 1972), 571–95; reprinted in idem, *Études sur la poésie latine tardive d'Ausone à Prudence* (Paris, 1980), 241–65.

Foucault, Michel, 'What Is an Author?' in Josué V. Harari (ed.), *Textual Strategies: Perspectives in Post-structuralist Criticism* (Ithaca, 1979), 141–60.

Frend, W. H. C., 'Paulinus of Nola and the Last Century of the Western Empire', *JRS* 59 (1969), 1–11.

———— 'The Two Worlds of Paulinus of Nola', in J. W. Binns (ed.), *Latin Literature of the Fourth Century* (London/Boston, 1974), 100–133.

Frye, Northrop, *The Great Code* (reissued: Harmondsworth, 1990).

Gamble, Harry Y., *Books and Readers in the Early Church* (New Haven / London, 1995).

Ghellinck, J. de, *Pour l'histoire du mot 'sacramentum'* Vol. I: *Les Anténicéens* (Louvain/Paris, 1924).

Gill, Christopher, *Personality in Greek Epic, Tragedy, and Philosophy* (Oxford, 1996).

Goldschmidt, Rudolf Carel, *Paulinus' Churches at Nola: Texts, Translations and Commentary* (Amsterdam, 1940).

Goppelt, Leonhard, *Typos: The Typological Interpretation of the Old Testament in the New*, trans. Donald H. Madvig (Grand Rapids MI, 1982; first published 1939).

Gorce, Denys, *Les voyages, l'hospitalité, et le port des lettres dans le monde chrétien des IVe et Ve siècles* (Paris, 1925).

Grabar, André, *Christian Iconography: A Study of Its Origins* (Princeton NJ, 1968).

Green, R. P. H., *The Poetry of Paulinus of Nola. A Study of his Latinity* (Brussels, 1971).

———— 'Paulinus of Nola and the Diction of Christian Latin Poetry', *Latomus* 32 (1973), 79–85.

———— 'The Christianity of Ausonius', *SP* 28 (1993): Latin Authors, 39–48.

Hadot, Pierre, 'De Tertullien à Boèce: le développement de la notion de personne dans les controverses théologiques', in Ignace Meyerson (ed.) *Problèmes de la Personne*, Colloque du centre de recherches de psychologie comparative XIII, (Paris, 1973), 123–134.

———— *Exercices spirituels et philosophie antique* (Paris, 1981).

Hagendahl, Harald, *Augustine and the Latin Classics* (Göteborg, 1967).

Hoek, Annewies van den, 'Paulinus of Nola, Courtyards and Canthari', unpublished paper delivered at the International Medieval Congress, Kalamazoo (May 1999).

Hunter, David, 'Vigilantius of Calagurris and Victricius of Rouen: Ascetics, Relics, and Clerics in Late Roman Gaul', *JECS* 7 (1999), 401–30.

Jantzen, Grace, *Becoming Divine: Towards a Feminist Philosophy of Religion* (Manchester, 1998).

Judge, E. A., 'The Earliest Use of Monachos for "Monk" (P. Coll. Youtie 77) and the Origins of Monasticism', *JbAC* 20 (1977), 72–89.

Junod-Ammerbauer, Helena, 'Les constructions de Nole et l'esthétique de Saint Paulin', *RÉAug* 24 (1978), 22–57.

Kamptner, Margit, 'Paulinus' Poem 18: Sources, Models and Structure', unpublished paper delivered at the International Medieval Congress, Kalamazoo (May 1999).

Kaster, Robert A., *Guardians of Language: The Grammarian and Society in Late Antiquity* (Berkeley/Los Angeles/London, 1988).

Kessler, Herbert, ' "Pictures Fertile with Truth": How Christians Managed to Make Images of God Without Violating the Second Commandment', *Journal of the Walters Art Gallery* 49/50 (1991/92).

Konstan, David, 'Problems in the History of Christian Friendship', *JECS* 4 (1996).

———— *Friendship in the Classical World* (Cambridge, 1997).

Lambot, C., 'Lettre inédite de S. Augustin relative au *De Civitate Dei*', *RBen* 51 (1939), 109–21.

Lawless, George, *Augustine of Hippo and his Monastic Rule* (Oxford, 1987).

Leeman, D., *Orationis Ratio: The Stylistic Theories and Practice of the Roman Orators, Historians and Philosophers* (Amsterdam, 1963).

Lehmann, Tomas, 'Lo sviluppo del complesso archeologico a Cimitile/Nola', *Boreas* 13 (1990), 75–93.

Lienhard, Joseph T., *Paulinus of Nola and Early Western Monasticism*, Theophaneia 28: Beiträge zur Religions- und Kirchengeschichte des Altertums (Cologne/Bonn, 1977).

Lietzmann, Hans, 'Zur Entstehungsgeschichte der Briefsammlung Augustins', in *Kleine Schriften*, Texte und Untersuchungen zur Geschichte der altchristlichen Literatur 67 (Berlin, 1958).

Llewelyn, S. R., *New Documents Illustrating Early Christianity* vol. 7 (Sydney, 1994).

Lubac, Henri de, *Exégèse Médiévale: les quatre sens de l'écriture* (4 vols.: Paris, 1959–64).

Macaulay, Rose, *Letters to a Friend*, ed. Constance Babington Smith (2 vols.: London, 1961 and 1962).

McEvoy, James, ' "Philia" and "Amicitia": the Philosophy of Friendship from Plato to Aristotle', *Sewanee Mediaeval Colloquium Occasional Papers* (1985), 1–24.

———— '*Anima una et cor unum*: Friendship and Spiritual Unity in Augustine', *Recherches de théologie ancienne et médiévale* 53 (1986), 40–92.

McGowan, Andrew, *Ascetic Eucharists: Food and Drink in Early Christian Ritual Meals* (Oxford, 1999).

McGuire, Brian Patrick, *Friendship and Community: The Monastic Experience 350–1250* (Kalamazoo, 1988).

McLynn, Neil B., *Ambrose of Milan: Church and Court in a Christian Capital* (Berkeley/Los Angeles/London, 1994).

Mâle, Emile, *The Early Churches of Rome*, tr. David Buxton (London, 1960).

Malherbe, Abraham J., *Ancient Epistolary Theorists*, Society of Biblical Literature Sources for Biblical Study 19 (Atlanta, 1988).

Markus, R. A., *The End of Ancient Christianity* (Cambridge, 1990).

Marrou, H.-I., 'La technique de l'édition à l'époque patristique', *VChr* 3 (1949), 208–224.

———— *Saint Augustin et la fin de la culture antique* (4th edn. Paris, 1958).

———— *Histoire de l'éducation dans l'antiquité* (6th edn., Paris, 1965).

Matter, E. Ann, *The Voice of My Beloved: The Song of Songs in Western Medieval Christianity* (Philadelphia, 1990).

Matthews, John, 'The Letters of Symmachus', in J. W. Binns (ed.), *Latin Literature of the Fourth Century* (London/Boston, 1974).

Meeks, Wayne A., *The First Urban Christians. The Social World of the Apostle Paul* (New Haven CT, 1983).

Miles, Margaret, *Image as Insight. Visual Understanding in Western Christianity and Secular Culture* (Boston, MA 1985).

Momigliano, A., 'Christianity and the Decline of the Roman Empire', in idem, *Paganism and Christianity in the Fourth Century* (Oxford, 1963), 1–16.

O'Donnell, J. J., review of R. P. H. Green (ed. and trans.), *Augustine: On Christian Doctrine* (Oxford, 1995): *Bryn Mawr Review* 96.3.15.

Onians, John, 'Abstraction and Imagination in Late Antiquity', *Art History* 3 (1980), 1–24.

Osborne, Catherine, *Eros Unveiled: Plato and the God of Love* (Oxford, 1994).

Perler, Othmar, *Les Voyages de Saint Augustin* (Paris, 1969).

Perrin, Michel-Yves, ' "Ad implendum caritatis ministerium" '. La place des courriers dans la correspondance de Paulin de Nole', *MEFRA* 104 (1992), 1025–68.

Pétré, Hélène, *Caritas: étude sur la vocabulaire latin de la charité chrétienne* (Louvain 1948).

Pillinger, Renate, *Die Tituli Historiarum oder das sogenannte Dittochaeon des Prudentius* (Vienna, 1980).

Pizzolato, Luigi, *L'idea di amicizia nel mondo antico classico e cristiano* (Turin, 1993).

Price, A. W., *Love and Friendship in Plato and Aristotle* (Oxford, 1989).

Rebenich, Stefan, *Hieronymus und sein Kreis* (Stuttgart, 1992).

Reinelt, Paul, *Studien über die Briefe des hl. Paulinus von Nola* (Breslau, 1903).

Rist, John, *Augustine: Ancient Thought Baptized* (Cambridge, 1994).

Roberts, Michael, *Biblical Epic and Rhetorical Paraphrase in Late Antiquity* (Liverpool, 1985).

———— 'Paulinus Poem 11, Virgil's first *Eclogue*, and the limits of *amicitia*', *TAPhA* 115 (1985), 271–82.

———— *The Jeweled Style: Poetry and Poetics in Late Antiquity* (Cornell, 1989).

Saller, Richard P., *Personal Patronage in the Early Empire* (Cambridge, 1982).

Skeb, Matthias, *Christo vivere: Studien zum literarischen Christusbild des Paulinus von Nola* (Bonn, 1997).

Smalley, Beryl, *The Study of the Bible in the Middle Ages* (Oxford, 1952).

Stancliffe, Clare, *Saint Martin and his Hagiographer: History and Miracle in Sulpicius Severus* (Oxford, 1983).

Stock, Brian, *Augustine the Reader: Meditation, Self-Knowledge, and the Ethics of Interpretation* (Cambridge MA/London, 1996).

Stowers, Stanley K., *Letter-Writing in Greco-Roman Antiquity* (Philadelphia, 1986).

Struthers Malbon, Elizabeth, *The Iconography of the Sarcophagus of Junius Bassus* (Princeton, 1990).

Summers, Joanna Ceinwen, *Paulinus of Nola and the Renunciation of Wealth* (PhD thesis: King's College London, 1992).

Taylor, Charles, *Sources of the Self. The Making of the Modern Identity* (Cambridge MA, 1989).

Trout, Dennis E., *Secular Renunciation and Social Action: Paulinus of Nola and Late Roman Society* (PhD thesis: Duke University, 1989).

———'The dates of the ordination of Paulinus of Bordeaux and his departure for Nola', *RÉAug* 37 (1991), 237–60.

———'History, Biography, and the Exemplary Life of Paulinus of Nola', *SP* 32 (1997), 462–7.

———*Paulinus of Nola: Life, Letters, and Poems* (Berkeley/Los Angeles/London, 1999).

van Bavel, Tarsicius J., 'The Double Face of Love in St. Augustine. The Daring Inversion: Love is God', in *Congresso Internazionale su S. Agostino nel XVI centenario della conversione* (Rome, 1987) III. 81–102.

———'The Influence of Cicero's Ideal of Friendship on Augustine', in *Augustiniana Traiectina* (Paris, 1987), 59–72.

Verheijen, Luc, *Nouvelle Approche de la Règle de Saint Augustin*, Collection de Spiritualité Orientale et Vie Monastique 8 (Abbaye de Bellefontaine, 1980).

Vessey, Mark, *Ideas of Christian Writing in Late Roman Gaul* (DPhil thesis: Oxford, 1988).

———'Erasmus' Jerome: The Publishing of a Christian Author', *Erasmus of Rotterdam Society Yearbook* 14 (1994), 62–99.

———'The Forging of Orthodoxy in Latin Christian Literature: A Case Study', *JECS* 4 (1996), 495–513.

Veyne, Paul, *Bread and Circuses*, abridged Oswyn Murray; translated Brian Pearce (Harmondsworth, 1990).

———*A History of Private Life* vol 1 (Cambridge MA/London, 1992).

Volbach, Wolfgang Fritz, *Elfenbeinarbeiten der Spätantike und des frühen Mittelalters* (Mainz, 1976).

Walsh, P. G., 'Paulinus of Nola and the Conflict of Ideologies in the Fourth Century', in P. Granfield and J. A. Jungmann (eds.), *Kyriakon: Festschrift Johannes Quasten* (2 vols.: Münster, 1970), II. 565–71.

Weitzmann, Kurt (ed.), *Age of Spirituality: Late Antique and Early Christian Art, Third to Seventh Century* (New York, 1979).

White, Carolinne, *Christian Friendship in the Fourth Century* (Cambridge, 1992).

Williams, R. D., 'The Pictures on Dido's Temple (*Aeneid* I. 450–93)', *CQ* NS 10 (1960), 145–51; reprinted in S. J. Harrison (ed.), *Oxford Readings in Vergil's 'Aeneid'* (Oxford, 1990), 37–45.

Wills, Garry, *Saint Augustine* (Harmondsworth, 1999).

Wiman, Gerhard, 'Till Paulinus Nolanus' Carmina', *Eranos* 32 (1934), 98–130.

Witke, Charles, *Numen Litterarum: The Old and the New in Latin Poetry from Constantine to Gregory the Great*, Mittellateinische Studien und Texte vol. 5 (Leiden/Cologne, 1971).

INDEX LOCORUM

All specific *loci* mentioned in the text are listed. (Allusions to entire works are noted in the General Index.)

GENERAL INDEX

This index effectively combines the functions of a General Index and an Index of Latin Terms, to facilitate cross-referencing. A Latin term may be cited simply by virtue of its occurrence in a quotation; other entries indicate some discussion of the topic.
Those named in the text simply as a letter's addressee are not included.